THE VEGETARIAN MENU BOOK

THE VEGETARIAN MENU BOOK

A comprehensive guide to authentic Indian vegetarian cuisine

by

Vasantha Moorthy

UBSPD

UBS Publishers' Distributors Ltd.

New Delhi • Bombay • Bangalore • Madras
Calcutta • Patna • Kanpur • London

UBS Publishers' Distributors Ltd.
5 Ansari Road, New Delhi-110 002
Bombay Bangalore Madras
Calcutta Patna Kanpur London

© Vasantha Moorthy

First Published 1993
First Reprint 1993
Second Reprint 1994

Cover Design : UBS Art Studio.
Photos : Courtesy ITDC, VIMLA PATIL, ROHINI SINGH

Printed at Rajkamal Electric Press, B-35/9, G.T. Karnal Road Industrial Area, Delhi-110 033

In loving memory of my mother

In loving memory of my mother

ACKNOWLEDGMENTS

It takes more than a good cook to produce a book such as this, and I owe my thanks to many others who helped complete this project. Foremost is my son Girish Moorthy, who toiled endlessly to turn my ideas and recipes collected over 40 years into one integrated and consistent book. Without his determined efforts this book would never have seen the light of day.

Special recognition must go to all my family and friends, who contributed in no small measure with their assistance and suggestions to make this a successful venture.

Table of Contents

Foreword

It is quite astonishing to find that despite the large number of published cookbooks there are very few that deal explicitly with the subject of menus. This is particularly so in the field of Indian vegetarian cooking, where, given the varieties and subtleties of the different colours and flavours, it becomes important that the dishes being served complement and balance one another in these respects.

My wife, the author of this book, has attempted to fill this void by sharing with the reader her vast experience and expertise in this field. From her childhood spent in Karnataka and Orissa and through our years together spent in different parts of India from Bengal to Bombay, she has evolved and perfected the recipes contained in these pages. As the wife of an Indian Railway officer, both during the British Raj and later in independent India, she learned many a secret from the erstwhile khansammas (chefs) of the Railway kitchens whose reputations were legendary. She has further broadened her horizons to include the United States, where during three long visits over the last few years, she continued to delight guests at her sons' homes in the hospitable Indian tradition.

The practice of vegetarianism is growing all over the world, and Indian cuisine offers a variety unparalleled in the rest of the world. (A quick browse through the pages of this book should convince you of this.) This variety offers a seemingly inexhaustible challenge to the potential gourmet to create the most delectable, yet nutritious dishes from the most mundane of ingredients. While no doubt other excellent volumes on this subject abound, the uniqueness of this book lies in its approach. The recipes have been grouped into menus, thus simplifying the planning of a meal, a task sometimes as formidable as preparing the individual recipes themselves.

Whether you are cooking a simple meal for two or planning an elaborate dinner party, I am sure that you will find this book invaluable, and will be well satisfied with the results.

M.R.N. Moorthy

Introduction

This book is a collection of recipes arranged in the form of menus and consists of six parts. The first five parts contain the menus and the individual recipes that go to make them, while the last section is devoted entirely to pickles and chutneys.

Just for Two presents eight lunch or dinner menus ideally suited to couples, both in the recipes selected and the portions therein. It will be especially helpful to the novice cook, someone who is probably venturing into the kitchen for the first time.

Family Meals comprises eight menus for a family of 4-6 people, and has a varied assortment of both North Indian and South Indian fare. The number of servings of each dish has been appropriately specified.

Party Specials is designed for the more adventurous who like to entertain. Both the number and variety of the recipes reflect this. These lunch and dinner recipes typically serve 6-8 people, but you can always increase the quantities proportionately, if you are catering to a larger group.

Something Nice for Tea has eight elaborate menus for High Tea, often an appealing alternative to dinner. These menus contain four sweet and four savoury dishes, and can serve 6-8 guests. Your guests will be pleasantly surprised at the variety that these menus offer.

Breakfast Ideas incorporates well coordinated dishes from different regions of India, and has a choice of seven menus. This is an excellent source of recipes for a holiday breakfast or brunch, good for a large family or a small party (6 persons).

For those who like to do everything themselves, **Pickles and Chutneys** provides a chance to try these exotic preparations referred to in the other chapters of this book. These items usually keep for longer periods.

In compiling the menus, factors such as nutrition, variety, colour and cost have been taken into account. The menus are well balanced with a judicious mix of cereals (grains), dairy products and vegetables. While all the recipes are vegetarian, some do contain eggs. For those who do not wish to eat eggs, eggless alternatives have been offered. In the tea menus, there is a choice between Western and Indian sweets.

In the first four parts, the main recipes for the menus (except in the Western and Chinese menus) are listed on the left hand side, with the (optional) accompaniments on the right. While the items on the right hand side are more in the nature of embellishments, the items on the left hand side constitute a full menu by themselves. Further, if the item on the right is a pickle or a chutney, you will find the recipe for it in the last section. Needless to say, you may add, drop, substitute, mix or match recipes according to your taste.

Many of the herbs, spices, lentils and vegetables may not be available in American supermarkets, but all American cities and most large towns usually have a Middle Eastern or Indian grocery store where you should be able to find most, if not all of the ingredients you need. The names of these ingredients are sometimes not the same in different parts of India, and I have tried to be faithful to the regional term in my description of each dish. Consult the glossary for explanations of these terms, if they are unfamiliar to you.

It is always difficult to write a cookbook for audiences who use more than one system of measurement, and the problem is compounded by the necessity of keeping an accurate kitchen scale at hand. I have tried to simplify the reader's task by resorting to the average Indian teacup (200 ml or 6.7 fl oz.), teaspoon (5 ml or 1/6 fl oz.) and tablespoon (15 ml or 1/2 fl oz.) for most of the measurements. American readers must note that the standard American measuring cup is 8 fl oz., and I have thus provided a table below for easy conversion. Where greater precision is required, such as in baked items, and in the Pickles and Chutneys section, I have used metric measurements with the corresponding American equivalents of weights, lengths and volumes.

British readers must note that the American pint, quart and gallon are 83% (five-sixths) of the corresponding British units, and hence will need to make the appropriate adjustments, wherever these units are used. Also, the British tablespoon (17 fl oz.) is slightly larger than its American counterpart.

Indian	American
1 cup	0.8 cup
2 cups	1.6 cups
3 cups	2.4 cups
4 cups	3.2 cups
5 cups	4.0 cups

Finally, this table of oven temperatures will be very useful in the recipes which involve baking.

Oven Heat	Celsius	Fahrenheit
Moderate	190	375
Hot	220	430
Very Hot	240	465

I hope you will have as much fun trying out the various recipes as I have had putting them together.

Vasantha Moorthy

"A good menu is like a good story. It must have a proper balance of dramatic elements, sorted out and arranged in such an order that each new course fulfils the promise of one that came before, while setting the scene for the one to follow, and everything must be resolved in the end, for unlike some stories, all meals must have happy endings."

From *The Vegetarian Epicure*

By Anna Thomas

JUST FOR TWO

JUST FOR TWO

Menu 1

Vegetable or Egg Biryani
Moong Dal
Kachumber (Salad)
Curds (Yoghurt)

Serve With
Chilly Pickle, Potato Chips
Dessert
Mango or Orange Basundi

Menu 2

Stuffed Vegetable or
Stuffed Egg Parathas
Spicy Masoor Dal
Tomato Onion Raita or
Curds (Yoghurt)

Serve With
Mango Pickle (North Indian)
Dessert
Kesar Kheer

Menu 3

Spinach or Plain Kadhi
Dal Bhujjia
Rice
Bhindi (Okra) Fry or Green Banana Fry
Fresh Vegetable Salad (Optional)

Serve With
Khattal (Jackfruit) Kababs
or Pumpkin Kababs
Green Chutney
Dessert
Kulfi

Menu 4

Chapatis
Peas Ambat
Potato Cauliflower Dry Curry or
Greens With Coconut
One cup rice (optional)

Serve With
Capsicum - Tomato Raita
or Curds (Yoghurt)
Navaratna Pickle
Dessert
Carrot Kheer

JUST FOR TWO

Menu 5

Coconut Rice
Ginger Pachadi
Vegetable Kootu
Lemon Rasam (Optional)
Curd (Yoghurt) Rice

Serve With
Fried Sago or Rice Vadams
South Indian Lime Pickle
Dessert
Aval Payasam

Menu 6

Savoury Puris
Fried Moong Dal
Mixed Vegetable Stew or
Spicy Egg Curry

Serve With
Kela (Banana) Raita or Curds
(Yoghurt)
Sweet-Hot Mango Chutney
Dessert
China Grass Pudding or Ginger-
Cinnamon Slices With Cream

Menu 7

Moong Dal Khichadi (North Indian)
or Venn Pongal (South Indian)
Onion Chutney
Carrot Salad
Tomato Rasam (Optional)
Curds (Yoghurt)

Serve With
Mixed Vegetable Pakodas
Dessert
Coconut Poli

Menu 8

Spinach Soup With Cream
Vegetable Casserole or
Eggs in White Sauce

Serve With
Toasted Bread Slices with Butter
Salad with French Dressing
Dessert
Caramel Custard or
Baked Custard

—— *Menu 1* ——

Vegetable or Egg Biryani	**Serve With**
Moong Dal	Chilly Pickle, Potato Chips
Kachumber (Salad)	**Dessert**
Curds (Yoghurt)	Mango or Orange Basundi

Vegetable Biryani

Ingredients

1 1/2 cups rice
1/2 cup peas, shelled
1 small potato
1 small carrot
a dozen beans
1 large onion, sliced
2-3 green chillies, slit
1/2 coconut, grated
3/4 cup ghee
2-3 bay leaves
5-6 cashew nuts
1/2 teaspoon turmeric
salt to taste
2 slices bread (optional)
2 tablespoons ghee (to fry bread)

For the masala

1 large onion
3-4 garlic cloves
1.3 cm/0.5 inch piece ginger
2 green chillies
a handful of coriander leaves
a few mint leaves
1 teaspoon aniseeds
1 teaspoon of poppy seeds
2-3 cloves
2.5 cm/1 inch cinnamon stick
2-3 cardamoms

For the garnish

1 tablespoon chopped coriander

Method

1. Grind the ingredients for the masala to a paste.
2. Wash the rice and allow to dry on a clean cloth.
3. Prepare the vegetables by washing, peeling and cutting into small pieces as desired.
4. Add 2 cups of boiling water to the grated coconut and allow to stand for 10 minutes. When cool pass through a liquidiser and strain to get coconut milk. Repeat the process to make 3 1/2 cups of coconut milk in all.
5. Heat half the ghee in a cooker, add the cashew nuts, fry until golden and remove. Add the sliced onions, fry until crisp, remove and set aside.
6. Add the bay leaves and fry. When done, add the rice, fry for two to three minutes and remove from cooker.
7. Add the rest of the ghee and the green chillies, and fry for a minute. Add the vegetables and fry until they turn a little soft. Now add the ground paste and

turmeric, and stir for 3-4 minutes until the ghee surfaces.

8. Put the fried rice back into the cooker, add the coconut milk and salt, and cook on low heat until done. Take care to see that the rice is not overcooked. If a pressure cooker is used, do not use the weight.

9. Cut the bread into croutons (cubes) and fry in ghee until crisp.

To serve

Carefully transfer the biryani onto a rice platter, mix in three quarters of the croutons and fried onions. Garnish with the rest of the croutons, some chopped coriander leaves and pieces of lemon, if required. Serve hot.

Egg Biryani

Ingredients

Same as Vegetable Biryani, except for the addition of 2-3 eggs. Omit the vegetables except for a half-cup of shelled peas.

Method

1. Hard boil the eggs, shell and cut them lengthwise. Boil the peas and set aside.

2. Prepare the biryani as above, except use only 3 cups of coconut milk and water. Fry the eggs lightly in ghee, remove, set aside, and then proceed with the biryani.

3. While serving, place the eggs evenly all over the rice, mix in the peas, and garnish with fried onions and chopped coriander.

Moong Dal

Ingredients

1 cup moong dal	1 teaspoon aniseeds
1 onion, chopped	1/4 teaspoon garam masala
1 tomato, chopped	1/4 teaspoon turmeric
1-2 dry red chillies, broken into bits	1 bay leaf
salt to taste	2 tablespoons ghee

Method

1. Wash the dal. Add the turmeric, sufficient water and boil. Set aside.

2. Heat the ghee. Add the bay leaf, aniseed, red chillies and garam masala. When done, add the onions and fry until golden.

3. Add the tomatoes and fry till soft. Then add the salt, boiled dal, and a cup of water, if necessary. Cook for a few minutes.

4. Serve hot.

Kachumber (Salad)

Ingredients

1 onion	1 green chilly, minced
1 carrot	2 teaspoons coriander, chopped
2 tomatoes	juice of one lemon
1/2 cucumber	salt to taste

Method

1. Wash, scrape and cut the vegetables into small pieces. Add the salt, lemon juice, chilly and coriander, and mix well. Chill and serve.

Potato Chips

Ingredients

450 gm/1 lb potatoes	oil for frying
1/2 teaspoon chilly or pepper powder	salt to taste

Method

1. Wash, peel and cut the potatoes into very thin slices. Leave them in cold water for some time. Squeeze out all water by pressing the slices between your palms and leave on a cloth to dry.
2. Deep fry the potatoes, a handful at a time until they are golden brown. Stir continuously so that the pieces do not stick to each other.
3. While still warm, sprinkle salt and pepper or chilly powder and mix well. When cool, put in a tin and store.

Chilly Pickle

Refer to Chilly Pickle in Part Six.

Mango Basundi

Ingredients
1 mango
3 tablespoons sugar
a generous pinch of saffron

500 ml/1 pint milk
2-3 cardamoms, powdered

Method
1. Boil the milk on a slow fire with the sugar and saffron stirring all the while till it is reduced to about half the quantity. Chill.
2. Skin and cut the mango into cubes. Chill.
3. Mix the mango pieces with the thickened milk, and add cardamom powder. Serve chilled.

Orange Basundi

Ingredients
Same as above, except use 2 oranges instead of mangoes. Peel, clean and remove the pips and seeds. Break into small pieces and chill. Proceed as above.

—— *Menu 2* ——

Stuffed Vegetable or
Stuffed Egg Parathas
Spicy Masoor Dal
Tomato Onion Raita or
Curds (Yoghurt)

Serve With
Mango Pickle (North Indian)
Dessert
Kesar Kheer

Stuffed Vegetable Parathas

Ingredients
3 cups wheat flour
1 small potato
1 small carrot
a few florets cauliflower
1/2 cup shelled peas
1/2 teaspoon red chilly powder
1/2 teaspoon garam masala powder
salt to taste
ghee or oil for frying

Chop very fine
3-4 green chillies
1.3 cm/0.5 inch piece ginger
1 medium onion
a handful fresh coriander

Method
1. Knead the flour with a little salt, 3 teaspoons of oil and sufficient water to make a soft dough. Keep covered for at least 2-3 hours before making.
2. Wash and chop the vegetables. Add the shelled peas, a little salt and steam cook. While still hot, mash. Set aside.
3. Heat 2 tablespoons of oil, add the chopped ingredients (except the coriander) and stir fry until the onions turn brown. Then add the chilly and garam masala powders, and fry for a while. Add the cooked vegetables and fry till dry. Add the chopped coriander, mix well, and set aside to cool. Divide the mixture into balls.
4. Divide the dough into lemon-sized balls, twice the number in Step 3. Taking out 2 balls at a time, roll into 2 chapatis using a little oil while rolling instead of flour. (This will make the parathas crisp).
5. Take a ball of the vegetable mixture, spread evenly on one chapati, and cover with the other. Seal the edges firmly all around by pressing them with wet fingers.
6. Heat a skillet (tava) gently, put in the paratha, turn on both sides till done. Now add oil or ghee all around the edges, fry both sides, carefully turning over until evenly brown. Serve very hot.

Stuffed Egg Parathas

Ingredients
Same as above, except omit the vegetables and use instead 3 or 4 eggs and a pinch of turmeric powder.

Method
1. Beat the eggs thoroughly with a pinch of turmeric and salt.
2. Fry the chopped ingredients till the onions turn brown. Add the dry masala powders, then the eggs, and cook, stirring all the while until the eggs are done. See that there is no trace of water when removing from fire. Cool, add the chopped coriander, and mix well. Divide the mixture into balls.
3. Follow instructions 4-6 from the previous recipe.

Spicy Masoor Dal

Ingredients
1 cup masoor dal
1 chopped onion
1 tomato
1-2 green chillies, slit
1-1/2 tablespoons ghee
2 (large) cardamoms
1-2 bay leaves
salt to taste

Grind to paste
1 dried red chilly
1.3 cm/0.5 inch piece ginger
3-4 garlic cloves
2 cloves
1.3 cm/0.5 inch stick cinnamon
1 teaspoon cumin seeds
a few peppercorns
1.3 cm / 0.5 inch turmeric piece

Method
1. Boil the dal with sufficient water until soft.
2. Heat the ghee, add the bay leaves, cardamom, green chillies and onion, and fry until the onions turn brown. Add the tomatoes and keep frying until they turn soft.
3. Add the ground paste and fry further until quite dry and the ghee comes to the surface. Add the dal, salt, 1 1/2 cups of water, and simmer for a few minutes. Serve hot with the parathas.

Tomato Onion Raita

(Tomatoes and Onions in Seasoned Yoghurt)

Ingredients

2 tomatoes

1 onion

1 green chilly, finely chopped

1 tablespoon chopped fresh coriander

1 cup curds (yoghurt)

salt to taste

Method

1. Cut the tomatoes into small pieces. Chop the onions very fine. Beat the curds. Mix all the ingredients with the curds. Serve chilled.

Kesar Kheer

(Saffron Pudding)

Ingredients

1/2 cup long grain rice

1/2 cup sugar

a pinch of saffron (kesar)

3 cups milk

2-3 teaspoons ghee

silver foil for decoration

1 cup water

2 cloves

2 cardamoms

0.6 cm/0.25 inch stick cinnamon

1/4 tablespoon almonds

1/4 tablespoon raisins

1/4 tablespoon cashew nuts

1/4 tablespoon pistachio nuts

Method

1. Wash the rice, and drain on a cloth. Soak the saffron in one tablespoon of warm milk and keep aside. Blanch and slice the almonds, slice the pista, and break the cashew nuts into small pieces. Clean the raisins if necessary.

2. Heat the ghee in a cooker, and add the raisins and cashew nuts. Fry until golden, remove and set aside.

3. Add the rice and the whole spices to the cooker and fry for 1 minute. Add the milk, saffron soaked in warm milk and the water. Cook for a few minutes on moderate heat until the rice is done. Now add the sugar, and cook further on low heat until the sugar has blended, and the mixture thickens. Remove from fire and allow to cool, if you wish to serve it chilled.

4. When about to serve, add half of the nuts, and mix well. Pour the kheer into individual bowls. Garnish with the rest of the nuts and raisins. Decorate with the silver foil. Serve chilled or hot.

---- *Menu 3* ----

Spinach or Plain Kadhi	**Serve With**
Dal Bhujjia	Khattal (Jackfruit) Kababs
Rice	or Pumpkin Kababs
Bhindi (Okra) Fry	Green Chutney
or Green Banana Fry	**Dessert**
Fresh Vegetable Salad (Optional)	Kulfi

Spinach Kadhi

Ingredients

1 cup curds (yoghurt)
3 cups water
1 1/2 tablespoon gram flour
a small bunch of spinach
a pinch of turmeric
salt to taste
2 teaspoons oil
2 teaspoons ghee
1/2 teaspoon sugar

Seasonings

a pinch of asafoetida
1/4 teaspoon cumin seeds
1/4 teaspoon fenugreek seeds
1-2 red chillies
a pinch garam masala
a pinch pepper powder

For the masala paste

1 green chilly
0.6 cm/0.25 inch piece ginger
2-3 garlic cloves
1 small onion

Method

1. Boil the spinach with salt. Cool, and grind to a paste with the masalas given.
2. Beat the curds with water. Add some salt, turmeric powder, gram flour and sugar, and mix thoroughly.
3. Heat the oil and season with the ingredients given, except the garam masala and pepper. Add the cooked spinach and fry for a minute or two.
4. Add the buttermilk mixture, simmer for a while, and remove from fire.
5. Before serving, heat the ghee, add the pepper and garam masala powders, and stir for one minute. Pour into the kadhi and mix.

Plain Kadhi

1. The kadhi can be prepared plain if so desired (without spinach). For this omit only the first step. For the seasoning, include chopped green chillies and ginger. The rest is the same.
2. If desired, small pakodas may be added to the kadhi. Refer to Part 1, Menu 7 for the pakodas.

Dal Bhujjia

Ingredients

1 cup whole moong dal
a small bunch of methi leaves (fenugreek)
1-2 green chillies
1.3 cm/0.5 inch piece ginger
1-2 garlic cloves (optional)
1 medium onion
1/2 teaspoon turmeric powder
1/2 teaspoon garam masala powder

Seasonings

1-2 dry red chillies, broken into bits
a pinch of mustard seeds
a pinch of asafoetida
a pinch of cumin seeds
1-1/2 tablespoons oil
2-3 teaspoons ghee
salt to taste

Method

1. Soak the dal for a couple of hours. Cook with the turmeric powder and sufficient water. Set aside.
2. Chop the green chillies, garlic, ginger, onion and methi leaves.
3. Heat the oil and add the seasonings. When done add the chopped ingredients from Step 2 except the methi. Fry till the onions are brown. Add the methi, fry for a while, add the cooked dal and salt, and simmer for some time.
4. Just before serving, heat the ghee, add the garam masala powder, cook for half a minute, and pour into the dal.

Rice

Method

Cook 1 1/2 to 2 cups of rice, as desired.

Bhindi Fry

Ingredients

250 gm/9 oz. bhindi (okra)
3-4 tablespoons oil
1/2 tablespoon gram flour (besan)
3 teaspoons coriander powder
3 teaspoons cumin powder

1/2 teaspoon turmeric powder
1/2 teaspoon garam masala powder
1/2 teaspoon chilly powder
1/2 teaspoon amchoor
salt to taste

Method

1. Mix all the ingredients, except the bhindi and oil.
2. Wipe and cut the bhindi into long pieces. If small, keep them whole (after cutting off the ends). Cut each piece or whole bhindi half way through.
3. Stuff the bhindis with the above masalas.
4. Heat the oil in a kadai (wok), and add the stuffed bhindi along with the rest of the masala, if any. Fry on low heat for a couple of minutes.
5. If it appears too dry or about to get burnt, sprinkle some water. Cover and leave on a low flame for a while.
6. Remove the lid and fry the bhindis until they are crisp, adding some more oil if necessary.

Green Banana Fry

Ingredients

2 green bananas (plantains)
1 bay leaf
2 teaspoons chopped coriander
3/4 tablespoon gram flour
salt to taste
oil for frying

To be ground

1 tablespoon coriander powder
1/2 tablespoon cumin powder
1/2 teaspoon turmeric powder
1/2 teaspoon chilly powder
1/2 teaspoon garam masala powder
a pinch of amchoor

Method

1. Peel and cut the bananas into small pieces 0.6 cm/0.25 inch thick and 4 cm/1.5 inches long.
2. Grind the masala. Add the salt, gram flour and coriander leaves, and mix well. Smear the banana pieces with this masala.
3. Heat the oil, add the bay leaves, and fry. Add the banana pieces, and fry on low heat turning occasionally. If necessary, sprinkle some water, cover the vessel, and cook until done.

Fresh Vegetable Salad

Ingredients

1 tomato

1 onion

1 lemon

1/2 medium sized cucumber

3-4 red radishes

salt and pepper to taste

Method

1. Wash the vegetables. Peel the onion and cucumber. Cut the vegetables into slices and the lemon into fours. Arrange the vegetable slices artistically on a salad plate (you can use a few lettuce leaves). Sprinkle some salt and pepper, and serve at once.

Khattal (Jackfruit) Kababs

Ingredients

150 gm/5 oz. jackfruit pieces (with seeds)

1/2 cup gram dal (channa dal)

2 cloves

2 large cardamoms

2 small cinnamon sticks

2 tablespoons gram flour

1/2 teaspoon turmeric powder

1 teaspoon chilly powder

oil for frying

salt to taste

Chop very fine

1 onion

2-3 garlic cloves

1.3 cm/0.5 piece ginger

Method

1. Boil the jackfruit pieces and dal with very little water. Grind to a smooth paste with the cloves, cardamoms, cinnamon and salt.
2. Add the chopped ingredients as well as the turmeric and chilly powders, and mix thoroughly.
3. Form cylindrical kababs, roll in gram flour, and deep fry.

Pumpkin Kababs

Ingredients

250 gm/9 oz pumpkin
5 tablespoons gram flour
1 tablespoon chopped coriander
1 tablespoon curds (yoghurt)
salt to taste
oil for frying

Chop fine

3-4 green chillies
0.6 cm/0.25 inch piece ginger
3 garlic cloves

Seasoning

1/2 teaspoon turmeric powder
1/2 teaspoon garam masala
1/2 teaspoon chilly powder

Method

1. Grate the pumpkin. Add a pinch of salt, and set aside for a while. Now squeeze the gratings to remove all the water.
2. Heat 2 tablespoons of oil, add the finely chopped ingredients, and fry for half a minute. Add the pumpkin gratings, seasonings, and salt, and fry for another minute. Remove from fire, and cool.
3. Add the gram flour, curds and chopped coriander to the pumpkin mixture. Mix well.
4. Using a little oil on your palm, form rolls from the mixture, steam these rolls, and set aside to cool.
5. Cut the rolls into two thick slices and form each into a kabab. Roll these kababs in gram flour, and shallow fry in hot oil to golden. Serve very hot.

Green Chutney

Ingredients

green mangoes or
2 small green tamarind
1 medium onion
4-5 green chillies
a mint leaves
salt to taste

1 small piece of ginger
2 garlic cloves
a pinch of pepper
a pinch of cumin seeds
a pinch of coriander seeds
1/2 teaspoon sugar

Method

1. Scrape the tamarind or mango, chop into bits and grind to a paste with all the ingredients except the sugar. Add the sugar when ground and mix well.

Note

If neither mango nor tamarind is available, grind the chutney along with some fresh coriander, and add some lemon juice for sourness.

Kulfi

Ingredients

3 cups milk
3/4 cup sugar
a handful of almonds

a few drops of almond essence
a few strands saffron
4 kulfi moulds

Method

1. Blanch and skin the almonds and grind to a paste with some milk. Soak the saffron in 1 tablespoon of warm milk.
2. Boil the milk with sugar and stir till dissolved. Add the ground almonds and saffron, and cook on low heat stirring all the while until thick and creamy. Remove from fire, add the essence, cool and pour into the kulfi moulds. Set in the freezer.
3. When about to serve, remove the moulds from the freezer, immerse in water and open lid. Turn it upside down on a plate, remove the mould and serve at once.

—— *Menu* 4 ——

Chapatis
Peas Ambat
Potato Cauliflower Dry Curry or
Greens With Coconut
One cup rice (optional)

Serve With
Capsicum - Tomato Raita
or Curds (Yoghurt)
Navaratna Pickle
Dessert
Carrot Kheer

Chapatis

Ingredients
2 cups wheat flour
4 teaspoonsful ghee
salt to taste

Method
1. Mix together the wheat flour, 2 teaspoons ghee and salt. Add some water and mix to a smooth, pliable dough. Cover and leave aside for 30 minutes.
2. Take a small ball of dough, make into a smooth round and roll into a circle on a floured board, occasionally dusting with some flour when sticky. Roll as thin as possible.
3. Heat a skillet (tava) and place the chapati on it. Cook both sides, turning over when one side is done. While still hot, smear some ghee over it.

Note
After cooking on both sides, the chapatis can be placed directly on the flame till they puff up. These are 'phulkas'. They should be served immediately with some ghee smeared over them, if desired.

Peas Ambat

Ingredients
1 1/2 cups fresh peas or
1 cup dehydrated peas
1-2 chopped medium onion
2-3 garlic cloves (optional)
2-3 tablespoons ghee
1 tablespoon chopped coriander
1/2 teaspoon turmeric powder
salt to taste

Masala
1 red chilly
1/4 teaspoon pepper
1.3 cm/0.5 inch piece cinnamon
2 cloves
2 tablespoons grated coconut
a small lump tamarind

Seasoning
1/2 teaspoon mustard seeds
2 sprigs curry leaves
2 green chillies slit (optional)

Method
1. Cook the fresh peas with very little water and some salt. If dried peas are used, soak overnight and cook in a pressure cooker.
2. Heat 1/2 tablespoon ghee, fry the masalas (except the tamarind), and grind with the tamarind to a paste. Heat the rest of the ghee, add the mustard and when done, add the curry leaves and the chillies. Add the turmeric, chopped onion and garlic. Fry till the onions are brown.
3. Add the masala paste, cooked peas and chopped coriander. Simmer for a while. Serve hot.

Note
This dish can also be prepared with masoor or moong dal.

Potato Cauliflower Dry Curry

Ingredients
- 2-3 large potatoes
- 1 small cauliflower
- 1 tablespoon chopped coriander
- 2-3 tablespoons oil
- salt to taste

For the masala
- 2 dried red chillies
- 1/2 teaspoon turmeric
- 2 tablespoons coriander seeds
- a pinch of asafoetida
- 2 tablespoons grated coconut

Seasoning
- 1 teaspoon mustard seeds
- 2 sprigs curry leaves

Method
1. Boil, peel and cut the potatoes into large pieces. Break the cauliflower into florets and cook with very little water until soft.
2. Grind the ingredients for the masala to a very smooth paste. Smear the vegetable pieces with this.
3. Heat the oil, season with the mustard and curry leaves, and add the vegetables. Fry until all the water has been absorbed, and the vegetables are dry. Add some more oil while frying if you desire it crisp and brown. Garnish with the chopped coriander.

Greens With Coconut

Ingredients
- 1 large bunch greens of any kind (collard, spinach or kale)
- a handful of methi (fenugreek) leaves
- 1/2 teaspoon chopped ginger
- 1 tablespoon oil
- salt to taste

For the masala
- 2-3 tablespoons grated coconut
- 1-2 dried red chillies
- a small ball of tamarind

Seasoning
- 1 teaspoon mustard seeds
- 1-2 green chillies
- 2-3 crushed garlic cloves (optional)

Method
1. Wash and chop the greens. Boil with chopped ginger. Chop the green chillies and the garlic.
2. Fry the red chillies in a little oil. Add the coconut and tamarind, and grind to a paste.
3. Heat the rest of the oil, and season with the mustard, chopped green chillies and garlic until browned. Pour into the cooked greens, add the ground paste and salt, and mix well. Simmer for one to two minutes.

Capsicum-Tomato Raita

(Seasoned Green Peppers and Tomatoes in Yoghurt)

Ingredients

2 small tomatoes
2 small capsicums
1 cup curds (yoghurt)
1/2 teaspoon sugar
1 teaspoon chopped coriander
salt to taste

Seasoning

2 teaspoons oil
1/2 teaspoon mustard seeds
1 dried red chilly
1 sprig curry leaf

Method

1. Chop the capsicum and tomatoes.
2. Heat the oil and add the mustard. When the mustard is done, add the red chilly (broken into small pieces), curry leaf, and chopped vegetables. Fry until soft. Cool.
3. Beat the curds with salt and sugar, add to the vegetables and mix well. Pour into a bowl. Garnish with some chopped coriander. Serve chilled.

Carrot Kheer

(Carrot Pudding)

Ingredients

2 small carrots
500 ml/1 pint milk
3/4 cup sugar
1 tablespoon ghee
1/2 cup water

1/2 tablespoon cashew nuts
1/2 tablespoon raisins
4-5 cardamoms, powdered
a pinch of saffron
1/2 teaspoon rose
         or almond essence

Method

1. Wash, scrape and grate the carrots. Add the milk and water and cook till soft. Add the sugar and cook further until quite thick.
2. Add the saffron, and continue to stir for a few minutes.
3. Remove from fire, add the cardamom powder and essence, and mix.
4. Heat the ghee and fry the raisins and cashew nuts (broken into little pieces). Add half of this to the kheer and mix well.
5. Pour the kheer into a serving bowl and sprinkle the rest of the nuts and raisins on top. Serve hot or cold.

---- *Menu 5* ----

Coconut Rice	**Serve With**
Ginger Pachadi	Fried Sago or Rice Vadams
Vegetable Kootu	South Indian Lemon Pickle
Lemon Rasam (Optional)	**Dessert**
Curd (Yoghurt) Rice	Aval Payasam

Coconut Rice

Ingredients
1 cup rice
1-1/2 cups grated coconut
2-3 slit green chillies
a few cashew nuts
or
a few peanuts (groundnuts)
2 sprigs curry leaves
salt to taste

Seasoning
2-3 tablespoons oil
1 teaspoon mustard seeds
1/2 tablespoon black gram dal
1/2 tablespoon gram dal
a pinch asafoetida
1-2 dried red chillies

Method
1. Cook the rice so that each grain is separate. Leave it on a plate to cool, sprinkling two teaspoons of oil and some salt.
2. Heat a little oil. Fry the cashew nuts (broken into small pieces) or peanuts, remove and set aside.
3. Add the rest of the oil and the seasoning ingredients as given - first the mustard and when done, the dals, chillies and asafoetida. Fry until the dals turn golden brown.
4. Add the green chillies, curry leaves and coconut, and fry until the coconut turns light brown, adding some salt. Pour these seasonings onto the rice and mix lightly using only the tips of your fingers.
5. Transfer onto a plate, and sprinkle the cashew nuts or peanuts. Serve warm.

Ginger Pachadi
(Seasoned Ginger in Yoghurt)

Ingredients
2.5 cm/1 inch piece ginger
2 tablespoons grated coconut
1-2 green chillies
1 cup curds (yoghurt)
1-2 tomatoes (optional)
salt to taste

Seasoning
1 teaspoon oil
1/2 teaspoon mustard seeds
1 sprig curry leaf

Method
1. Wash, scrape and grind the ginger with the chillies, coconut and salt. Chop the tomatoes.
2. Beat the curds, and add the ginger paste and tomatoes. This mixture is the pachadi.
3. Heat the oil and season with the mustard and curry leaf. Add this to the pachadi and mix well. Serve chilled.

Vegetable Kootu

Ingredients
3/4 cup toovar dal
1/2 teaspoon turmeric powder
3 tablespoons grated coconut
500 gm/1.1 lb of any one of the
following vegetables or a
mixture of ones available:
Brinjal (eggplant), ash gourd,
snake gourd, beans, green banana
tamarind juice (optional)
salt to taste

Fry in 1 teaspoon oil and grind with coconut
1/2 tablespoon black gram
3-4 red chillies
1/4 teaspoon asafoetida

Seasoning
1 teaspoon oil
1/2 teaspoon mustard seeds
1 teaspoon black gram
1 sprig curry leaf

Method
1. Boil the dal with 1/4 teaspoon of turmeric, and set aside.
2. Wash and cut the vegetables into small pieces. Boil with 1/4 teaspoon turmeric, and some salt. Set aside.

3. Mix together the boiled dal, cooked vegetables and ground paste. Add some water if too thick, and simmer for a few minutes. Add a little tamarind juice to the mixture, if desired. Tamarind juice is made by squeezing a piece of tamarind soaked in water, and filtering. Alternatively bottled tamarind concentrate can be appropriately diluted.

4. Heat the oil, and when hot, add the mustard seeds, black gram and curry leaf. Pour the seasonings into the kootu. Serve hot.

Lemon Rasam

Ingredients

1/2 cup toovar or moong dal
1-2 medium tomatoes, chopped
2-3 split green chillies
1.3 cm/0.5 inch piece chopped ginger
2 teaspoons chopped coriander
1/4 teaspoon turmeric powder
juice of 1 lemon
salt and pepper to taste

Seasoning

2 teaspoons ghee
1/2 teaspoon mustard seeds
1/2 teaspoon cumin seeds
1 sprig curry leaf

Method

1. Boil the dal in water with the turmeric. When cooked add 1 1/2 cups of water, churn and set aside.

2. Heat the ghee, add the seasonings and when done add the chillies, ginger and tomatoes. Fry for a minute or so. Add half a cup of water, salt and half the chopped coriander. Cook till the tomatoes are soft.

3. Add the dal, and continue to heat until the rasam boils. Remove from fire, and add the lemon juice, along with the rest of the coriander. Serve very hot, either as an appetizer or with rice. If it is served as an appetizer, dilute it with an additional cup of water, and some salt and pepper.

Curd (Yoghurt) Rice

Ingredients

3/4 cup rice
1 1/2 cup curds (yoghurt)
1/2 cup milk
1/2 teaspoon chopped ginger
1 sprig curry leaves
salt to taste

Seasoning

2 teaspoons oil
1/2 teaspoon mustard seeds
1-2 cut red or green chillies
1 teaspoon black gram
1 sprig curry leaves

Method

1. Cook the rice and mash while still hot. Add the salt, chopped ginger, and curry leaves. Mix thoroughly. When cool, add the curds and milk.
2. Heat the oil, and when hot, add the mustard seeds, chillies, black gram and curry leaf. Add this to the mixed rice and chill. When serving, add some water or curds to the rice if found too thick.

Note

Since both the Coconut and Curd Rice require cooked rice, it may be cooked once and divided into two or three portions.

Aval Payasam
(Beaten Rice Pudding)

Ingredients

1 cup beaten rice, thin variety (aval)
3 cups milk
1/2 cup sugar
2 tablespoons ghee
1 tablespoon cashew nuts (broken into pieces)
1 – 1-1/2 tablespoon raisins
4-5 small cardamoms (white)
a few strands saffron (optional)

Method

1. Heat the ghee, fry the nuts and raisins in it and remove. To the same ghee add the aval, and fry to a light brown.
2. Add the milk and saffron, and cook for a while. Add the sugar, and keep cooking and stirring all the time on low heat until the payasam is thick and creamy.
3. Remove from fire. Add the powdered cardamom, fried nuts and raisins. Serve either hot or chilled.

Fried Sago and/or Rice Vadams

Purchase at any grocery store.

South Indian Lime Pickle

Refer to South Indian Lime Pickle in Part 6.

——— Menu 6 ———

Savoury Puris
Fried Moong Dal
Mixed Vegetable Stew or
Spicy Egg Curry

Serve With
Kela (Banana) Raita
or Curds (Yoghurt)
Sweet-Hot Mango Chutney
Dessert
China Grass Pudding
or Ginger-Cinnamon Slices
with Cream

Savoury Puris

Ingredients

2 cups maida (flour)
1/2 teaspoon chilly powder
1/4 teaspoon pepper powder
1/2 teaspoon cumin powder
1/2 teaspoon anardana (pomegranate seeds)
oil for frying

Grind to paste

a handful coriander leaves
2-3 green chillies
2-3 garlic cloves (optional)
salt to taste

Method

1. Sift the maida. (If preferred, a handful of wheat flour may be added and the maida reduced). Add the ground paste and all the other ingredients along with 1 table-spoon of oil and enough water to form a dough. The dough should be stiff.
2. Roll out the puris slightly thick, and fry in hot oil, turning over both sides.

Fried Moong Dal

Ingredients

1 cup moong dal
1 large chopped onion
2-3 cloves crushed garlic
2 tablespoons ghee
salt to taste

Grind to paste

2-3 red chillies
2.5 cm/1 inch small piece turmeric
1/2 teaspoon cumin seeds
1 small piece tamarind

Method

1. Wash the dal, and then soak it for a few minutes. Drain the water and set aside.
2. Heat the ghee, and fry the garlic for a minute or two. Then add the onions, fry until golden, add the masala paste, and continue to fry until done.

3. Add the dal and fry for two to three minutes. Then add some water and salt, and cook until done.

Mixed Vegetable Stew

Ingredients
1 carrot
1 potato
1 onion
1/2 cauliflower
1/2 cup shelled peas
a handful of beans
1 tablespoon maida
2 tablespoons ghee
1 cup milk
salt to taste

Seasoning
2-3 green chillies
1.3 cm/0.5 inch piece ginger,
   chopped fine
a handful of coriander leaves
2 cloves
2 cardamoms
1.3 cm/0.5 inch stick cinnamon
1/2 teaspoon peppercorns

Method
1. Wash and prepare the vegetables as follows: peel the potato and carrot. String the beans, slice the onions, cut the potatoes into 2.5 cm/1 inch pieces, carrots into rounds, beans into inch long pieces, cauliflower into sprigs, and the ginger into thin slivers. Slit the chillies lengthwise.
2. Heat the ghee, then add the whole spices and fry. When done, add the chilly and ginger, and fry for a minute or two. Add the onions and fry without letting them brown.
3. Add all the vegetables and fry for some time. Then add salt and a little water, cover and cook until nearly done. The vegetables should be soft, but not overcooked.
4. Blend the maida with milk, add the chopped coriander and pour this into the vegetables. Simmer for some time. Serve hot.

Spicy Egg Curry

Ingredients

2 hard-boiled eggs
2 onions
2 tomatoes
4-5 garlic cloves
1.1 cm/0.5 inch piece ginger
2-3 green chillies, slit
a handful coriander
1/2 cup oil
salt to taste

Powdered Masalas

1/2 teaspoon cumin powder
1/2 teaspoon chilly powder
1/2 teaspoon turmeric powder
1/2 teaspoon pepper powder
1 1/2 teaspoon coriander powder

Whole Spices

2 cloves
2 cardamom
2 cinnamon
2 bay leaves

Method

1. Cut the eggs lengthwise, fry in 1 tablespoon of oil to golden brown, remove, and set aside.
2. Grind the garlic, ginger, and one onion to a paste. Chop the other onion, and the tomatoes and coriander leaves.
3. Heat the rest of the oil, add the bay leaf and whole spices and when done, the green chillies.
4. Add the garlic, ginger paste, and fry until dry. Then add the tomatoes and continue frying until they turn soft. Add the powdered masalas and fry. If necessary, sprinkle some water while frying, so that the masalas do not get singed.
5. Add two cups of water, salt, half of the chopped coriander and cook on slow heat until the gravy is thick. Add the eggs and simmer for a couple of minutes.
6. Carefully transfer the curry to a bowl and garnish with the rest of the chopped coriander.

Note

The garlic, ginger, and onion can be minced very fine instead of being ground.

Kela Raita

(Bananas in Seasoned Yoghurt)

Ingredients
2 bananas
1 1/2 cups curds/yoghurt

2 minced green chillies
2 teaspoons finely chopped mint or coriander leaves
salt to taste

1/2 teaspoon chilly powder
1 teaspoon cumin seeds, broiled
    and powdered
a pinch sugar (optional)

Method
1. Beat the curds with water to a smooth consistency. Add the salt, sugar, chilly powder and minced chillies. Cut the bananas into round slices, add to the curds and mix thoroughly. Pour into a glass bowl.
2. Sprinkle the mint or coriander leaves, and powdered cumin. Chill.

China Grass Pudding

Ingredients
500 ml/1 pint milk
3/4 cup sugar
3 tablespoons china grass broken into bits

a few almonds, blanched and
    chopped
3-4 cardamoms powdered
a few drops of almond essence
    (optional)

Method
1. Boil the milk. Add the sugar and stir until all the sugar has dissolved.
2. Add the china grass pieces, and cook, stirring all the while until the china grass dissolves and the milk starts to thicken. When it attains a custard-like consistency, remove from fire, and add the cardamom, essence and half the nuts.
3. Pour into a flat dish and cool. Sprinkle the rest of the nuts all over and refrigerate. Serve chilled.

Ginger-Cinnamon Slices with Cream

Ingredients

2 cups flour	1 teaspoon cinnamon powder
1 cup jaggery	1 teaspoon lemon juice
1/2 cup powdered sugar	2 teaspoons ginger juice
3/4 cup oil	1/4 teaspoon salt
2 eggs	1/2 teaspoon baking soda
1 cup fresh cream	a loaf tin

Method

1. Sift together the flour, soda, salt and cinnamon powder.
2. Separate the egg whites from the yolks, and beat the whites until light. Add the yolks, beat some more, and keep aside.
3. Bring 1 cup of water to a boil. Add the jaggery, and continue to boil until a syrup is obtained. Strain the syrup and pour while still warm into a mixing bowl .
4. Add the powdered sugar, ginger and lemon juices and oil. Beat the mixture slowly at first and then vigorously until well blended. Add the eggs a little at a time, continuing to beat. Now add the sifted flour, beating all the while. About 200-250 strokes should be sufficient.
5. Grease a loaf tin with oil. Pour in the batter and bake at 190°C/375°F for 35-40 minutes.
6. When done (the cake will have left the sides of the tin), switch off the oven and leave the cake in it for a few more minutes. Remove, cool and transfer to a serving plate.

To serve

Cut the loaf into slices. Beat the cream lightly and pour over each slice. Serve chilled.

```
┌─────────────────────────────────────────────────────────────┐
│                    ──── Menu 7 ────                            │
│                                                                │
│   Moong Dal Khichadi (North Indian)   Serve With              │
│   or Venn Pongal (South Indian)       Mixed Vegetable Pakodas │
│   Onion Chutney                       Dessert                 │
│   Carrot Salad                        Coconut Poli            │
│   Tomato Rasam (Optional)                                     │
│   Curds (Yoghurt)                                             │
└─────────────────────────────────────────────────────────────┘
```

Moong Dal Khichadi (Kedgeree)

Ingredients

1 cup rice   1 chopped onion
1/2 cup moong dal   1.3 cm/0.5 inch piece of ginger
2 cardamoms   1 or 2 slit green chillies
2 cloves   3 tablespoons ghee
1 stick cinnamon   1/4 teaspoon turmeric powder
1/4 teaspoon peppercorns   salt to taste
1/4 teaspoon cumin seeds
a few cashew nuts (optional)

Method

1. Wash the rice and dal together and set aside.
2. Heat 2 tablespoons of ghee in a pressure cooker. Add the whole spices and when done, add the slit chillies, chopped onion and ginger. Fry until the onions are light brown in colour.
3. Add the rice and dal, and continue to fry adding the turmeric powder, salt and four cups of water. Then cook using the weight.

To serve

Transfer the khichadi to a bowl. Heat 1 tablespoon ghee, fry the cashew nuts to golden, pour on to the khichadi and mix well. Serve hot.

Venn Pongal
(Khichadi South Indian Style)

Ingredients	Seasoning
1 cup rice	1 teaspoon pepper
1/2 cup moong dal	1 teaspoon cumin seeds
3 tablespoons ghee	1 inch piece ginger
6-8 cashew nuts	2 sprigs curry leaves
salt to taste	

Method

1. Wash the rice and dal together and cook (preferably in a pressure cooker) with 4 1/2 cups of water and salt. When cooked, the mixture must not be dry.
2. Break the cashew nuts into small pieces and cut the ginger into thin slivers.
3. Heat 2 tablespoons of ghee and fry the cashew nuts to a golden colour. Remove. Add the seasonings in the order given and fry for 1 1/2 minutes. Pour this seasoning into the rice-dal mixture and mix thoroughly, adding some of the cashew nuts.
4. Transfer the mixture onto a bowl. Garnish with the rest of the nuts. Serve piping hot with the rest of the ghee.

Onion Chutney

Ingredients

5-6 onions	2-3 tablespoons oil
8-10 green chillies	1/2 teaspoon turmeric powder
(according to taste)	1/2 teaspoon mustard seeds
1 sprig curry leaf	1 teaspoon black gram dal
a large piece of tamarind	1/2 teaspoon chilly powder
a small piece of jaggery	(optional)
salt to taste	1/4 teaspoon asafoetida
	1/4 teaspoon fenugreek seeds

Method

1. Boil the tamarind with some water. When cool, squeeze to extract as much pulp as possible, and set aside.
2. Cut the chillies into 2-3 pieces each. Chop the onions.
3. Heat the oil. Add the asafoetida, fenugreek, mustard, and gram dal. When the dal turns brown, add the green chillies, curry leaf and fry until the chillies turn a little soft.
4. Now add the onions and fry, adding turmeric powder until the onions turn brown.

5. Add the tamarind extract, jaggery, salt, chilly powder and a little water, if too thick. Cook until the oil comes to the surface and the chutney is done. Cool and bottle.

Note

Refrigerated, it will last a week.

Carrot Salad

Ingredients

2 carrots
1 teaspoon chilly powder
1/2 teaspoon turmeric powder
salt to taste
juice of 1 lemon

2 teaspoons oil
1/2 teaspoon mustard seeds
a pinch of asafoetida
1/4 teaspoon fenugreek

Method

1. Wash and dice the carrots.
2. Place the carrot pieces in a bowl, and put the turmeric and chilly powder in the centre.
3. Heat the oil, and fry the asafoetida and fenugreek. Remove from fire and powder.
4. In the same oil, fry the mustard and pour this along with the oil on to the chilly and turmeric powder. Add the salt, lemon juice, asafoetida and fenugreek powder. Mix well.
5. Serve after a couple of hours. Can be stored in a refrigerator for two to three days.

Tomato Rasam

Ingredients

4-5 medium tomatoes
1-2 cloves garlic (optional)
a pinch of sugar
salt to taste
2 teaspoons chopped coriander
1-2 sprigs curry leaves

For the rasam powder

Roast dry and powder:
1 tablespoon coriander seeds
1/2 tablespoon gram dal
1/2 tablespoon toovar dal
1/2 teaspoon pepper
1/4 teaspoon cumin (seeds)

Seasoning

1 teaspoon ghee
1/2 teaspoon mustard seeds
a pinch asafoetida
1-2 red chillies

Method

1. Boil the tomatoes in 2 cups of water. Peel the skin and extract the juice. To this add 2 teaspoons of rasam powder, sugar, salt, crushed garlic, curry leaf, half of the coriander leaves, and enough water to make 4-5 cups in all. Boil for a few minutes.

2. Season the ingredients given in ghee and pour into the hot rasam. Sprinkle the rest of the coriander leaves. Serve hot with rice or as an appetizer.

Note

You may store any remaining rasam powder for future use.

Mixed Vegetable Pakodas

Ingredients

1 small potato
1 small onion
a few sprigs cauliflower
1/2 carrot
a few spinach leaves
a 1/4 head cabbage

Green Masala

3-4 green chillies
1.3 cm/0.5 inch piece ginger
a handful coriander leaves
1-2 sprigs curry leaves
1-2 cloves garlic (optional)

For the batter

1 cup gram flour
2 tablespoons rice flour
salt to taste

oil for frying
water and oil to mix

Dry Masala

1 1/2 teaspoons chilly powder
1/2 teaspoon turmeric powder
1/2 teaspoon crushed coriander seeds
    or 1 teaspoon ajwain

Method

1. Mince the vegetables and the ingredients for the green masala very fine.
2. In a large bowl add the gram flour, rice flour, 4 teaspoons of oil, minced ingredients, dry masala and salt. Mix thoroughly. Add just enough water to make a fairly stiff dough.
3. Break pieces of the dough the size of gooseberries, and drop in hot oil. Fry to a golden brown. Serve hot.

Coconut Poli

(A Sweet Paratha)

For the outer covering

1 cup maida (flour)
1/4 teaspoon salt
1/4 teaspoon turmeric powder
2-1/2 tablespoons oil (for mixing)
ghee for frying

For the filling

1/2 cup gram dal
1 cup grated coconut
1-1 1/2 cups jaggery
3-4 cardamoms
1/2 cup water

Method

1. Knead all the ingredients for the covering (except the ghee) and 1 - 1 1/2 tablespoons of water to a smooth dough. Cover and set aside.
2. Boil the dal and cool. Add the ingredients for the filling, and grind to a smooth paste adding just enough water.
3. Heat 2 tablespoons of ghee, add the ground mixture, and fry over very low heat

until quite dry, stirring all the while. Cool, make lemon-sized balls and keep aside.

4. Make lemon-shaped balls of the dough and with a little oil rubbed on your palms, shape them into a cup. Put some of the filling into the cup and seal it by bringing the edges together at the top. Pat the cup and keep it aside. Use up all the dough and the filling in this manner.

5. Using a little flour or oil, roll out the filled cups into thin rounds (polis), making them as thin as possible.

6. Heat a skillet (tava), and cook the polis on either side, turning over carefully when one side is done. Add some ghee and fry both sides until light brown in colour. Serve hot with ghee or milk.

Note

If you find it difficult to roll the polis very thin with the stuffing inside, then make two very thin polis and spread some of the filling over one up to 1/2 inch from the edge. Carefully place another poli on top. With wet fingers press the two together all around, sealing well.

```
──── Menu 8 ────
```

Spinach Soup With Cream	**Serve With**
Vegetable Casserole	Toasted Bread Slices with
or	Butter
Eggs in White Sauce	Salad with French Dressing
	Dessert
	Caramel Custard or
	Baked Custard

Spinach Soup With Cream

Ingredients

a large bundle of spinach	1 tablespoon flour (maida)
1 medium onion, chopped	2 tablespoons butter
1 potato	salt to taste
0.6 cm/0.25 inch piece ginger, chopped (optional)	

To serve

Fresh cream

Method

1. Wash and chop the potatoes and spinach. Keep separate.
2. Melt the butter on low heat. Fry the onions to a light pink, add the flour and fry for a minute or two.
3. Add the ginger, spinach and potatoes, and fry for a couple of minutes. Add 2 cups of water, some salt and cook, preferably in a pressure cooker.
4. When the mixture is cool, puree in a blender. When about to serve, reheat the soup to boiling point adding some salt (if necessary) and pepper.
5. Beat the cream lightly.
6. Pour into soup bowls, add a dollop of cream and serve immediately.

Vegetable Casserole

Ingredients
2 cups boiled vegetables
(a mixture of potato, cauliflower,
peas, carrots and french beans)
1 to 1 1/2 cups grated cheese
a little extra butter
a greased casserole dish (oven proof)

For the white sauce
2 tablespoons butter
2 tablespoons flour
2 1/2 cups milk
a pinch of grated nutmeg (optional)
salt and pepper to taste

Method
1. Melt the butter in a saucepan on low heat. Add the flour and stir on low heat until slightly fried but not browned.
2. Remove from fire, and add the milk gradually, blending it into the flour to form a smooth paste. Make sure that there are no lumps.
3. Return the saucepan to the fire and cook on low heat stirring all the while until the mixture attains a thick consistency. This is the white sauce.
4. Add salt, pepper, nutmeg, half of the cheese and mix thoroughly. Add the boiled vegetables and mix.
5. Pour the vegetable-sauce mixture into the greased casserole dish. Sprinkle the rest of the cheese on top, dot with butter and bake for 30 minutes at 375°F/190°C or until the top is nicely browned.

Eggs in White Sauce

Ingredients
1/2 cup milk (for step 3)
2 or 3 hard-boiled eggs
finely chopped herbs
(a mixture of parsley, dill weed,
etc. or coriander)
salt and pepper to taste

For the white sauce
2 1/4 cups milk
2 tablespoons flour
2 tablespoons butter
1 tablespoon cheese (optional)
a few peppercorns for garnish
1 medium onion
salt and pepper to taste

Method
1. Hard boil the eggs, shell and cut into two halves lengthwise.
2. Carefully scoop out the yolks and keep the whites aside.
3. Mash the yolks with the milk, salt, pepper and mixed herbs to a smooth paste.
4. Fill the hollows of the eggs with the above mixture, and set aside.
5. Thinly slice the onions. Melt the butter over low heat and fry the onions until light brown. Add the flour and fry until light pink. Prepare the white sauce as in the above recipe, adding the cheese if desired.

6. Pour the white sauce carefully into the oven proof dish. Arrange the eggs in a circle in the white sauce. Garnish the eggs with whole peppers.
7. Keep the dish warm in the oven until ready to serve.

Salad with French Dressing

Ingredients
- 1 carrot
- 2 tomatoes
- 1/4 cucumber
- a few lettuce leaves (optional)

French Dressing
- juice of 1 lemon
- 3 teaspoons olive oil
- salt, pepper and sugar to taste
- 1 teaspoon white vinegar (optional)
- mustard to taste (optional)
- chopped herbs to taste (optional)

Method
1. Wash, scrape and cut the vegetables into the desired shape. Keep separate, chilled.
2. Mix thoroughly the ingredients for the dressing and chill. Pour over the salad just before serving.

Note
If you are adding white vinegar, reduce the lemon juice accordingly.

Caramel Custard

For the custard
- 2 cups milk
- 2 eggs
- 2 tablespoons sugar
- 1/4 teaspoon vanilla essence

For the caramel
- 3 tablespoons sugar
- 1/2 cup water
- a deep mould for steaming

Method for the caramel

1. Melt the sugar on low heat until it turns a deep brown. Remove from fire, add the water carefully, then put back on fire and cook on slow heat until a thick honey-like syrup is obtained. This is the caramel.
2. While still hot, pour the caramel into the mould (rinsed in cold water) and gradually turn the mould so that the sides also get coated with the caramel. Leave aside.

For the custard

1. Beat the eggs with the sugar thoroughly.
2. Boil the milk. While still boiling, pour into the egg-sugar mixture and beat vigorously until well blended. There should be no lumps.
3. Add the essence, beat once again and pour into the mould.
4. Cover the mould with a piece of aluminium foil. Bring down the foil on all sides and tie at the rim of the mould with a piece of string.
5. Steam cook the custard on very low heat for 30-45 minutes. (A fine needle pierced through should come out clean). Remove the foil. Cool, and refrigerate until ready to serve.
6. Just before serving, cover the mouth of the mould with a plate. Quickly turn the mould over on to the plate and remove the mould. Serve immediately.

Note

If you have no aluminium foil, cut a thick brown paper into a circle 5 cm (2 inches) larger than the mould. Grease well on both sides with some butter or refined oil.

Baked Custard

Ingredients

4 slices bread	1/4 cup red jam or jelly
2 tablespoons butter	2 tablespoons custard powder
1/4 cup sugar	1/4 teaspoon vanilla essence
2 cups milk	1 tablespoon chopped nuts

Method

1. Remove the crusts from the bread, cut into fours, and shallow fry in butter to golden. Cool. Spread a little jam or jelly on each alternate square, and sandwich two squares together (one plain, one with the jam).
2. Grease a flat pie dish with butter, and spread the sandwich squares covering the entire bottom of the dish. Sprinkle half of the nuts over the surface.
3. Mix the custard powder with some of the cold milk to form a smooth paste. Set aside.
4. Boil the rest of the milk with sugar until the sugar has dissolved and the milk is quite thick.
5. Add the custard paste, and stir over low heat until a thick consistency is formed. Add the essence and stir.
6. Pour this over the bread slices, sprinkle the rest of the nuts, and keep aside for a few minutes.
7. Bake in a moderate oven for 20-30 minutes.

Note

If a cold pudding is desired, cover the custard with a foil or plate and leave in the refrigerator to set.

FAMILY MEALS

FAMILY MEALS

Menu 1

Moong, Masoor or Egg Pulav	**Serve with**
Sindhi Besan	Carrot Pickle
Mughlai Potatoes	Salad
Chapatis (optional)	**Dessert**
Curds (Yoghurt)	Fruit Salad with Jelly and Cream

Menu 2

Methi (Fenugreek) Roti	**Serve with**
Rice (optional)	Stuffed Tomatoes with
Rajma Urad Dal Rasedar	a. Paneer
Aloo Gobi	b. Eggs
Onion Raita	North Indian Lime Pickle
	Dessert
	Phirni

Menu 3

Vegetable Masala Rice	**Serve with**
Tomato Pachadi (Raita)	Capsicum Bhajjis or
Rice - Rasam	Fried Appalams (Papadams)
Beans or Cabbage Curry	Mango Thokku
Curds (Yoghurt)	**Dessert**
	Semia Payasam

Menu 4

Dal-stuffed Puris	**Serve with**
Cauliflower Peas Kheema	Capsicum Onion Chutney
Yellow Rice with Cheese or Eggs	Dahi Aloo
Garnished Salad	**Dessert**
	Orange Trifle or Orange Jelly

FAMILY MEALS

Menu 5

Rice or Chapatis
Tuvar Dal
Sindhi Palak
Aloo Posto

Serve with
Cabbage-Groundnut Salad
Baigan Raita
Garlic Chutney (optional)
Radish Pickle
Dessert
Pantua

Menu 6

Sprouted Bean Pulav
Tomato-Coconut Kurma
Masala Brinjal (Eggplant)
or Drumstick Fry
Chapatis

Serve with
Capsicum Raita
Mixed Vegetable Pickle
Dessert
Biscuit Pudding or Biscuit Fudge

Menu 7

Rice - Morkuzhambu
Cabbage or Beans Paruppu Curry
or Colocasia Roast
Mysore Rasam
Curds (Yoghurt)

Serve with
Banana Chips
Bitter Gourd Chutney (Gojju)
Dessert
Coconut Rice Payasam

Menu 8

Mixed Vegetable Soup
served with Dumplings (optional)
Capsicum Noodles
Potato Eggs

Serve with
Fresh Bread Rolls and Butter
Cucumber Cups
Dessert
Hot Chocolate Pudding with Sauce
Chocolate Blancmange

```
     ——— Menu 1 ———
Moong, Masoor or Egg Pulav   Serve with
Sindhi Besan                 Carrot Pickle
Mughlai Potatoes             Salad
Chapatis (optional)          Dessert
Curds (Yoghurt)              Fruit Salad
                             with Jelly and Cream
```

Moong or Masoor Pulav

Ingredients

2 cups rice
1 cup dal
6+1 tablespoons ghee
1/2 teaspoon chilly powder
1/2 teaspoon turmeric powder
2 medium onions, sliced
1 cup shelled peas (optional)
salt to taste

Seasoning

6 peppercorns
2 large cardamoms
2 cloves
2 bay leaves

For the garnish

1 tablespoon chopped coriander
8 cashew nuts (optional)

For the masala liquid

4 tablespoons grated coconut
1 large onion
1.3 cm/0.5 inch piece ginger
4 garlic cloves
3 green chillies
a handful of coriander leaves
1 teaspoon aniseeds
1 teaspoon khus-khus
2 cloves
2 small cardamoms
1.3 cm/0.5 inch cinnamon stick

For the masala paste (alt.)

1 tablespoon grated coconut
Rest same as above

Method

1. Wash the dal and rice together, and drain on a cloth.
2. To prepare the masala liquid, grind all the ingredients, add two cups of boiling water, strain and set aside the extract. Repeat the process twice with 2 cups of boiling water each time until 6 cups of masala liquid in all are obtained. Alternately, grind the masala with only 1 tablespoon of coconut to a very fine paste. Set aside until required.

3. Heat 4 tablespoons of ghee in a pressure cooker. Add the spices and bay leaf, and when done, add the onions. Fry till crisp. Remove only the onions from the cooker and set aside.

4. Add 2 tablespoons of ghee, then the rice and dal, and fry for a while, adding the turmeric and chilly powders. Fry for half a minute. Add the masala liquid, peas and salt. Cover the cooker, and cook on low heat without using the weight until done.

Alternate Method

Fry the masala paste along with the turmeric and chilly powders in two tablespoons of ghee on low heat till masala is done. Add the rice and dal, and fry for a few minutes. Add the peas, salt and 6 cups of boiling water. Cover the cooker and cook on low heat till done.

To serve

Remove the pulav from the cooker on to a rice dish. Smoothen the surface. Heat 1 tablespoon of ghee, fry the cashew nuts and sprinkle over the pulav. Garnish with fried onions and chopped coriander.

Egg Pulav

Ingredients
2 cups rice
4 eggs
4 tablespoons ghee
1/4 teaspoon turmeric
1 chopped onion
2 green chillies, slit
1 tablespoon lemon juice
salt to taste

Grind to paste
1 large onion
2.5 cm/1 inch piece ginger
5 garlic cloves
a handful of coriander leaves
a few leaves of mint
2 green chillies

Seasoning
3 cardamoms
3 cloves
2 small pieces cinnamon
chopped coriander for garnish

Method

1. Boil the rice with a little salt, 1/2 tablespoon of ghee and a pinch of turmeric. Take care that the rice is not overcooked, and the grains are separate. Cool on a plate.

2. Heat the ghee and fry the whole spices. Then add the slit chillies and chopped onions, and fry until the onions are browned. Add the ground masala and a pinch of turmeric powder. Fry till the masalas are done.
3. Beat the eggs with a pinch of salt, pour into the cooked masala, and stir on low heat. Add the rice carefully, mixing in the masala and eggs. Remove and add lemon juice.
4. Transfer on to a plate, and garnish with chopped coriander.

Alternate Method

Prepare as before till the masalas are cooked. Add the rice, mixing it in carefully. Transfer on to a serving plate. Hard boil the eggs, cut lengthwise, and arrange on the rice. Sprinkle chopped coriander and lemon juice before serving.

Sindhi Besan

(A Mixed Vegetable Curry from Sind)

Ingredients

2 potatoes	1 teaspoon mustard seeds
2 brinjals (eggplant)	1 teaspoon cumin seeds
2 drumsticks	1/4 teaspoon fenugreek seeds
6 pieces bhindi (okra)	1/2 teaspoon turmeric powder
1 small piece suran (yam)	1/2 teaspoon chilly powder
3 green chillies	1 small piece tamarind
2 sprigs curry leaves	1 small piece jaggery
2 teaspoons chopped coriander	3 tablespoons gram flour
salt to taste	4 tablespoons oil

Method

1. Wash and cut the vegetables into pieces 4 cm (1.5 inches) long. Chop the chillies.
2. Heat the oil and add the mustard, cumin seeds and fenugreek. When done, add the green chillies, curry leaf, and fry for half a minute. Add the vegetables, and fry for a while. Remove the bhindi and set aside. Add 1 cup of water, and cook until the vegetables are slightly soft.
3. Mix the gram flour with 3 cups of water to a smooth consistency. To this add the turmeric, chilly powder, and salt. Add this mixture to the vegetables. Keep cooking on slow heat till they are nearly done, stirring occasionally.
4. Boil the tamarind in water, and squeeze to extract the pulp. Add this along with the jaggery and the bhindi, and cook for some more time. Remove from fire, and add the chopped coriander.

Mughlai Potatoes

Ingredients
4 large potatoes
3 chopped onions
a handful of coriander leaves
4 green chillies, slit
1 cup curds (yoghurt)
1 teaspoon cumin seeds
1/2 teaspoon chilly powder
1/4 teaspoon turmeric powder
2 teaspoons chopped coriander
6 tablespoons oil or ghee
1/2 teaspoon garam masala (optional)
salt to taste

Grind to paste
2.5 cm/1 inch piece ginger
3 cloves garlic
6-8 cashew nuts

Method
1. Boil the potatoes and cut into thick slices.
2. Heat half of the oil, and fry the potatoes until light brown in colour. Remove from vessel and set aside.
3. Heat the rest of the oil, and add the cumin seeds. When done, add the chillies and onions, and fry till they are browned.
4. Add the masala paste, turmeric, chilly, and garam masala powders, and fry till the oil surfaces.
5. Beat the curds, add the salt and some of the chopped coriander, and pour this into the masala. Add the potatoes and simmer gently till well blended. Serve garnished with the rest of the chopped coriander.

Chapatis

Ingredients
3 teaspoons oil for mixing
3 cups wheat flour
salt to taste
ghee for smearing

Method
1. Mix all the ingredients except the ghee with some water to form a soft, pliable dough. Cover and set aside for at least half an hour before making the rotis.
2. Divide the dough into lemon-sized balls. Flatten on the palm of your hand, and roll into thin rounds, dusting with flour as needed.
3. Heat a tava (skillet), place the roti on it and cook till both sides are done. After the roti is cooked place it over direct heat allowing it to puff up. Remove from fire, smear some ghee on one side and serve immediately.

Salad

Ingredients
1 apple
2 slices pineapple
1 cucumber
2 large tomatoes
a piece of cabbage
1 carrot
50 gm/1.75 oz. cheese
a handful of assorted nuts

Dressing
1 lemon
salt to taste
a pinch of sugar

Method
1. Grate the cabbage and carrot. Leave in cold water for a few minutes.
2. Cut the apple, pineapple, cucumber, tomatoes and cheese into cubes, and mix.
3. Extract juice from the lemon, and mix along with salt and sugar. Chill.
4. When ready to serve, drain the water from the carrot and cabbage, and spread over salad plate. Place the rest of the fruits and vegetables in the centre. Pour the dressing, sprinkle chopped nuts and serve chilled.

Fruit Salad with Jelly and Cream

Ingredients

2 bananas

2 apples

2 oranges

1 musambi (sweet lime)

1 tablespoon lemon juice

3/4 cup sugar

a pinch of yellow colour

1 packet red jelly (jello)

1 cup cream

2 tablespoons chopped dry fruits

1/2 teaspoon vanilla essence

Method

1. Set the jelly according to the instructions on the packet. Refrigerate until ready to serve.
2. Peel and cut the fruits into small cubes. Add the lemon juice, mix well and set aside.
3. Boil the sugar with one cup of water until a thick syrup is formed. Cool. Add the essence and colour, and mix in the fruits and nuts. Refrigerate.

To serve

Beat the cream until smooth and set aside. Remove the jelly from the refrigerator, and use a cold knife to cut it into irregular shapes. Pour the fruit salad into a glass serving bowl and cover with jelly pieces. Pour the cream and serve immediately.

—— *Menu 2* ——

Methi (Fenugreek) Roti	**Serve with**
Rice (optional)	Stuffed Tomatoes with
Rajma Urad Dal Rasedar	a. Paneer
Aloo Gobi	b. Eggs
Onion Raita	North Indian Lime Pickle
	Dessert
	Phirni

Methi Roti
(Fenugreek Bread)

Ingredients

1 1/2 cups methi leaves, chopped fine	1/2 teaspoon turmeric powder
3 teaspoons oil for mixing	1/2 teaspoon chilly powder
3 cups wheat flour	salt to taste
	ghee for frying

Method

1. Mix all the ingredients except the ghee with some water to form a soft, pliable dough. Cover and set aside for at least an hour before making the rotis.
2. Divide the dough into lemon-sized balls. Flatten on the palm of your hand, and roll into thin rounds, dusting with flour as needed.
3. Heat a tava (skillet), place the roti on it and fry till both sides are done. Now pour a teaspoon of ghee all around the roti, and fry once again on both sides till slightly browned.

Note

Alternately, after the roti is cooked place it over direct heat allowing it to puff up. Remove from fire, smear some ghee on one side and serve immediately.
Cook two cups of plain white rice, preferably in a rice cooker.

Rajma Urad Dal Rasedar
(Red Kidney Beans and Lentils in Gravy)

Ingredients

1 cup rajma (kidney beans)

1/2 cup urad dal

1 large onion, chopped

1 chopped tomato

4 tablespoons ghee

1 tablespoon butter or cream

salt to taste

2.5 cm/1 inch piece ginger, minced

4 garlic cloves, minced

1 teaspoon chilly powder

2 teaspoons coriander powder

1 teaspoon cumin powder

1/2 teaspoon turmeric powder

1/2 teaspoon garam masala

1/2 teaspoon pepper, optional

2 bay leaves

Method

1. Soak the rajma overnight, urad dal for 3-4 hours. Wash the dals together and set aside.
2. Heat 1 tablespoon of ghee, add the minced ginger and garlic, and fry. Add the onions and continue to fry until they are browned.
3. Add the dals, turmeric powder, enough water and cook until soft, preferably in a pressure cooker. When cool, mash thoroughly and set aside.
4. Heat the rest of the ghee. Add the bay leaves, chopped tomatoes and fry until the tomatoes turn soft. Add the powdered masalas and salt, and fry for a couple of minutes.
5. Pour the mashed dal into the mixture and simmer until blended.

To serve

Transfer the dal into a deep bowl. Add fresh butter or cream, and sprinkle some pepper on top if desired.

Aloo Gobi
(Potato and Cauliflower Curry)

Ingredients
- 5 medium potatoes
- 1 large cauliflower
- 1 teaspoon chilly powder
- 4 teaspoons cumin powder
- 4 teaspoons coriander powder
- 1/2 teaspoon turmeric powder
- 6 tablespoons oil
- salt to taste

Chop very fine
- a handful of coriander leaves
- 2 onions
- 2 tomatoes
- 3 green chillies
- 2.5 cm/1 inch piece ginger
- 4 garlic cloves

Method
1. Peel and cut the potatoes into large pieces. Break the cauliflower into florets.
2. Heat the oil. Add the chillies, ginger and garlic, and fry for a minute. Add the onions and turmeric powder and fry until brown. Add the tomatoes and continue to fry until they turn soft.
3. Add all the powdered masalas, and fry. Then add the vegetables and stir fry until they turn soft. Add the salt, sprinkle some water, cover and cook on low heat for a while.
4. Garnish with coriander leaves. Serve hot.

Onion Raita
(Onions in Seasoned Yoghurt)

Ingredients
- 1 large onion, minced
- 2 green chillies, minced
- a few sprigs fresh coriander, minced
- a few sprigs chopped mint, minced
- 2 cups curds (yoghurt)
- 1 teaspoon cumin seeds
- 1/2 teaspoon chilly powder
- salt to taste
- 1/4 teaspoon pepper (optional)

Method
1. Broil the cumin seeds until they turn dark, and powder.
2. Beat the curds till smooth. Add the salt, chilly powder, and the minced ingredients. Mix well and pour into a bowl.
3. Sprinkle the cumin powder, and some pepper if desired. Serve chilled.

Stuffed Tomatoes

Ingredients

8 tomatoes	1 large onion
1 cup paneer (Indian cream cheese)	2 green chillies
1 cup boiled peas	a handful of coriander leaves
2 tablespoons ghee	1/2 teaspoon turmeric powder
2 tablespoons melted butter	1/2 teaspoon chilly powder
oil for frying (optional)	bread crumbs
a shallow oven proof dish	salt to taste

For the sauce

1 finely chopped onion	1 tablespoon oil
1/2 teaspoon chilly powder	1/2 tablespoon flour (maida)
1/2 teaspoon sugar	salt to taste

Method

1. Select firm, red, ripe tomatoes. Cut out the tops of the tomatoes and scoop out as much pulp as possible. Smear the insides with some salt and set aside, keeping the pulp for the sauce.

2. Chop the onions, green chillies and coriander very fine. Heat the ghee, add the chopped onions and chillies, and fry till the onions are lightly browned. Add the turmeric and chilly powder, and fry for a while. Add the peas and paneer, and cook till dry. Add the chopped coriander and mix well. Remove from fire, and allow to cool.

3. Just before filling the tomatoes, invert them to remove any juice still left. Fill with the paneer-peas mixture and press a few bread crumbs on this. Put a little butter on top of the crumbs.

4. Smear each tomato on the outside with some melted butter, and set it in a greased oven-proof dish. Place the dish in the oven at 150°C (300°F) until the tomatoes turn soft.

Note

As an alternative to baking, the tomatoes may be shallow fried, preferably in a non-stick pan. Pour some oil in the pan, put the tomatoes with the cut side down, reduce the heat, cover with a tight fitting lid, and cook for 2-3 minutes. Then remove the cover, and baste some oil on the tomatoes. When browned, turn over carefully, and fry the other side until the tomatoes are done.

For the sauce

1. In 1 tablespoon of oil, fry the onions till brown. Add the tomato pulp (which was set aside) along with seasonings.

2. Mix the flour with some water, add to the tomato pulp and simmer until a sauce-like consistency is obtained. If too thick, add some water while boiling.

For the paneer

Boil 1.5 litres (1.6 quarts) of milk and while still on fire, add some lemon juice gradually until the milk starts to curdle. Boil for another minute and remove from fire. When cool, strain through a muslin cloth. Take out the paneer, knead into a smooth dough, wrap in a cloth, place a heavy flat weight on top and leave for an hour. When the paneer block has flattened out, remove the weight and crumble the paneer. Set aside.

175 gm (6 oz.) of paneer may be purchased if you do not have the time to make it. Ricotta cheese is a suitable substitute.

To serve

Remove the baked tomatoes from the oven, pour the hot sauce, and serve at once. (The sauce can be served separately, if desired.)

Stuffed Tomatoes (With Eggs)

Ingredients

8 tomatoes	1 large onion
4 eggs	2 chopped green chillies
1/2 cup grated cheese	a handful of coriander
1/2 cup boiled peas	1/2 teaspoon turmeric powder
2 tablespoons melted butter	1/2 teaspoon chilly powder
oil for frying (optional)	salt and pepper to taste
a shallow oven proof dish	

Method

1. Heat the butter or oil. Add the chopped chillies and onion, and fry till brown.
2. Beat the eggs with turmeric powder. Add the salt, pour into the onions and fry until the eggs are cooked, adding the chilly and pepper powders.
3. Add the peas and cook until all the water has evaporated and the mixture is quite dry.
4. Remove from fire. Add the cheese and chopped coriander, mix and allow to cool. Stuff this mixture into the tomatoes and follow the steps from the previous recipe for the rest.

To serve

Remove the tomato dish from the oven, pour the warm sauce carefully onto the tomatoes and serve at once.

Phirni
(Rice Blancmange)

Ingredients
    4 cups milk
    1 cup sugar
    1 tablespoon rice flour
    1/2 teaspoon rose essence
    6 pistachio nuts
    6 almonds
    a few rose petals for garnishing

Method
1. Blanch the almonds. Chop or cut into thin slivers along with the pistachio. Keep aside.
2. Make a smooth paste of the rice flour with some milk. Add to the rest of the milk. Cook over a slow fire stirring constantly. See that no lumps are formed while cooking.
3. Add the sugar and cook until the sugar has dissolved and the mixture starts thickening. When quite thick and creamy (the consistency of a custard) remove from fire, add the essence and half the chopped nuts.
4. Pour into a transparent glass bowl, garnish with rose petals and the rest of the nuts. Serve chilled.

---- ℳenu 3 ----

Vegetable Masala Rice
Tomato Pachadi (Raita)
Rice - Rasam
Beans or Cabbage Curry
Curds (Yoghurt)

Serve with
Capsicum Bhajjis or
Fried Appalams (Papadams)
Mango Thokku
Dessert
Semia Payasam

Vegetable Masala Rice

Three cups of rice are sufficient for both rice dishes in this menu.

Ingredients
1 1/2 cups rice
3 tablespoons oil
1 small lump of tamarind
1 brinjal (eggplant)
1 potato
1 capsicum (green pepper)
1 tomato
1 carrot
a few beans
1/2 cup shelled peas
salt to taste
1/2 cup copra gratings
2 sprigs curry leaves
1/2 teaspoon turmeric powder

Fry in 2 teaspoons oil and powder
1 tablespoon Bengal gram dal
1/2 tablespoon black gram dal
1 1/2 tablespoons coriander seeds
3 dried red chillies
1/4 teaspoon asafoetida
1 small cinnamon stick (optional)
3 cloves (optional)

Seasonings
1 teaspoon mustard seeds
2 teaspoons Bengal gram dal
2 teaspoons black gram dal

Method
1. Cook the rice, and cool on a plate, sprinkling a little oil. Cook the peas and keep separately. Boil the tamarind in water and squeeze to extract the pulp.
2. Cut the vegetables into pieces 3 cm (1 1/2 inches) long. Prepare the masala as indicated above, and add some copra gratings while powdering.
3. Heat the oil, and add the mustard, dal and curry leaves. When the seeds have popped, add first the potato, then the carrots and beans. Fry for a minute or two, and then add the capsicum and brinjals, and fry for a few minutes before adding the tomatoes. Fry until the vegetables turn soft.
4. Add the turmeric, salt and approximately half a cup of water. Cover and cook until done.

5. Remove the lid, add the peas and the tamarind extract, and cook until the water has evaporated. Add the masala powder, mix well, and remove from fire.
6. Pour this mixture on to the rice and mix well. Add a little oil if the rice is dry.
7. Add the chopped coriander and the rest of the copra gratings, and mix well. Serve hot.

Tomato Pachadi
(Tomatoes in Seasoned Yoghurt)

Ingredients

3 medium tomatoes
1 1/2 cups curds (yoghurt)
1 teaspoon chopped coriander
salt to taste

Seasoning

2 teaspoons oil
1/2 teaspoon mustard seeds
2 sprigs curry leaves
2 green chillies

Method

1. Cut the tomatoes into small pieces. Chop the chillies into 2-3 pieces each.
2. Beat the curds and season with the given ingredients. Add the salt and tomatoes. Garnish with chopped coriander before serving.

Paruppu Rasam
(Lentil-based Mulligatawny Soup)

Ingredients

1 cup tuvar dal
1 lemon-sized ball tamarind
1/2 teaspoon turmeric powder
a pinch of asafoetida
1 medium tomato (optional)
2 sprigs curry leaves
a few coriander leaves
salt to taste

For the rasam powder

1 teaspoon oil
1 tablespoon coriander seeds
1 teaspoon cumin seeds
1/4 teaspoon fenugreek seeds
1/2 teaspoon mustard seeds
1 teaspoon pepper
1 teaspoon tuvar dal
1 teaspoon gram dal
1 sprig curry leaf
2-3 red chillies
1/4 teaspoon asafoetida

For the seasoning

1 teaspoon ghee
1 teaspoon mustard seeds

Method

1. Fry the red chillies and the asafoetida in oil, and dry roast the other ingredients for the powder. Mix, powder and store in an air-tight bottle. If stored properly, this powder will last up to 6 months.

2. Boil the dal with the turmeric. When done, add 2 cups of water, and churn to make smooth. Set aside. Chop the tomatoes, and set aside.
3. Add a little boiling water to the tamarind and squeeze to extract the pulp. Add 1-1 1/2 cups of water. To this add 3 teaspoons of rasam powder, turmeric powder, salt, curry leaf, asafoetida and tomato. Cook this on a slow flame until the smell of raw tamarind disappears. By this time more than half the water will have evaporated.
4. Now add the dal water, coriander leaves and boil till it simmers. Remove from fire. Season the mustard in ghee, and add it to the rasam. Serve hot with rice.

Beans or Cabbage Curry

Ingredients
500 gm/1.1 lb beans
or 1 medium cabbage
or a mixture of both
1 1/2 tablespoons grated coconut
a pinch of turmeric powder
salt to taste

Seasoning
1 sprig curry leaf
2 teaspoons oil
1 teaspoon mustard
1 teaspoon black gram dal

Method
1. Wash and cut the vegetables into small pieces. Boil with just sufficient water, salt and turmeric powder, or steam cook in a pressure cooker with very little water, without using the weight.
2. Heat the oil, and add the seasonings. When done add the cooked vegetable, and fry for a while. Add the grated coconut, mix well, and remove from fire.

Capsicum Bhajjis
(Green Pepper Fritters)

Ingredients
4 large capsicums (green peppers)
1/2 teaspoon turmeric powder
1 cup gram flour (besan)
1 teaspoon chilly powder
1/2 cup rice flour

oil for frying
salt to taste
a pinch of ajwain
water to mix
a pinch of baking soda (optional)

Method
1. Cut the capsicums (removing the seeds) into thin circular slices.

2. Mix the gram flour, turmeric, chilly powder, salt, rice flour, ajwain, baking soda and 2 teaspoons of oil. Add a little water and beat thoroughly.
3. Add some more water and mix well to form a thick batter.
4. Dip the capsicum slices in batter, and deep fry to a golden colour. Remove, and serve immediately.

Semia Payasam
(Vermicelli Pudding)

Ingredients

1 litre/1 quart milk

1 cup sugar

1 cup semia (vermicelli), broken

2 tablespoons ghee

2 small cardamoms, powdered

6 cashew nuts, broken into pieces

2 tablespoon raisins

a few drops of rose essence

Method

1. Fry the cashew nuts and raisins in ghee. Remove from pan and set aside. Break the semia into pieces.
2. Fry the semia in the same ghee on low heat till light brown in colour. Add the milk, half a cup of water, and cook until the semia is done.
3. Now add the sugar and continue cooking on slow heat until the payasam is quite thick. Remove from fire.
4. Add the cardamom powder, nuts, raisins and essence.
5. Serve hot or cold.

Fried Appalams (Papadams)

These are best purchased from a store, and fried according to the instructions on the packet.

Mango Thokku

The recipe for this pickle is in the chapter on Pickles and Chutneys (Part 6).

---- *Menu 4* ----

Dal-stuffed Puris	**Serve with**
Cauliflower Peas Kheema	Capsicum Onion Chutney
Yellow Rice with Cheese or Eggs	Dahi Aloo
Garnished Salad	**Dessert**
	Orange Trifle or Orange Jelly

Dal-stuffed Puris

Ingredients

1 cup tuvar dal or Bengal gram dal
2 tablespoons oil
1/4 teaspoon turmeric powder
3 cups wheat flour
1/2 teaspoon chilly powder
1/2 teaspoon garam masala
oil for frying

Grind to a fine paste

4 green chillies
1.3 cm (1/2 inch) piece ginger
3 garlic cloves
a handful of coriander leaves
1 medium onion
salt to taste

Method

1. Boil the dal with turmeric powder and sufficient water so that when cooked it is dry but not overdone. Mash it while still hot.
2. Heat 1 tablespoon of oil and fry the ground paste until it is done. Add the chilly and garam masala powders, mashed dal and salt, and continue to fry until the mixture is quite dry. Cool.
3. Knead the flour with 1 tablespoon of oil, a little salt and enough water to form a stiff dough.
4. Take a small portion of the dough, and make a circle with your hand to form a cup. Put a little of the mixture inside, cover by bringing the edges together and closing the cup. Pat into shape and roll very carefully into a puri.
   Alternately, make two puris of the same size. Put a little of the mixture in the centre of one, and cover with the other. Seal the edges with wet fingers.
5. Fry the puris in hot oil, carefully turning over when one side is done. Drain on absorbent paper before serving.

Note

If desired, puris may be substituted by parathas.

Cauliflower Peas Kheema
(Cauliflower and Peas in a Spicy Gravy)

Ingredients

1 large cauliflower	6 tablespoons oil
1 1/2 cups shelled peas	1 teaspoon chilly powder
4 tomatoes	1 teaspoon garam masala powder
3 large onions	1/2 teaspoon turmeric powder
3 green chillies	salt to taste
1 inch piece ginger	**Seasoning**
5 garlic cloves	1/4 teaspoon fenugreek seeds
a handful of fresh coriander	1 teaspoon cumin seeds
3/4 cup curds (yoghurt) or cream	

Method

1. Chop the cauliflower, tomatoes, green chillies, coriander and 1 onion. Boil the peas with some salt and set aside.
2. Grind 2 onions, garlic and ginger to a paste.
3. Heat half of the oil in a kadai (wok), add the chopped cauliflower, and fry to a golden colour, stirring constantly. Remove from the kadai, and set aside.
4. Pour the rest of the oil into the kadai along with the fenugreek and cumin seeds and fry. When done, add the chopped onions and green chillies, and fry for a minute. Add the ground paste, garam masala, turmeric and chilly powders, and fry until the oil surfaces.
5. Add the chopped tomatoes and fry until soft. Add 1 1/2 cups of water, and simmer until the gravy is formed. Now add the fried cauliflower, cooked peas, half of the chopped coriander and some more water if too thick. Cook for another 3-4 minutes.
6. If curds are used, beat, then add to the curry, simmer just once, and remove. Serve garnished with the rest of the chopped coriander. Alternatively, if you use cream, pour the curry into a serving bowl, then pour the cream on top and garnish with chopped coriander.

Yellow Rice with Cheese or Eggs

As a variation from the usual pulavs, this rice has cheese or eggs included in the preparation. However, it can also be made plain. It is usually served with a garnished salad.

Yellow Rice with Cheese

Ingredients

2 cups rice
2 medium onions
5 green chillies
a handful of fresh coriander
1.3 cm/0.5 inch piece ginger
4 garlic cloves
1 cup shelled peas
salt to taste

1/2 teaspoon turmeric powder
1/2 teaspoon chilly powder
1/2 teaspoon pepper powder
1 teaspoon cumin seeds
2 cloves
2 cardamoms
2 bay leaves
5 tablespoons ghee
3/4 cup grated cheese

For the garnish

2 tomatoes
1/2 medium cucumber
1 lemon
1/4 teaspoon pepper (optional)

Method

1. Wash the rice and allow it to dry on a clean muslin cloth.
2. Grind one onion, ginger, garlic and half the chillies to a paste.
3. Chop the other onion and the coriander leaves. Slit the rest of the chillies.
4. Heat the ghee in a pressure cooker. Add the cloves, bay leaves, cardamom and cumin seeds, and fry for a minute. Add the green chillies and chopped onions. Fry until the onions turn brown. Remove only the onions from the cooker. Add the ground paste, turmeric and chilly powders and fry until done. Now add rice and fry for 2-3 minutes.
5. Add the peas, half of the chopped coriander, salt and 3 cups of water. Cover the cooker and cook without using the weight. This dish may also be made in an electric rice cooker.

To serve

Mix 3/4 of the grated cheese and fried onions with the pulav, and transfer it to a rice platter. Garnish with sliced tomatoes, cucumbers, the rest of the cheese, and chopped coriander. Sprinkle pepper if desired.

Yellow Rice with Eggs

The methods and ingredients used are exactly the same as above, except that half the cheese is replaced by two to three eggs. Also, the tomato and cucumber garnish is to be omitted; instead, these salad vegetables are served separately.

Method 1

Poach the eggs until they are half-done, and carefully place over the rice in an oven-proof dish. Sprinkle the cheese and coriander, and bake in a moderate oven (175°C/ 350°F) until the eggs are set. Serve immediately.

Method 2

1. Beat the eggs, and add salt, pepper and one chopped onion.
2. Pour a little oil into a frying pan (preferably non-stick), and pour the egg batter. Tilt the pan so that the eggs spread evenly. Cover and cook on low heat until the eggs are done.
3. Transfer the eggs on to a plate, and cut into small pieces. Mix with the rice, cheese and chopped coriander. Serve hot.

Garnished Salad

This is described under Yellow Rice.

Capsicum Onion Chutney

Ingredients

500 gm/1.1 lb capsicum (green peppers)
250 gm/9 oz. onions
1 small piece tamarind
1 small piece jaggery
2 sprigs curry leaves
4 garlic cloves
salt to taste

2 teaspoons chilly powder
1/4 teaspoon turmeric powder
4 tablespoons oil

Broil and grind to paste

1 1/2 tablespoons sesame seeds
1 tablespoon coriander seeds
1 teaspoon cumin seeds
1 tablespoon copra gratings

Method

1. Chop the onion and garlic. Cut the capsicums lengthwise. Boil the tamarind in a little water, and squeeze to extract the pulp.
2. Heat the oil, add the curry leaves, onion and garlic, and fry until browned. Add

the ground paste and fry, adding the chilly and turmeric powders till the masala is done. Add the capsicums and fry until it turns soft.

3. Now add the tamarind extract, jaggery and salt. Cover the vessel and cook on low heat till a chutney consistency is obtained. Remove, cool and bottle.

Note

This chutney can be stored in a refrigerator for a week.

Dahi Aloo
(Curried Potatoes in a Yoghurt Sauce)

Ingredients	Chop very fine
250 gm/ 9 oz. small potatoes	1 large onion
2 cups curds (yoghurt)	2 green chillies
1/2 teaspoon chilly powder	1 or 2 garlic cloves (optional)
1/2 teaspoon turmeric powder	a small piece of ginger
1/2 teaspoon pepper	a handful of coriander leaves
1/2 teaspoon garam masala	
salt to taste	
4 tablespoons oil	

Method

1. Boil the potatoes in water. Drain the water, allow to cool, and then peel. If large potatoes are used, cut into small pieces.
2. Heat half of the oil in a kadai (wok). Fry the potatoes to a golden brown, sprinkling a little salt. Remove and set aside to cool.
3. Pour the rest of the oil into the kadai, and fry the chopped ingredients (except the coriander) until the onions are browned. Add all the masala powders except the pepper. Fry until done, remove the kadai from the heat, and allow to cool.
4. Add half of the chopped coriander, potatoes and some salt, if necessary. Mix well. Beat the curds and add to mixture.
5. Pour the mixture into a deep bowl, and garnish with the rest of the coriander. Sprinkle the pepper. Serve chilled, if desired.

Orange Trifle

Ingredients

1 two-egg sponge cake	1 tablespoon chopped walnuts
4 cups milk	1 tablespoon slivered almonds
3 tablespoons custard powder	1 tablespoon raisins
2 + 1 tablespoons sugar	1 teaspoon orange essence
3 medium oranges	1 medium-sized pudding bowl

Method

1. Grease the pudding bowl and cover the entire base of the mould with the sponge cake. Warm 1 cup of milk, pour over the cake, and allow it soak.
2. Skin the orange, and peel it into sections, removing the seeds and pips. Mix in half of the nuts and raisins, and spread it over the cake layer. Sprinkle a tablespoon of sugar and 1/2 teaspoon of the orange essence. Refrigerate.
3. Mix the custard powder with half a cup of milk to a smooth paste. Set aside. Boil the rest of the milk with 2 tablespoons of sugar until the sugar dissolves and the milk starts to thicken. Now add the custard powder, stirring all the while so that no lumps are formed. Mix in the rest of the essence. Cool.
4. When the custard is sufficiently cold, pour it over the oranges and shake the vessel to ensure an even spread. Refrigerate.
5. Before serving, sprinkle the rest of the nuts and raisins on the custard layer.

Note

For the sponge cake, refer to Part 3, Menu 7.

Orange Jelly

Ingredients
1 packet gelatine (jello) crystals, orange flavour
2 oranges
1 cup heavy cream
1 tablespoon chopped nuts
2 teaspoons lemon juice

Method
1. Set the jelly according to the instructions on the packet in a round mould. Chill.
2. Skin, peel and break the oranges into small pieces.
3. When the jelly is about to set, remove from the refrigerator, add the lemon juice, orange pieces, and some of the nuts. Mix thoroughly and set once again.
4. When about to serve, invert the jelly onto a glass dish, and sprinkle some of the nuts. Beat the cream lightly and pour over the jelly. Serve at once. Alternately, serve the cream separately.

```
──── Menu 5 ────
```

Rice or Chapatis	**Serve with**
Tuvar Dal	Cabbage-Groundnut Salad
Sindhi Palak	Baigan Raita
Aloo Posto	Garlic Chutney (optional)
	Radish Pickle
	Dessert
	Pantua

Rice or Chapatis

Cook three cups of rice or make chapatis using three cups of wheat flour.

Tuvar Dal
(A Gujarati Style Dal)

Ingredients

1 cup tuvar dal
1/4 teaspoon turmeric powder
salt to taste
1 small piece of tamarind (optional)
    or 1 tablespoon lemon juice
1/2 teaspoon jaggery

Seasoning

a pinch of asafoetida
1 tablespoon ghee
2 dried red chillies
3/4 teaspoon cumin seeds
5 garlic cloves (optional)

Method

1. Wash and boil the dal with turmeric in a pressure cooker. Break each red chilly into two or three pieces. Mash the dal after it has been cooked.

2. Heat the ghee in a kadai (wok), and add the cumin seeds, red chilly pieces, cloves and garlic. When the cumin seeds turn dark brown, add the dal, two cups of water, and salt. Cook for a few minutes.

3. If a little sourness is desired, add extract of tamarind and then the jaggery. Cook for a few more minutes. Otherwise, add lemon juice just before serving. To obtain the tamarind extract, add boiling water to the tamarind, squeeze and strain. Use the resulting liquid.

Note

If chapatis are made, the dal must be thicker.

Sindhi Palak
(Curried Spinach from Sind)

Ingredients

3/4 cup channa dal (Bengal gram dal)
a large bunch of spinach (palak)
1 potato
1 tomato
1 brinjal (eggplant)
1 carrot
1 onion
salt to taste

1.3 cm/0.5 inch piece ginger
2 green chillies
1 teaspoon chilly powder
1/2 teaspoon garam masala
1 tablespoon ghee
a pinch of pepper (optional)

Method

1. Wash and chop the vegetables into small pieces. Cook all the ingredients together except for the garam masala, ghee and pepper in a pressure cooker along with salt and very little water.
2. When cooked, mash the dal and vegetables slightly.
3. Just before serving, heat the ghee, add the garam masala powder, pepper and pour into the dal. Serve immediately.

Aloo Posto
(A Spicy Potato Preparation from Bengal)

Ingredients

1 kg/2.2 lb potatoes
1 cup oil
2 green chillies, slit
1 bay leaf

Grind to a fine paste

4 green chillies
1/2 teaspoon turmeric powder
3 tablespoons poppy seeds
  (khus khus)
salt to taste

Method

1. Boil, peel and cut the potatoes into 1 cm (1/2 inch) thick slices.
2. Mix the ground paste with 1/2 tablespoon water, and smear the slices with this. Set aside.
3. Heat the oil. Add first the bay leaves, then the potatoes and the chillies. Fry on low heat until browned, stirring all the while.
4. Serve hot.

Cabbage-Groundnut Salad

Ingredients

1 small cabbage	2 green chillies
1 large lemon	a handful of chopped coriander
1 tablespoon grated coconut	salt to taste
1 tablespoon groundnuts (peanuts)	

Method

1. Cut the cabbage into very thin strips and place in a bowl of cold water.
2. Roast the groundnuts and grind to a rough powder. Fry the coconut gratings to a light brown, and mix with the groundnuts. Extract the lemon juice.
3. Since this dish has to be served immediately, keep all the ingredients ready, and mix only when ready to serve.

To serve

Drain all water from the cabbage, and place in a large mixing bowl. Add all the ingredients except half of the chopped coriander. Mix well and transfer to a serving bowl. Garnish with the rest of the chopped coriander, and serve immediately.

Baigan Raita
(Spiced Eggplant in Yoghurt)

Ingredients

	Mince very fine
2 medium brinjals (eggplant)	1 teaspoon coriander leaves
1 cup curds (yoghurt)	2 green chillies
2 teaspoons oil	1 small onion
1/2 teaspoon cumin seeds	2 garlic cloves (optional)
1/2 teaspoon chilly powder	
salt to taste	

Method

1. Smear some oil on the brinjal. Place over a medium gas flame and cook, turning occasionally until the skin gets soft and wrinkled. Remove from fire and cool.
2. Peel, remove the stalk and mash with a fork.
3. Beat the curds and add to the mashed brinjal along with salt and chilly powder.
4. Season the cumin in oil and pour over mixture.
5. Add all the minced ingredients except the garlic. Mix and serve chilled.

Note

If garlic is used, brown minced garlic along with the cumin.

Garlic Chutney

Ingredients

1 whole garlic
6 dried red chillies
2 teaspoons cumin seeds
1 teaspoon coriander seeds
1 teaspoon poppy seeds
1 tablespoon dry copra (coconut) gratings
salt to taste

Method

1. Dry roast all the ingredients except for the garlic and salt.
2. Add the garlic and salt, and grind to a fine paste with some water.

Note

If desired, a small lump of tamarind may be added while grinding.

Pantua
(Bengali Milk Pastry in Cardamom Syrup)

Ingredients

1 litre/1 quart milk
1 large lemon
1 1/2 cups sugar
1 cup water
1 1/2 tablespoons flour
1/2 cup extra milk

1/2 teaspoon cardamom powder
a dozen raisins
1 teaspoon ghee
additional ghee for frying
a pinch of baking soda

Method

1. Boil the milk briskly, gradually adding the lemon juice until the milk starts to curdle. Add 1 or 2 more drops of lemon juice, and allow to boil once more. Turn off the heat and allow the paneer that has formed to remain for 10-15 minutes. When sufficiently cool, strain the whey and tie the resulting paneer block in a thick muslin cloth. Hang this cloth for a few hours until not a trace of water is left.
2. Transfer the paneer onto a plate and divide it into 3 equal portions. To one portion, add an equal quantity (by volume) of sugar. To the second portion, add an equal quantity (by volume) of flour. To the third portion, add 1 teaspoon of ghee, a pinch of baking soda, and the cardamom powder.

3. Mix all the portions together, and knead the dough gently until it is very soft and forms a round smooth ball. Divide the dough into 12 equal portions. Knead each piece into a ball, and then form it back into a cup. Place a raisin in the centre of each cup, close, and smoothen the ball.

4. Prepare the sugar syrup by boiling the sugar with 1 cup of water until a thick syrup is obtained. Add 1/4 cup of milk and boil further until a thick layer coats the surface. Remove the syrup from the fire, strain and put back in the vessel. Continue to boil until the syrup is of a one thread consistency. Keep the syrup warm.

5. Deep fry the balls from Step 3, 3-4 at a time on a very slow flame, stirring constantly. Fry to a golden colour and while still hot, soak them in the syrup. Allow them to soak for at least an hour before serving.

```
──── Menu 6 ────
```

Sprouted Bean Pulav
Tomato-Coconut Kurma
Masala Brinjal (Eggplant)
or Drumstick Fry
Chapatis

Serve with
Capsicum Raita
Mixed Vegetable Pickle
Dessert
Biscuit Pudding or
Biscuit Fudge

Sprouted Bean Pulav

Ingredients
2 cups rice
1 cup rajma (red kidney beans)
or 1 cup chowlai (black-eyed peas)
1 cup ghee
1/2 cup curds (yoghurt)
2 large cardamoms
2 cinnamon sticks
3 cloves
2 large tomatoes
a handful of chopped mint
  and coriander leaves

Chop fine
2 onions
3 green chillies
1 inch piece ginger
3 garlic cloves

Powdered masala
1/4 teaspoon turmeric powder
1 teaspoon chilly powder
2 teaspoons coriander powder
1 teaspoon cumin powder
1/2 teaspoon garam masala

For the garnish
1 tablespoon grated coconut
1 tablespoon chopped coriander

Method
1. To sprout the beans, soak the beans in water for a whole day keeping the vessel tightly covered. At night remove all water, tie the beans loosely in a thin muslin cloth, and leave overnight in a large covered vessel. By morning most of it will have sprouted. Gently remove the outer skin and cook very carefully in just enough water with turmeric and salt. If there is any water left, strain it and use while cooking the masala. Set the beans aside.
2. Cook the rice with just sufficient water and salt such that the grains are separate. Cool on a plate, and sprinkle hot ghee. Set aside.
3. Blanch the tomatoes in boiling water. Remove. When cool, peel skin and mash to a puree. Set aside.

4. Heat 3 tablespoons of ghee and fry the whole spices. Add the chopped ingredients and continue to fry for a while. Add the powdered masalas and fry along with tomato puree, curds, coriander and mint until the oil surfaces. Add the beans and stir gently, adding one cup of water. Simmer for a couple of minutes. Remove from fire and set aside.
5. Grease a large serving bowl with ghee. Divide the rice into two equal portions. Place one portion at the bottom of the bowl, covering the entire surface. Pour the beans curry all over, spreading it evenly. Spread the remainder of the rice over this. Sprinkle grated coconut, chopped coriander and some more ghee.
6. Cover and place in a moderate oven for about fifteen minutes until the pulav is steaming hot.

Note

This recipe may also be prepared without sprouting the beans. For this, the beans must be soaked overnight, and pressure cooked the next day. They may then be added to the fried masalas in Step 4. The rest is the same as above.

Tomato-Coconut Kurma

Ingredients

1 kg/2.2 lb tomatoes	1/2 teaspoon mustard seeds
500 gm/1.1 lb potatoes	1/4 teaspoon turmeric powder
1 large onion, thinly sliced	2 cloves
4 green chillies, slit	1/2 teaspoon cumin seeds
1 small piece ginger, chopped	2 cinnamon sticks
a handful of chopped coriander	2 cardamoms
1 cup shelled peas (optional)	3 tablespoons ghee
1 large coconut, grated	salt to taste

Method

1. Boil the potatoes and peas. Cut the potatoes into thick pieces, tomatoes into fours, and set aside.
2. Add one cup of boiling water to the grated coconut and take out thick milk by squeezing the gratings and straining the resultant mixture. Set aside. Add some more water and extract as much thin milk as you can. Strain. Keep the 'milks' separate.
3. Heat the ghee, and add the whole spices, mustard, and cumin seeds, then the slit chillies, ginger and onions. Fry till the onions turn light brown in colour. Do not allow to brown too much.
4. Add the tomatoes and fry until they turn soft. Add the potato pieces and fry for some time. Now add the turmeric powder.

5. Add the thin milk, salt, and cook for 3-5 minutes or until the gravy is thick. Then add the thick milk, peas, some of the chopped coriander, and cook for a minute or two. Remove from fire.

6. Serve garnished with the rest of the chopped coriander.

Masala Brinjal
(Curried Eggplant)

Ingredients

500 gm/1.1 lb brinjals (eggplant)
3 tablespoons oil
1 teaspoon mustard seeds
1 sprig curry leaf
salt to taste
1/4 teaspoon turmeric powder
a lemon-sized piece of tamarind

Roast in 1 teaspoon oil and powder

2 tablespoons sesame seeds
1 tablespoon gram dal
1 tablespoon coriander seeds
4 dried red chillies
1/4 teaspoon asafoetida

Method

1. Wash and cut the brinjals into fours. Extract the pulp from the tamarind by boiling it in some water, and then squeezing.

2. Heat the oil, and add the mustard and curry leaf. When done, add the brinjals and turmeric, and fry on a low fire. Sprinkle a little water, cover the vessel and cook on low heat until the brinjals turn soft.

3. Add the tamarind extract, salt and cook for some more time until almost all the water has evaporated. Add the masala powder and stir for a few minutes. Remove and serve hot.

Drumstick Fry

Ingredients

8 drumsticks
1 large onion, chopped fine
a pinch of sugar
salt to taste
3 tablespoons oil
a lemon-sized ball of tamarind

1/2 teaspoon turmeric powder
2 teaspoons chilly powder
1 tablespoon flour
1/2 teaspoon mustard
2 sprigs curry leaves

Method

1. Cut the drumsticks into 2 inch long pieces. Cook with salt and very little water till tender and all the water has evaporated. Do not overcook.

2. Obtain the tamarind extract by adding 3 tablespoons of boiling water, and squeezing the pulp. To this, add the flour, chilly and turmeric powders, sugar and salt to make a smooth paste. Coat the drumstick pieces with this paste.
3. Heat the oil, and add the mustard and curry leaves. When done add the chopped onions and fry until brown. Now add the drumstick pieces, and fry for a few minutes more.

Chapatis

Refer to the recipe in Part 2, Menu 1.

Capsicum Raita
(Green Peppers in a Yoghurt Sauce)

Ingredients

4 capsicums (green peppers)	1/2 teaspoon mustard seeds
1 1/2 cups curds (yoghurt)	1 tablespoon oil
salt to taste	1/2 teaspoon sugar
1 sprig of curry leaves	

Method

1. Chop the capsicums.
2. Heat the oil and add the mustard. When done, add the curry leaves and the capsicums, and fry until soft. Cool. Beat the curds with sugar and salt, add to the capsicums, and mix well. Serve chilled.

Biscuit Pudding

Ingredients

200 gm/7 oz. Arrowroot/Marie biscuits	1 teaspoon instant coffee
2 tablespoons custard powder	2 tablespoons sugar
3 cups milk	1 tablespoon chopped nuts
2 tablespoons cocoa	1/4 cup boiling water

Method

1. Mix the custard powder and cocoa with a small amount of the milk to a smooth paste.
2. Boil the rest of the milk with sugar for 3-5 minutes or until the sugar has dissolved and the milk thickens.

3. Add the custard powder and cook stirring all the while till a thick creamy consistency is formed. Cool.
4. Mix the coffee in boiling water. Have a serving bowl ready before proceeding to the next step.
5. Dip a biscuit in hot coffee, shake out the excess water and arrange at the bottom of the bowl covering the entire surface. Continue until the entire surface has been covered, using smaller pieces if necessary. Pour half of the custard onto the biscuit layer, and sprinkle half the chopped nuts.
6. Repeat the biscuit and custard layers. Carefully shake the bowl so that the custard layer gets evened out. Sprinkle all the nuts. Also crumble any biscuit left over and sprinkle this on the surface. Refrigerate until ready to serve.

Biscuit Fudge

Ingredients

5 tablespoons cocoa
1/2 cup margarine or butter
1/2 cup milk
1 1/4 cup sugar
200 gm/7 oz. Arrowroot/Marie biscuits
1 loaf tin

1 tablespoon walnuts, chopped
a few walnuts, halved
1 tablespoon raisins
1/2 teaspoon vanilla essence
1 egg

Method

1. Grease the loaf tin thoroughly with a few drops of salad or refined oil.
2. Mix the cocoa and sugar. Melt the margarine or butter in a sauce-pan over very low heat. Remove from fire when melted. Beat in the cocoa-sugar mixture along with the egg.
3. Put back on fire and cook over gentle heat for 10 minutes (preferably in a double boiler) until the mixture is smooth and starts coating the back of the spoon. Do not allow to boil. Remove from flame. Add the chopped nuts, raisins, vanilla and mix thoroughly.
4. Pour some of the mixture into the greased tin to cover the entire base. Keep the rest warm.
5. Dip a biscuit in milk, shake out the excess milk, and cover the chocolate layer with the biscuits. The biscuits should be kept in an overlapping manner with each biscuit covering one half of the other. When the biscuit layer is complete, pour some more chocolate and repeat the process, topping with a chocolate layer.
6. Cover with waxed paper, press down lightly, leave in cool place for a few hours.
7. When ready to serve, place the tin in warm water, and loosen the edges with a sharp knife. Invert the fudge very carefully on to a plate. Mark the top and sides of the fudge with squares. Press a halved walnut in each square. Cut into squares using a saw-edged knife.

---- *Menu 7* ----

Rice - Morkuzhambu	**Serve with**
Cabbage or Beans Paruppu Curry	Banana Chips
or Colocasia Roast	Bitter Gourd Chutney (Gojju)
Mysore Rasam	**Dessert**
Curds (Yoghurt)	Coconut Rice Payasam

Morkuzhambu
(South Indian Kadhi)

Ingredients
250 gm/9 oz. ash gourd or
250 gm/9 oz. bhindi (okra)
2 cups curds (yoghurt)
2 sprigs curry leaves
1/2 teaspoon turmeric powder
3 tablespoons grated coconut
2 tablespoons oil (optional)
salt to taste

Seasoning
1 teaspoon mustard seeds
1 teaspoon oil

Roast in 1 teaspoon oil
1 tablespoon Bengal gram dal
1/4 teaspoon asafoetida
1/4 teaspoon fenugreek seeds
2 dried red chillies
2 green chillies

Soak in water
1 tablespoon tuvar dal
1 teaspoon cumin seeds

Method
1. Remove excess water from the dal and cumin seeds. Grind these along with the roasted ingredients and coconut gratings.
2. Churn the curds with two cups of water to a smooth consistency. Add the ground paste, turmeric, a little salt, and some of the curry leaves.
3. Peel and cut the ash gourd into 4 cm(1 1/2 inch) lengths, and cook with a pinch of turmeric and some salt in sufficient water till tender. Add the buttermilk, coconut mixture, and boil just once. Remove from fire. Season in oil with the mustard seeds and the remainder of the curry leaves.

If bhindi is used, cut these into 4 cm(1 1/2 inch) lengths. Heat 2 tablespoons of oil and add the mustard. When done, add the bhindi pieces and fry until crisp. Boil the buttermilk mixture once, and add the fried vegetable. Remove from fire.

Cabbage or Beans Paruppu Curry
(Cabbage or Beans Curry with Lentils)

Ingredients
500 gm/1.1 lb beans or cabbage
1/2 cup tuvar dal or moong dal
1/2 teaspoon turmeric
salt to taste

Seasoning
1 1/2 tablespoons oil
1 teaspoon mustard seeds
2 teaspoons black gram
1 sprig curry leaf
2 tablespoons coconut gratings
2 dried red chillies, broken
    into pieces

Method
1. If moong dal is used, soak for a couple of hours. If tuvar dal is used, boil this with just enough water and a pinch of turmeric such that when cooked, the dal is dry.
2. Cut the vegetable into small pieces. Steam cook with some salt and a sprinkling of water. This can be done by cooking the vegetable with very little water and some salt in a pressure cooker without the weight until the water has evaporated. Do not allow the vegetables to get soggy.
3. Heat the oil and add the mustard. When done, add the black gram and the red chillies. When the dal turns brown, add the curry leaves and either the cooked dal or the soaked dal (after removing the water) and fry for one minute. Now add the vegetable and grated coconut and fry for a while until the water has evaporated.

Note
This curry can be made with any variety of green beans.

Colocasia Roast
(Crisp, Spicy Yam Fries)

Ingredients
750 gm/1.7 lb colocasia
3/4 cup oil
2 teaspoons chilly powder
2 teaspoons coriander powder
1/2 teaspoon turmeric powder
salt to taste
1 small piece tamarind

Seasoning
1 teaspoon mustard seeds
2 teaspoons black gram
2 sprigs curry leaves
2 dried red chillies, broken into
    pieces

Method

1. Soak the tamarind in boiling water, and squeeze to extract the pulp. Boil the colocasia, peel the skin, and cut into rounds.
2. Mix together the chilly, turmeric, and coriander powders along with some salt.
3. Smear the pieces with this masala.
4. Heat the oil and add the mustard. When done, add the dal, red chillies, and the curry leaves. Add the colocasia pieces, tamarind extract, and fry on high, turning occasionally. If additional crispness is desired, add some more oil while frying.

Mysore Rasam
(Thick Mulligatawny Soup, Mysore Style Served with Rice)

Ingredients

1 cup tuvar dal
1 lemon-sized ball tamarind
2 sprigs of curry leaves
2 teaspoons coriander leaves, chopped
1/2 teaspoon turmeric powder
salt to taste

Fry in 2 teaspoons ghee and grind to fine paste

1 tablespoon coriander seeds
1 teaspoon cumin seeds
1/2 teaspoon pepper
2 red chillies
1/4 teaspoon asafoetida
2 tablespoons coconut gratings
1 piece cinnamon (optional)

Seasoning

2 teaspoons ghee
1 teaspoon mustard seeds
1 dried red chilly, broken into pieces (optional)

Method

1. Boil the dal with some turmeric powder. Set aside.
2. Boil the tamarind with some water, and squeeze to extract the pulp. Add 1 1/2 cups of water, salt, turmeric powder, curry leaves and boil until the quantity is reduced to less than half.
3. Mix the masala paste with some water and add to the tamarind extract along with the dal. Allow to simmer for a while.
4. Season the mustard and red chilly in ghee, and pour into the rasam. Add the chopped coriander and serve steaming hot with rice.

Bitter Gourd Chutney (Gojju)

Ingredients

250 gm/9 oz. bitter gourd
8 green chillies
1 lemon-sized ball tamarind
1 small piece jaggery
1/4 teaspoon turmeric powder
3 tablespoons oil
salt to taste
2 sprigs curry leaves

Roast dry and powder

1 tablespoon sesame seeds
1/4 teaspoon fenugreek seeds
1/2 teaspoon cumin seeds

Seasoning

1/2 teaspoon mustard seeds
1 1/2 teaspoons black gram
1 1/2 teaspoons Bengal gram dal

Method

1. Cut the bitter gourd into small pieces. Chop the chillies.
2. Heat the oil and add the seasonings. When done, add the chillies and fry for a minute or two. Add the gourd pieces along with the turmeric and fry until soft.
3. Boil the tamarind with a little water, and squeeze to extract the pulp. Add this to the vegetable along with salt and jaggery. Cook till the chutney is thick. Add the powdered masala, cook for a few more minutes, and remove from fire. This chutney should keep for a few days.

Banana Chips

Ingredients

4 large unripe bananas (plantains)
oil for frying
salt and chilly powder to taste

Method

1. Peel the skin of the bananas, and leave in water for some time. Then remove and cut into very thin wafer-like rounds.
2. Heat the oil to smoking point, put in a handful of the slices and fry, stirring all the while. When golden and crisp, remove from oil and drain in a colander.
3. When all the chips are ready, sprinkle some salt and chilly powder.

Coconut Rice Payasam

Ingredients

1 tablespoon rice
1/2 coconut, grated
1 cup jaggery, grated
1 1/2 cups milk
1 tablespoon ghee

a pinch of camphor (optional)
1 tablespoon cashew nuts
1 tablespoon raisins
4 cardamoms

Method

1. Soak the rice for 2-3 hours. Grind to a very smooth paste with coconut. Add 2 1/2 cups of water and mix well. Bring the milk to a boil, and set aside.
2. Cook the ground mixture on slow heat stirring all the while so that lumps are not formed. When cooked, add the jaggery and cook further until it is dissolved, and a thick consistency is obtained.
3. Add the boiled milk, stir, and remove from fire. Fry the cashew nuts and raisins in ghee, and add to the payasam along with powdered cardamom and camphor. Serve hot in cups.

Rice

Cook 2 cups of rice, preferably in a rice cooker.

---- *Menu 8* ----

Mixed Vegetable Soup   **Serve with**
served with Dumplings (optional)   Fresh Bread Rolls and Butter
Capsicum Noodles   Cucumber Cups
Potato Eggs   **Dessert**
                              Hot Chocolate Pudding
                              with Sauce or
                              Chocolate Blancmange

Mixed Vegetable Soup

Ingredients

1 potato	2 cups milk
1 small carrot	30 gm/1 oz. butter
1/4 cabbage	salt to taste
1 piece bottle gourd	a pinch grated nutmeg
a few florets cauliflower	a few peppercorns
1 large onion, chopped	1 bay leaf
1/2 cup shelled peas	
a few celery leaves (optional)	

Method

1. Chop the vegetables into small pieces.
2. Melt the butter, and add the bay leaf, pepper and onion. Fry until the onion turns pink. Now add all the vegetables except for the peas, and fry for a minute or two.
3. Add 3 cups of water and salt, and cook until the vegetables are done. Cook the peas separately.
4. When the vegetables are cooked, remove and discard the bay leaf. Take out some of the boiled vegetables and pass the rest through a sieve or a mixer, setting aside this thick puree until it is needed.
5. Prepare the batter for the dumplings, and set aside.
6. Get the soup ready a quarter of an hour before serving. To the pureed vegetables, add the milk and nutmeg. Add the peas and the vegetables, and bring the soup to a boil.
7. When the soup is boiling, drop as many marble-sized balls of the dumpling batter as the vessel can hold. Cook after covering and simmer. When cooked, the dumplings will become fluffy and come to the top. Remove from heat. Carefully ladle out the soup into bowls, and serve steaming hot.

Dumplings

Ingredients

3/4 cup flour
1 1/2 teaspoons baking powder
2 tablespoons butter

1/2 cup milk
a pinch of salt
a pinch of pepper

Method

1. Mix thoroughly all the ingredients except for the milk.
2. Add the milk to form a smooth consistency. When the soup (above recipe) is boiling, drop marble-sized balls and simmer till the dumplings are cooked.

Capsicum Noodles

Ingredients

100 gm/3.5 oz. noodles
1 large potato, cut into cubes
1 large onion, chopped
2 capsicums (green peppers), chopped
1 cup shelled peas
a few cauliflower florets
2 cups milk
2 eggs
salt to taste

3 green chillies, chopped
1 tablespoon chopped coriander
4 tablespoons grated cheese
1/2 teaspoon chilly powder
1/2 teaspoon pepper
3 tablespoons oil
1 tablespoon butter
2 tablespoons bread crumbs

Method

1. Boil the noodles in water with 1 teaspoon of oil and some salt. Drain and set aside, sprinkling some oil.
2. Chop the onions, capsicum and green chillies. Boil the potatoes, cauliflower and peas with just enough water and some salt. Set aside.
3. Heat the oil, add the chopped chillies, capsicum and onions, and fry till the onions turn soft. Add the boiled potatoes, peas and cauliflower, and fry for a while. Add the chopped coriander, 3/4 of the cheese, and noodles. Mix thoroughly. Add half of the milk as well.
4. Beat the eggs, and add the rest of the milk, salt, pepper and chilly powder. Add this to the noodles, and mix. Pour this egg-noodle-vegetable mixture into a well-greased casserole bowl. Sprinkle the rest of the cheese and bread crumbs on top, dot with butter, and bake in a moderate oven at 190°C (375°F) for 20 minutes or until the top is nicely browned.

5. Alternately, the mixture can be poured into a deep greased pan or loaf tin and steam cooked in a pressure cooker (without the weight) for 30 minutes.

Note

If you do not wish to use eggs, follow the recipe up to Step 3, and then as described below.

Alternate Method (Eggless)

Additional Ingredients

2 tablespoons flour
2 tablespoons butter
4 cups milk
2 tablespoons cheese

4. Fry 2 tablespoons of flour in 2 tablespoons of butter to a light pink, and gradually add 4 cups of milk. Stir on low heat until a custard-like consistency is obtained. Pour this into the vegetable-noodle mixture and mix thoroughly, adding 4 tablespoons of cheese.

5. Transfer the mixture into a well-greased casserole bowl, and sprinkle 2 tablespoons cheese and bread crumbs. Dot with butter. Bake in a moderate oven (190°C/375°F) for 20 minutes until the top is nicely browned.

Potato Eggs

Ingredients

500 gm/1.1 lb potatoes	1 tablespoon coriander, minced
1 cup shelled peas	4 green chillies, minced
1 cup grated cheese	1/2 tablespoon mint, minced
oil for frying	2 tablespoons flour (maida)
bread crumbs	1 cup water to mix
salt and pepper to taste	

Method

1. Cook the potatoes. Cool, peel the skins, and mash thoroughly.
2. Cook the peas separately. Mash roughly, add half of the cheese, and some salt and pepper. Make small balls the size of egg yolk, and set aside.
3. Add all the seasonings and the rest of the cheese to the mashed potatoes, and mix well. Take a little of this mixture and form into a small cup. Keeping the pea ball in the centre, close the cup, and pat into shape like an egg. Form all 'eggs' thus.

4. Mix the flour with water to form a thin paste, and add a pinch of salt and pepper. Dip the egg in this, roll in bread crumbs, and deep fry to golden brown.

Note
If a yellow yolk is desired, substitute two carrots for the peas.

Egg Cutlets

Additional Ingredients
3 hard-boiled eggs
1 hard-boiled egg for coating

Shell and chop the eggs into small pieces. Add this to the mashed potatoes along with the seasonings and cheese. Mould the mixture into egg shapes. Brush with the beaten eggs, roll in bread crumbs and deep fry in hot oil till golden.

Note
For this recipe, omit peas or carrots, and use only 300 gm (11 oz.) potatoes.

Fresh Bread Rolls

Ingredients
3 cups flour (maida)
1 1/2 teaspoons sugar
1 teaspoon salt
2 tablespoons butter (or margarine)
1 teaspoon dry yeast
or 2 teaspoons fresh yeast

6 tablespoons warm water to mix
2 tablespoons warm milk
2 tablespoons butter (to serve)

Method
1. Add the sugar to the milk, add yeast, and set aside. Do not shake the vessel as it will disturb the yeast. Leave for 10 to 15 minutes or until the yeast has risen.
2. Rub the butter into the sifted flour and lightly mix till the flour looks like bread crumbs. Mix the salt with warm water.
3. Make a well in the centre, pour in the yeast mixture, add warm water and gradually mix the dough to a smooth consistency. Keep the dough covered with a wet cloth till it rises to twice its original size.
4. Knead the dough again, and make eight to ten round balls. Leave for ten minutes.
5. Shape the dough into balls or rolls as desired, place on a greased tray and leave for 30 minutes or till it doubles in size.

6. Sprinkle some water on the rolls and bake at very high temperature (230°C/ 450°F) for 7-10 minutes and till the top is nicely browned.
7. Serve hot with melted butter smeared on top.

Cucumber Cups

Ingredients	**Seasonings**
1 large cucumber	salt, pepper, mustard to taste
4 tomatoes	1 teaspoon lemon juice
2 onions	1 teaspoon sugar
a few lettuce leaves	

Method
1. Peel the cucumber and cut into as many two-inch pieces as desired. Scoop out the inside, wash thoroughly, and leave these cups in cold water.
2. Chop the rest of the cucumber along with 2 of the tomatoes and one onion. Add the seasonings to this and fill the cups with the mixture. Wash the lettuce leaves, and arrange them on a salad plate. Slice the tomatoes and onions, and arrange these as well. Place the cucumber cups on each tomato slice. Serve chilled.

Hot Chocolate Pudding with Sauce

For the pudding	**For the sauce**
3 eggs	2 cups milk
3/4 cup butter or margarine	4 level tablespoons sugar
3/4 cup sugar	1 tablespoon cocoa
2 cups flour	1 tablespoon cornflour
2 tablespoons cocoa	1/2 teaspoon vanilla essence
1 teaspoon instant coffee	
a pinch of salt	pudding bowl
	grease proof paper

Method
1. Sift together the flour, cocoa, coffee and salt.
2. Beat the butter and sugar till creamy. Add the eggs one at a time, and beat till the mixture is well blended.
3. Add the flour gradually along with the essence. Pour into a greased pudding mould, tie double grease paper (or aluminium foil) and steam cook (in a pressure cooker without weight) for about an hour. When done, a needle passed through should come out clean. Keep the pudding hot.

Note

Grease-proof paper can be made from thick brown paper as follows: Cut brown paper into two circular sheets, 5 cm (2 inches) larger (on each side) than the diameter of the pudding bowl. Grease thoroughly.

Chocolate Sauce

1. Mix the cocoa and cornflour to a paste with a little cold milk.
2. Boil the rest of the milk with sugar, add the cocoa mixture, and cook on low heat till a thick consistency is obtained. Remove and add the essence.

To serve

Remove the grease-proof paper carefully, and invert the pudding on to a serving bowl. Pour the hot chocolate sauce over the pudding. Serve hot. Alternately, the sauce can be kept in a separate bowl and spooned over the pudding slices.

Chocolate Blancmange

Ingredients

2 level tablespoons custard powder
2 level tablespoons cocoa
4 tablespoons sugar
4 cups milk
a few drops of vanilla essence
120 gm/4 oz. whipping cream
1 teaspoon gelatine

Method

1. Mix the custard powder and cocoa to a smooth paste in some of the milk. Soak the gelatine in hot water.
2. Bring the rest of the milk to a boil, adding the sugar. When the sugar has dissolved and the milk is slightly thick, add the custard powder, cocoa mixture, and stir over low heat until it thickens.
3. Remove from fire, add the essence, and cool. Add the gelatine and mix thoroughly.
4. Rinse a pudding mould with some cold water, pour the custard into it, cover and set in a refrigerator.
5. When about to serve, dip the mould in warm water, and quickly invert on to a glass dish. Beat the cream lightly, pour over the blancmange and serve immediately. Alternately, serve the cream separately.

PARTY
SPECIALS

PARTY SPECIALS

Menu 1

Pudina-Peas Pulav
Lauki-Moong Dal Kofta
Mixed Vegetable Kurma
Aloo Puris with Coriander Chutney
Curds (Yoghurt)

Serve with
Salad
Stuffed Capsicum
   a. with Vegetables
   b. with Eggs
Dessert
Cabbage Rabdi

Menu 2

Plain or Egg Parathas
Dal Stew with Cream
Dum Gobi with Potato Fingers
Methi Garlic Pulav
Cucumber Raita

Serve with
Bhagara Tomato
Stuffed Brinjals
Dessert
Pumpkin Halwa

Menu 3

Savoury Idlis
Onion Sambar
Capsicum Rice
Carrot Pachadi (Raita)
Jeera Rasam (optional)
Curds (Yoghurt) Semia

Serve with
Cabbage Vadas
Coconut Chutney
Tomato Thokku
Dessert
Pal Polis

Menu 4

Cheese Parathas
Malai Dal
Vegetable Delight
Brinjal or Egg Moillee
Caramel Rice

Serve with
Cabbage Raita
Green Banana Tikki
Vinegar Mangoes
Dessert
Ras Malai

Menu 5

Cauliflower Pulav with Whey
Shahi Dal
Paneer or Egg Korma
Bhagara Baigan
Palak Puris

Serve with
Pumpkin Raita
Stuffed Cabbage Rolls
Sweet-Hot Mango Chutney
Dessert
Custard Souffle or
Apricot or Guava Stew with Custard

PARTY SPECIALS

Menu 6

Puris	**Serve with**
Potato Curry (Aloo Palya)	Dahi Vadas
Chitranna	Cucumber Kosamalli
Vegetable Sagu	Capsicum Chilly Gojju
Milagu (Pepper) Rasam	**Dessert**
Curd (Yoghurt) Rice	Badam Kheer

Menu 7

Tomato Rice	Serve with
Chutney Raita	Boiled Vegetable Salad
Potato Cheese Balls in Spinach Gravy	Dal-Vegetable or Egg Kabab
Bread or Chapatis	Brinjal (Eggplant) Pickle
	Dessert
	Jelly-Cake Fiesta

Menu 8

Cabbage Soup	Serve with
Carrot Cups	Lentil Rissoles (Dal Cutlets)
Three layered Macaroni	Cucumber Mould (salad)
or Potato-Egg Casserole (optional)	**Dessert**
	Steamed Date Pudding or
	Baked Date Loaf (eggless)

Menu 9

Tomato Cream Soup	Serve with
Cheese Croutons	Mexican Salad
Cottage Cheese Casserole	Spaghetti Rolls
Baked Savoury Omelette (optional)	**Dessert**
	Apple Walnut Loaf served with
	Cream or Crumble Top Apple Pie

Menu 10

Sweet Corn Soup	Serve with
Vegetable Fried Rice or	Chillies in Vinegar
Egg Fried Rice	Chilly Sauce
Sweet and Sour Carrots	Egg Fuyong with Hot Sauce or
Cauliflower Manchurian	Green Chilly Sauce or
	Vegetable Cakes with Tomato Sauce
	Dessert
	Eight Treasure Pudding or Fresh Fruit

---- Menu 1 ----

Pudina-Peas Pulav	**Serve with**
Lauki-Moong Dal Kofta	Salad
Mixed Vegetable Kurma	Stuffed Capsicums
Aloo Puris with Coriander Chutney	a. with Vegetables
Curds (Yoghurt)	b. with Eggs
	Dessert
	Cabbage Rabdi

Pudina-Peas Pulav

Ingredients
2 cups rice
1 cup boiled peas
1 tablespoon lemon juice
1 tablespoon chopped mint
2 slices bread (optional)
4 tablespoons ghee
2 tablespoons extra ghee
    for frying the bread
salt to taste

Grind to paste
4 tablespoons grated coconut
1 tablespoon chopped mint (pudina)
1 tablespoon chopped coriander
2 green chillies
1.3 cm/0.5 inch piece ginger
1 medium onion
2 teaspoon khus khus
4 cloves
2 - 1.3 cm/0.5 inch cinnamon sticks

Seasoning
1 teaspoon mustard seeds
2 bay leaves
2 slit green chillies

Method
1. Cook the rice and allow it to cool on a plate, sprinkling some oil so that each grain is separate.
2. Grind the masala with very little water. Cut the bread into cubes (croutons).
3. Heat 2 tablespoons of ghee. Fry the bread cubes until crisp and set aside.
4. Add 4 tablespoons of ghee, mustard, bay leaves and then the chillies. Fry for a minute. Add the ground masala and salt, and stir on a slow fire until all the water evaporates. Add the boiled peas, fry, remove, and cool.
5. Mix the masala with the rice very lightly using only the tips of your fingers, adding the lemon juice, half of the bread cubes and the chopped mint.

To serve

Transfer the rice on to a serving plate and smoothen the surface. Garnish with the rest of the bread cubes and chopped mint. Serve hot.

Lauki-Moong Dal Kofta
(Squash-Lentil Balls in Spicy Gravy)

For the kofta

2 tablespoons gram flour
1/2 cup moong dal
2 cups grated lauki (squash)
3 green chillies
a handful coriander leaves
1 small piece ginger
1/4 teaspoon turmeric powder
salt to taste
oil for frying

For the gravy

1 green chilly, slit
1 teaspoon chilly powder
2 teaspoons cumin powder
2 teaspoons coriander powder
1 teaspoon garam masala powder
1/2 teaspoon turmeric powder
2 large onions, chopped
3 garlic cloves
2.5 cm/1 inch piece ginger
3 medium tomatoes, chopped
salt to taste

Garnish

1 cup light cream
1 tablespoon chopped coriander

This makes 16 koftas.

Method

1. Peel and grate the lauki. Add a pinch of salt, turmeric powder, and set aside.
2. Soak the dal for three to four hours, and drain. Grind to a thick paste with the ginger, green chillies and salt, taking care not to add too much water.
3. Squeeze out all the water from the lauki, and keep this water aside for the gravy. Add the lauki to the dal paste along with the chopped coriander, and mix well. Form balls, roll in the gram flour, and deep fry in a kadai (wok) on very low heat to a brown colour. Set aside.
4. Grind to paste 1 onion, ginger and garlic. Remove the excess oil from the kadai, leaving only 3-4 tablespoons. To this, add the slit chilly and, after a minute, the chopped onion. Fry to a brownish colour. Add the ground paste and fry, adding the dry masala powders. Continue frying on low heat until the oil comes to the surface.

5. Add the tomatoes, and fry till they turn soft. Now add the lauki water, 1 cup of water (if necessary) and cook until the gravy is thick. Add the koftas, simmer for a couple of minutes, and remove from fire.

To serve

Heat the gravy and pour it into a deep bowl. Beat the cream slightly, and pour this over the koftas. Garnish with chopped coriander.

Mixed Vegetable Kurma

Ingredients
2 potatoes
2 carrots
2 tomatoes
2 onions
1 small cauliflower
1 cup shelled peas
a handful of beans
3/4 cup ghee or vanaspati
a pinch of turmeric powder
3/4 cup curds/yoghurt (optional)
salt to taste

Seasoning
2 bay leaves
4 cashew nuts (optional)
1-2 green chillies, slit

Garnish
2 tablespoons chopped coriander

Grind to a fine paste
4 tablespoons grated coconut
6 cashew nuts
2 teaspoons khus khus
1 teaspoon aniseed
3 small cardamoms
2 cinnamon sticks
4 cloves
1/2 teaspoon cumin seeds
3 dried red chillies
1 tablespoon mint
1 tablespoon coriander leaves
2.5 cm/1 inch piece ginger
2 garlic cloves (optional)

Method
1. Wash and cut the vegetables (except the onion and tomatoes) into medium-sized pieces. Steam cook with some salt and a pinch of turmeric powder. Set aside.
2. Chop the onions and tomatoes into small pieces.
3. Heat the ghee, add the bay leaves and cashew nuts (broken into pieces), and fry until the nuts turn golden in colour. Add the slit chillies and onions, and fry till brown. Then add the chopped tomatoes, and fry until they are soft. Now add the ground paste and continue to fry until the ghee rises to the surface.

4. Add the steamed vegetables, a little water (if necessary), and some of the chopped coriander. Cover and cook for a few minutes. If you are adding curds, do so at this stage and simmer for some time. When done, add the rest of the chopped coriander and serve.

Note

Instead of steam cooking the vegetables, they can be stir-fried in a little extra ghee or oil before frying the masala, and added during Step 3.

Aloo Puris

Ingredients

4 level cups flour	1 1/2 teaspoon cumin seeds
2 medium potatoes (150 gm)	1/2 teaspoon turmeric powder
oil for frying	1/2 teaspoon garam masala
salt to taste	

Method

1. Boil and mash the potatoes (while still hot) to a smooth dough, ensuring that no lumps are formed.
2. Add 4 teaspoons of oil to the mashed potatoes, and the rest of the ingredients to make a stiff dough.
3. Take small balls of this dough and roll out into puris. Deep fry to golden.
4. Serve hot with chutney.

Coriander Chutney

Ingredients

1 medium onion	1/2 teaspoon cumin seeds
1.3 cm/0.5 inch piece ginger	5 peppercorns
5 garlic cloves	1 large bundle fresh coriander
4 green chillies	juice of 1 lemon
salt to taste	

Method

1. Grind all the ingredients to a smooth paste with a little water. Add the lemon juice, salt and mix.

Salad

Ingredients

2 large onions

2 large tomatoes

1 large carrot

1/2 large cucumber

a few cabbage leaves

1/2 teaspoon chopped mint

juice of 1 lemon

salt and pepper to taste

a pinch of sugar

Method

1. Slice the onions, tomatoes and cucumber. Grate the carrots. Shred the cabbage leaves.
2. Arrange the vegetables on a salad plate and leave in a refrigerator. Mix together the lemon juice, salt, pepper and sugar. Refrigerate until ready to serve.
3. When about to serve, sprinkle this juice on top of the vegetables along with the chopped mint.

Stuffed Capsicum (Green Peppers)

Ingredients

8 large capsicums

8 small eggs (optional)

2 medium onions

1 cup cooked peas

1/2 small cabbage

2 medium potatoes

1 carrot

2 green chillies, chopped

2 tablespoons chopped coriander

1/2 teaspoon garam masala

1/2 teaspoon chilly powder

50 gm/2 oz. cheese

3 slices bread

oil for frying

salt to taste

For the eggs

salt and pepper to taste

2 slices bread

Method

1. Prepare the capsicums for stuffing thus: cut the stalks of the capsicums and carefully remove the seeds. Smear the insides with salt and leave them upside down for some time. Boil some water and immerse the capsicums in this for about 5 minutes or till they turn soft. Remove the capsicums, shake off all water and set aside.

   Alternately place the capsicums on a trivet with the cut sides down in a pressure cooker. Allow to cook for 5-7 minutes without using the weight. When cool, remove the lid, and take out the capsicums carefully.

Filling

1. Chop the onions, green chillies, potatoes and cabbage. Grate the carrots and cheese.
2. Heat 4 tablespoons of oil, and add the chillies and onions. When browned, add the potatoes and fry for a while. Then add the cabbage and carrot, and continue to fry, adding the garam masala, chilly powder and salt. Sprinkle some water, cover and cook on low heat. When done, add the chopped coriander, cooked peas and stir for some time until all the water has evaporated. Allow to cool, add the cheese, and mix thoroughly.
3. Stuff the capsicums with this mixture. Crumble the bread slices. Taking small portions, place this on top of the filling and press down with wet fingers so that the crumbs are moist. Set aside until needed.
4. Pour a little oil in a frying pan (preferably non-stick). Place the capsicums upside down (the filling side should be at the bottom), reduce the heat, cover with a tight fitting lid, and allow to cook for 2-3 minutes. Then remove the cover and fry by basting some oil on top of the capsicums. Carefully turn and fry the other side as well until the capsicums are done.

   Alternately, grease a baking tray, smear the capsicums with some butter/ghee, and put them on the tray with the filling at the bottom. Bake in a moderate oven (190°C/375°F) for 15 minutes. Remove the tray, invert the capsicums and leave them in the oven for another ten minutes.

Stuffed Capsicum with Eggs

Method

1. Prepare the capsicums as before. Carefully break an egg into each hollow, and season with salt, pepper and cheese.
2. Crumble the bread slices, press the top with crumbs, and smear capsicums with butter/ghee. Place on a greased tray and bake in a moderate oven (190°C/375°F) for 15-20 minutes or until the eggs are set.

   Alternately, place the capsicums on a trivet, and steam cook in a pressure cooker without the weight until the eggs are set.

Note

For this recipe, omit all the vegetables except for the capsicums.

Cabbage Rabdi
(A Thick Delicious Cabbage Pudding)

Ingredients

2 litres/2.1 quarts milk	10 almonds, skinned
2 cups chopped cabbage	10 cashew nuts
1 cup sugar	1 teaspoon cardamom powder
1 cup light cream	
a pinch of green colour (optional)	

Method

1. Grate half of the nuts and chop the other half.
2. Boil the milk, add the cabbage and cook on a very slow fire stirring constantly until the mixture is thick. Do not allow cream to form on the surface.
3. Now add the grated nuts and the sugar and continue to cook until the mixture is very thick and creamy. Cool.
4. Add the cream and the cardamom powder, stir, and pour into a bowl. Garnish with the chopped nuts coloured green. Serve chilled.

To colour the nuts

Chop or cut the almonds and cashew nuts into thin slivers. Sprinkle some green colour (optional) and very little water, and delicately mix the nuts and colour. Allow to dry before use.

---- *Menu* 2 ----

Plain or Egg Parathas	**Serve with**
Dal Stew with Cream	Bhagara Tomato
Dum Gobi with Potato Fingers	Stuffed Brinjals
Methi Garlic Pulav	**Dessert**
Cucumber Raita	Pumpkin Halwa

Plain or Egg Parathas

Ingredients (plain)
- 4 cups wheat flour
- 4 teaspoons oil (to mix in dough)
- 1/2 teaspoon salt
- oil for frying

Ingredients (egg)
- 8 small eggs
- a pinch of turmeric powder
- 1/2 teaspoon chilly powder
- salt to taste

Method (plain)

1. Mix all the ingredients for the parathas with some water to make a soft dough. Leave covered for at least three hours.
2. Take out a large lemon-sized ball and flatten it with a rolling-pin into a thick circle. Apply some oil and fold into half (semicircle). Apply some oil and fold again to form a triangle.
3. Flatten the triangle further with a rolling pin using very little flour or oil.
4. Heat a tava (skillet), place the paratha on it, and allow to cook on both sides. Now pour a few drops of oil all around and on top and cook until brown on both sides.
5. Make all the parathas thus.

Method (egg)

Beat the eggs with a pinch of turmeric and salt. Add the chilly powder. Place a cooked paratha on a tava (skillet), and taking a tablespoon of the egg mixture, spread it all over the paratha. Turn over the paratha carefully. Cover with a plate and leave for a minute or two on a slow fire until the egg is cooked. Turn over and repeat this process till both sides are coated with the egg. Serve hot.

Dal Stew

Ingredients

1 cup gram dal	1/2 teaspoon turmeric powder
2 medium onions	1/2 teaspoon chilly powder
2 medium potatoes	1/2 teaspoon cumin seeds
2 medium tomatoes	3/4 cup light cream
3 green chillies, slit	1 teaspoon garam masala powder
1.3 cm/0.5 inch piece ginger (minced)	
2 tablespoons ghee	
salt to taste	

Method

1. Chop one onion and slice the other. Cut the potatoes and tomatoes into cubes.
2. Wash the dal, and cook in water with the turmeric. When half cooked, add the chopped onion, potatoes and tomatoes, chilly powder and salt. Cook until the dal and vegetables are done. Remove from fire.
3. Heat the ghee in a kadai (wok). Add the cumin seeds and when done, add the sliced onion, slit chillies and minced ginger. Fry until the onions are browned. Pour the cooked dal into this and simmer for a minute or two. Remove from fire and pour into a serving bowl.
4. Beat the cream lightly, pour over the dal and sprinkle the garam masala. Serve hot.

Dum Gobi with Potato Fingers

Ingredients

1 large cauliflower
6 medium potatoes
1 cup boiled peas
3 chopped tomatoes
2 cups curds (yoghurt)
1/2 teaspoon pepper
1 tablespoon chopped coriander
2 tablespoons ghee
oil for frying potatoes
salt to taste

Grind to paste

2 medium onions
5 garlic cloves
1 small piece ginger
2 teaspoons coriander powder
2 teaspoons cumin powder
1 teaspoon chilly powder
1/2 teaspoon turmeric powder
1/2 teaspoon garam masala
1 tablespoon chopped mint
1 tablespoon coriander

Seasoning

5 cashew nuts, broken
3/4 teaspoon caraway seeds
3 green chillies

Method

1. Cut the potatoes into finger lengths and leave in water to which a little salt has been added. After some time remove the pieces, squeeze out all the water and allow to dry on a cloth before frying.
2. Heat the oil in a kadai (wok). Fry the potato fingers, a handful at a time until fairly crisp and browned. After frying all the potatoes, sprinkle some salt while still warm and set aside.
3. Chop the tomatoes, boil the peas, and cut the chillies into small pieces. Remove the stem of the cauliflower and wash thoroughly in warm water, especially between the florets. Smear some salt and pepper, place the cauliflower on a trivet in a pressure cooker and steam for 10 minutes without using the weight until it is almost cooked. Remove carefully and transfer it on to a flat oven-proof dish.
4. Leave two tablespoons of oil in the kadai (after frying the potatoes), and add 2 tablespoons of ghee to it. Heat the mixture and add the caraway seeds and cashew nuts. When the nuts are browned, add the green chillies, then the ground paste and fry until the oil rises to the surface.
5. Add the tomatoes and fry until they turn soft. Now beat the curds and add it to the masalas, along with half of the cooked peas. Simmer on slow heat until the gravy is thick. Pour this over the cauliflower.
6. Surround the cauliflower with the potato fingers. Sprinkle the rest of the peas and chopped coriander all over. If desired, a little grated cheese may also be sprinkled.
7. Leave the cauliflower in an oven at 100°C/210°F until ready to serve.

Methi Garlic Pulav

(Fenugreek and Garlic Flavoured Fried Rice)

Ingredients

2 cups rice	1/2 teaspoon asafoetida
3 or 4 medium tomatoes	1/2 teaspoon cumin seeds
12 garlic cloves	1/2 teaspoon turmeric powder
2.5 cm/1 inch piece ginger	1 1/2 teaspoons chilly powder
2 large bundles methi(fenugreek) leaves	3 tablespoons oil
3 green chillies	3 tablespoons ghee
1 cup peas, shelled	salt to taste

Method

1. Wash the rice and spread on a cloth to dry. Crush the garlic, slit the green chillies, and chop the ginger and tomatoes. Keep each of these separate. Wash and chop the methi leaves.
2. Heat the ghee-oil mixture in a pressure cooker. Add the asafoetida, cumin, garlic, ginger and chillies. When the garlic is browned, add the methi leaves and fry for a couple of minutes.

3. Add the chopped tomatoes and continue to fry until they turn soft. Add the turmeric and chilly powders, and fry for a minute or two.
4. Now add the rice and fry for a few more minutes. Then add the salt, peas, four cups of boiling water and cook covered without using the weight.

Cucumber Raita

Ingredients
1 medium cucumber
1 1/2 cups yoghurt
2 teaspoons chopped coriander
salt to taste

Seasoning
1/2 teaspoon chilly powder
1/2 teaspoon cumin powder
1 green chilly, minced fine

Method
1. Grate the cucumber and set aside.
2. Beat the curds and add the salt, green chilly, half the chopped coriander, and grated cucumber. Mix well and pour into a bowl.
3. Sprinkle the chilly and cumin powders, and garnish with the rest of the chopped coriander.

Stuffed Brinjals (Eggplant)

Ingredients
8 brinjals (round variety)
2 medium onions
4 green chillies
1.3 cm/0.5 inch piece ginger
2 garlic cloves
1 tablespoon chopped coriander
2 teaspoons vinegar (optional)

1/2 cup grated cheese
3/4 teaspoon pepper powder
3/4 teaspoon garam masala
4 slices bread
6 tablespoons oil or vanaspati
salt to taste

Method
1. Cut the brinjals into halves, and parboil (boil until they are almost but not quite done) in salted water. Do not overcook. Remove the brinjals carefully from the water and leave on a plate to cool. When cold, scoop out the pulp carefully, and set aside both the pulp and the cases.
2. Chop the onions and mince the ginger, garlic and green chillies. Heat 2 table-spoons of oil and add the minced and chopped ingredients. Fry until the onions turn pink. Add the brinjal pulp, salt, pepper, and garam masala. Mix well and cook for a minute. If you are using vinegar, add it at this stage. Remove from fire, add the cheese and chopped coriander, and mix.

3. Stuff the brinjal cases with the above filling, and smoothen out the surface. Discard the edges of the bread slices, and break the slices into crumbs. Take a little of this and press down on the stuffing all over. Sprinkle some water and moisten the crumbs so that they hold. Fill all the cases thus and set aside.
4. When ready to serve, fry the brinjals in a shallow frying pan (preferably non-stick) with the stuffed sides downwards using some oil. Carefully turn over and fry the other side too, adding a little oil. Transfer the fried brinjals on to a plate and serve immediately.

Alternately

Grease a baking tray and place the stuffed brinjals in them with the stuffed side upwards. Brush the tops and sides with oil, and bake in a moderate oven (190°C/375°F) for 20 minutes until the top is nicely browned.

Bhagara Tomato

Ingredients

500 gm/1.1 lb tomatoes	1 1/2 tablespoons sesame seeds
1 large onion	2 tablespoons coriander seeds
2.5 cm/1 inch piece ginger	2 tablespoons cumin seeds
4 garlic cloves	2 teaspoons chilly powder
5 green chillies	1/2 teaspoon turmeric powder
2 sprigs curry leaves	1/2 cup oil
2 tablespoons grated coconut	salt to taste
1 tablespoon chopped coriander	

Method

1. Wash, wipe and cut the tomatoes and chillies into small pieces. Chop the onions.
2. Dry roast first the sesame seeds, then the coconut until reddish in colour, then the coriander and cumin seeds, all separately. Grind the roasted ingredients along with the garlic and ginger to a fine paste adding very little water.
3. Heat the oil. Add the curry leaves, onions and cut chillies, and fry for 1 minute. Then add the ground paste and continue to fry adding the chilly and turmeric powders, until the oil rises to the surface. Add the tomatoes and fry until they turn soft. Now add the salt, coriander leaves and some water if necessary. Simmer on low heat until the tomatoes are cooked, and the gravy is thick. Cool, bottle and store in the refrigerator.

Note

This dish keeps well, and can be prepared in advance of the party, if necessary to save time.

Pumpkin Halwa

Ingredients

2 cups grated red pumpkin
1 cup grated coconut
2 cups milk
4 tablespoons heavy cream
4 tablespoons ghee
1 cup sugar

1 tablespoon almonds
1 tablespoon chopped cashew nuts
1/2 tablespoon sultanas
1 teaspoon powdered cardamom
a few drops almond or rose essence
a pinch yellow colour (optional)

Method

1. Steam cook the pumpkin gratings with very little water. Cool. Grind (preferably in a mixer) with the coconut and some of the nuts, along with some milk.
2. Put the mixture in a thick-bottomed vessel, and add the rest of the milk along with the sugar. Stir over low heat.
3. When the sugar has dissolved, and the mixture starts to thicken, add the colour (optional), and continue to cook until the mixture is quite thick.
4. Setting aside 2 tablespoons of ghee, add the rest gradually to the halwa, stirring all the while until the mixture starts to leave the sides of the vessel.
5. Remove from the fire, add the cardamom powder and essence, and mix well. Fry the nuts and sultanas in the remainder of the ghee, and add half of them to the halwa.

To serve

Transfer the halwa onto a serving bowl. Smoothen out the surface, and garnish with the remaining nuts. Serve hot or cold.

---- Menu 3 ----

Savoury Idlis	**Serve with**
Onion Sambar	Cabbage Vadas
Capsicum Rice	Coconut Chutney
Carrot Pachadi (Raita)	Tomato Thokku
Jeera Rasam (optional)	**Dessert**
Curds (Yoghurt) Semia	Pal Polis

Savoury Idlis

(Steam-cooked Lentil Cakes)

Ingredients
1/2 cup green gram dal
1/2 cup black gram dal
2 cups semolina (cream of wheat)
2 tablespoons ghee
2 tablespoons oil
1/4 teaspoon baking soda
1 cup curds (yoghurt)
salt to taste
1 dozen cup moulds

Chop very fine
3 green chillies
1.3 cm/0.5 inch piece ginger
2 sprigs curry leaves
1 tablespoon chopped coriander

Powder roughly
1 teaspoon pepper
2 teaspoons cumin seeds

To serve
Some ghee

Method
1. Soak the dals in water for a few hours and grind to a smooth paste with the addition of a little water.
2. Dry roast the semolina in a kadai (wok) to a light brown colour stirring continuously. Remove from fire and cool. Then add to the ground dal with some salt and set aside for at least eight hours, thereby allowing sufficient time for fermentation to take place.
3. Before making the idlis check to see if the batter is fermented. Otherwise add either the soda or the baking powder and mix thoroughly before setting aside.
4. Heat 2 tablespoons of ghee and add powdered pepper and cumin seeds. When done, add the chopped ingredients (except the coriander leaves) and fry for one minute. Pour the seasoning into the batter and mix well.
5. Beat the curds and add the chopped coriander leaves (and some more salt if

necessary) along with one tablespoon of oil. Pour this mixture into the batter and mix thoroughly.

6. Grease the cup moulds with some oil and pour some of the batter into each cup. Steam cook for eight to ten minutes until the idlis are done.

7. Remove from cups and serve hot with ghee and coconut chutney.

Note

If you do not have sufficient cups to make idlis, use the idli stand instead.

Onion Sambar

Ingredients

1 cup tuvar dal
1 teaspoon turmeric powder
2 sprigs curry leaves
1 1/2 cup spring onions, peeled
2 green chillies, slit
1 lemon-sized ball tamarind
3 tablespoons oil
salt to taste

For the masala

1/4 teaspoon asafoetida
1/2 teaspoon fenugreek seeds
1 tablespoon gram dal
3 dried red chillies
2 tablespoons coriander seeds
3 tablespoons grated coconut

Seasoning

1 teaspoon mustard seeds

Method

1. Heat 1 tablespoon of oil in a kadai (wok). Fry the asafoetida and the fenugreek seeds until they turn dark brown. Remove both from the kadai. Add the gram dal and the red chillies and fry until the dal turns golden brown. Remove. Add the coriander seeds and fry for a minute or so. Add the coconut gratings and fry until the coconut turns light brown. Remove. Grind all these ingredients together to a fine paste.

2. Cook the dal in water with half a teaspoon of turmeric powder in a pressure cooker.

3. Boil the tamarind in boiling water, and squeeze to extract the pulp.

4. Heat the rest of the oil and add the mustard. When done, add the curry leaves, green chillies, onions and turmeric powder, and fry until the onions are soft and brown.

5. Add the tamarind extract and salt, and cook for 5-8 minutes.

6. Now add the cooked dal, ground masalas and some water if the mixture is too thick. Simmer for a few minutes. Serve hot.

Capsicum Rice

Ingredients
1 1/2 cups rice
4 capsicums (green peppers)
2 potatoes
2 tomatoes
4 green chillies, slit
1.3 cm/0.5 inch piece ginger, minced
1 cup shelled peas
1 large lemon
2 tablespoons chopped coriander
2 sprigs curry leaves
1 large onion

Seasoning
1 teaspoon mustard seeds
2 teaspoons black gram dal
2 teaspoons Bengal gram dal
1/2 teaspoon turmeric powder
2 tablespoons oil
2 tablespoons ghee
salt to taste
1/2 teaspoon garam masala
    (optional)

Garnish
2 tablespoons grated coconut

Method
1. Cook the rice so that each grain is separate. Spread on a plate to cool, sprinkling some oil.
2. Chop the onions. Cut the potatoes into inch-long finger chips. Cut the capsicums into thin strips and tomatoes into quarters. Boil the peas.
3. Heat the oil and ghee together in a kadai (wok). Add the mustard seeds, and when done, add both the dals and fry till they turn golden. Add the slit chillies, minced ginger and curry leaves. Fry for a minute, adding the chopped onion at this time. Add the turmeric and garam masala powders, and fry until the onions turn brown.
4. Add the capsicums and fry until they turn soft. Next add the potatoes and tomatoes, and fry for a few minutes. Now add half a cup of water, salt and cook in a covered vessel until the vegetables are done. Add the peas and stir for a while until all the water evaporates. Remove from fire and allow to cool. Add the lemon juice and some of the chopped coriander.
5. Pour this mixture into the rice and mix lightly using only the tips of your fingers.

Note
A tablespoon of sambar powder can be added to the vegetables to enhance the taste.

To serve
Transfer the rice onto a serving plate. Smoothen the surface, and garnish with the grated coconut and the rest of the coriander.

Carrot Pachadi

(Seasoned Yoghurt with Carrots)

Ingredients

3 medium carrots

1 1/2 cups curds (yoghurt)

2 green chillies, chopped fine

1 tablespoon chopped coriander

2 teaspoons oil

1 teaspoon mustard seeds

2 sprigs curry leaves

salt to taste

Method

1. Wash, grate and cook the carrots in sufficient water until they are cooked and all the water has evaporated.
2. Heat the oil and add the mustard, chillies and curry leaves. Pour this into the cooked carrots. Cool.
3. Beat the curds and add to the carrots along with some of the chopped coriander. Pour into a bowl and garnish with the rest of the coriander. Serve chilled.

Note

The carrots may be grated after they are cooked.

Jeera Rasam

(Cumin Flavoured Mulligatawny Soup)

Ingredients

1 teaspoon rasam powder
(see Paruppu Rasam)

1 lemon-sized ball tamarind

salt to taste

Grind to paste

1 teaspoon tuvar dal

1/2 teaspoon cumin seeds

2 sprigs curry leaves

Seasoning

2 teaspoons ghee

1 teaspoon mustard seeds

1 dried red chilly

1 sprig curry leaf

Method

1. Boil the tamarind in water, and squeeze to extract the pulp. Add 1 cup of water, rasam powder, salt, and boil until the quantity is reduced by half.
2. To the ground paste, add 2-3 cups of water and mix well. Add this to the boiling mixture, and allow to simmer for a while.
3. Season the given ingredients in ghee and pour into the rasam. Serve very hot as an appetizer. (Serves 4.)

Note

For rasam powder refer to Part 2, Menu 3.

Curds (Yoghurt) Semia
(Seasoned Vermicelli in Yoghurt)

Ingredients

2 cups vermicelli, broken
4 cups curds (yoghurt)
1 small piece ginger, chopped
2 green chillies, cut into pieces
1 tablespoon coriander, chopped
salt to taste

Seasoning

1 1/2 tablespoons oil
1 teaspoon mustard seeds
2 teaspoons Bengal gram dal
2 teaspoons black gram dal
2 sprigs curry leaves

Method

1. Boil 4 cups of water with 2 teaspoons of oil and a little salt. Add the vermicelli and cook until it is done. Remove from fire, strain and cool.
2. Heat the oil. Add the seasonings and when done, add the green chillies and ginger, and fry for a minute. Remove from fire and allow to cool.
3. Beat the curds with salt. Add the chopped coriander, cooked vermicelli, and seasonings, and mix well. Serve chilled.

Cabbage Vadas
(Spicy Cabbage Fritters)

Ingredients

1 1/2 cups black gram dal
1 cup cabbage, chopped
4 green chillies, chopped
2.5 cm/1 inch piece ginger
1 chopped onion (optional)

3 sprigs curry leaves
2 tablespoons chopped coriander
oil for frying
salt to taste

Method

1. Soak the dal in sufficient water for 3-4 hours. Drain the water and grind to a smooth paste, adding the chillies, ginger, curry leaves and salt. (Take care not to add too much water while grinding.) Add the chopped cabbage and coriander. Add 1 chopped onion if you desire.
2. Make small balls of the batter, flatten using the palms of your hands, and deep fry. Serve immediately.

Coconut Chutney

Ingredients

1/2 large coconut
1/2 cup curds (yoghurt)
1 1/2 tablespoons Bengal gram dal
1/4 teaspoon asafoetida
2 sprigs curry leaves
salt to taste

4 green chillies
2 tablespoons chopped coriander
3 teaspoons oil
1 teaspoon mustard seeds
2 teaspoons black gram

Method

1. Fry the asafoetida and Bengal gram dal in a little oil. Add the green chillies, half of the curry leaves, half of the coriander leaves, salt and coconut. Grind to a paste.
2. Heat the oil. Add the mustard and black gram dal. When the dal turns brown, add the remainder of the curry leaves. Pour this seasoning into the chutney.
3. Beat the curds and add half a cup of water as well as the rest of the chopped coriander. Pour into the chutney and mix well.

Note

Instead of curds, juice of one lemon can be added.

Pal Polis
(Flour and Semolina Dumplings in Milk)

Ingredients

1/2 cup semolina (cream of wheat)

2 cups flour (maida)

4 teaspoons ghee (for mixing)

a pinch of salt

ghee or ghee/vanaspati mixture for frying

7 cups milk

1 1/2 cups sugar

a pinch of saffron

4 cardamoms, powdered

Method

1. Mix the flour and semolina with ghee, adding a pinch of salt. Form a fairly stiff dough by kneading, adding very little water. Cover the dough and set aside.
2. Boil the milk with sugar until the milk thickens slightly. Add the saffron and cardamom and boil for a few more minutes. Remove from fire.
3. Divide the dough into small balls, and roll them out into very small puris using ghee while rolling instead of flour.
4. Heat the ghee in a kadai (wok), and fry two or three puris at a time on medium heat until golden brown. Fry both sides.
5. While still hot, soak the puris in warm milk. After a few minutes, remove the puris from the milk so that they do not get too soggy.
6. Just before serving, warm the milk (from Step 5) and pour it over the puris. Serve hot.

Tomato Thokku

Refer to Tomato Thokku in Part 6, Pickles and Chutneys.

---- *Menu 4* ----

Cheese Parathas	**Serve with**
Malai Dal	Cabbage Raita
Vegetable Delight	Green Banana Tikki
Brinjal or Egg Moillee	Vinegar Mangoes
Caramel Rice	**Dessert**
	Ras Malai

Cheese Parathas

Ingredients

4 cups wheat flour
200 gm/7 oz. grated cheese
1 tablespoon chopped coriander
2 green chillies, minced

1/2 teaspoon pepper powders
1/2 teaspoon chilly powder
salt to taste
oil for frying

Method

1. Add 4 teaspoons of oil to the flour along with salt and sufficient water. Mix to form a soft dough. Cover and set aside for two to three hours.
2. Add all the other ingredients to the grated cheese, and mix well.
3. Divide the dough into lemon-sized balls, adding a little oil during the process. Gradually work each ball into a cup, using some oil while doing so. Fill each ball with some of the cheese filling, and close. Roll out carefully into a paratha.
4. Cook the parathas on a griddle, until browned on the underside. Turn it over, add a little oil, and repeat the process.

Malai Dal

Ingredients

1 1/2 cups whole black gram dal
2 medium onions, chopped
3 green chillies, chopped fine
2.5 cm/1 inch piece ginger
6 garlic cloves
1/2 teaspoon garam masala

1 tablespoon unsalted white butter
4 tablespoons light cream
2 cups milk
3 tablespoon ghee
salt to taste

Method

1. Wash and soak the dal in sufficient water for at least 2 hours. Boil (preferably in a pressure cooker) with chopped ginger, garlic and green chillies. When cooked, mash gently with a ladle.
2. Add the milk and cook further until the mixture is well blended. Add the salt at this time, and some water if too thick.
3. Fry the onions in ghee until browned. Add the garam masala powder, stir for a minute, and pour into the dal.
4. Just before serving, heat the dal, add the butter and mix well. Transfer into a serving bowl, pour the cream and serve immediately.

Vegetable Delight

Ingredients

4 medium potatoes
1 small cauliflower
150 gm/5 oz. green beans
2 medium carrots
1 cup shelled peas
1/2 small cabbage
2 large onions
3 medium tomatoes
4 green chillies, slit
1 tablespoon chopped coriander
5 tablespoons oil or vanaspati
salt to taste

1/2 teaspoon turmeric powder
2 tablespoons coriander-cumin powder
2 teaspoons chilly powder
1 teaspoon garam masala

Grind to paste

4 tablespoons grated coconut
2 teaspoons khus khus
2.5 cm/1 inch piece ginger
1 large onion
1 tablespoon chopped coriander
1 tablespoon chopped mint
4 garlic cloves

Method

1. Prepare the vegetables as follows: peel and cut the potatoes into large pieces; scrape the carrots and cut into rounds or inch-long pieces; break the cauliflower into small florets; cut the cabbage into large pieces; cut the beans into 4 cm (1.5 inch) pieces; cut the onions into thick slices; slice the tomatoes into quarters.
2. Heat the oil, and fry the chillies and onion slices until browned. Add the ground paste, turmeric powder and continue to fry until the masalas are done. Add the tomatoes, and fry for a while. Now add all the vegetables and fry until they turn a little soft.
3. Add the dry masala powders and stir fry the vegetables for a few minutes. Now add the salt, sufficient water to cover the vegetables, and cook covered on slow heat until a thick gravy is formed. Garnish with chopped coriander before serving.

Brinjal or Egg Moillee

Note
The same method is used in either recipe with the main ingredient being either brinjal or eggs. Also since American brinjals are much larger than other varieties, a smaller number must be used, if you are cooking in the US.

Ingredients
6 medium brinjals (round variety)
1 small coconut, grated
6 tablespoons ghee or oil
1/2 teaspoon turmeric powder
4 green chillies, slit
salt to taste

Egg Moillee
6 medium eggs

Chop fine
2 large onions
3 tomatoes
a handful chopped coriander

Grind to paste
6 garlic cloves
2.5 cm/1 inch piece ginger

Seasoning
3 cloves
3 cardamoms
3 cinnamon sticks
2 bay leaves

Method
1. Add one cup of boiling water to the grated coconut and take out thick milk by first squeezing and then straining the resultant liquid. Set aside. Add some more water and extract as much thin milk as you can. Strain. Keep the milks separate.
2. Cut the brinjals into slices, and smear some salt and a little turmeric powder. Set aside for some time. After a while, press the slices between the palms of your hands and squeeze out all the water.
3. Fry the brinjal slices in approximately 3 tablespoons of ghee, and set aside. (You may find it easier to fry the vegetable in smaller portions, using the ghee in proportionately smaller quantities.)
4. Heat the rest of the ghee, and add the seasonings. When done, add the slit chillies and fry for a minute. Add the onions and fry until brown in colour.
5. Now add the ground paste and fry until the ghee separates. Then add the tomatoes and fry until they are done. Add the thin coconut milk, some of the chopped coriander, brinjal slices and salt, and simmer for a few minutes before removing from the fire.
6. Just before serving, add the thick milk, the rest of the chopped coriander, boil once and remove from fire. Serve immediately.

Egg Moillee

Hard boil the eggs, shell when cold, and cut into two halves. Fry lightly in ghee, turning over carefully so as not to break them. Pour the curry (prepared the same way) into a serving bowl, add the eggs, sprinkle chopped coriander and serve.

Caramel Rice

Ingredients
2 cups rice
3/4 cup curds (yoghurt)
2 sliced onions
2.5 cm/1 inch piece ginger, chopped
4 green chillies, slit
2 tablespoons sugar
1/2 cup ghee
salt to taste

Seasoning
4 cloves
4 cardamoms
3 small cinnamon sticks
8 cashew nuts, broken
2 tablespoons raisins
2 teaspoons coriander powder
1 teaspoon chilly powder

Method
1. Wash the rice and dry on a cloth or paper towel.
2. Heat half of the ghee in a pressure cooker and add the cashew nuts and raisins. Fry to a golden colour and remove from the cooker. Add the sliced onions, fry until crisp, remove and set aside.
3. Pour the rest of the ghee in the cooker, add the cloves, cinnamon and cardamoms, and fry until done. Add the sugar and when it turns dark brown in colour, add the rice, green chillies, ginger, coriander and chilly powders, and continue to fry. Add the curds, and stir for a few minutes.
4. Now add 4 cups of boiling water and salt, close the lid of the cooker and cook on low heat without the weight until the rice is cooked.

To serve
Take half of the nuts, raisins and fried onions, and mix well with the rice. Transfer the rice to a serving plate, garnish with the rest, and serve.

Cabbage Raita

(Cabbage in Seasoned Yoghurt)

Ingredients

300 gm/10 oz. cabbage
2 green chillies, chopped
1 chopped onion (optional)
2 cups curds (yoghurt)

1/2 teaspoon chilly powder
1 teaspoon cumin seeds
salt to taste
1 tablespoon chopped coriander

Method

1. Chop the cabbage, and steam cook with salt, or cook with very little water on medium heat. Remove from fire. Cool.
2. Dry roast the cumin seeds, powder and set aside.
3. Beat the curds, add the chillies and onions, cooked cabbage, chilly powder and some of the cumin powder. Pour into a bowl, sprinkle the chopped coriander and the rest of the cumin. Serve chilled.

Green Banana Tikki

(Savoury Plantain Fritters)

Ingredients

4 unripe bananas (plantains)
2 potatoes
2 large onions
2.5 cm/1 inch piece ginger
6 green.chillies, chopped
1 tablespoon chopped coriander
salt to taste
oil for frying

1/2 teaspoon turmeric powder
1 teaspoon chilly powder
1 tablespoon coriander powder
1/4 tablespoon cumin powder
1 teaspoon garam masala
3 tablespoons gram flour

Method

1. Boil the bananas and potatoes with their jackets. Peel and mash while still warm.
2. Grind the onions and ginger to a paste. Heat 1 tablespoon of oil, and add the chopped chillies. Fry for a minute, add the ground paste along with the dry masalas, and stir for a few more minutes.
3. Add the mashed vegetables, salt and some of the chopped coriander, and mix thoroughly. Remove from fire and allow to cool.
4. Divide the dough into lemon-sized balls. Flatten on the palm of your hand, roll in gram flour and shallow fry.

Note

If preferred, the tikkis can be made with potatoes only.

Ras Malai
(Indian Cream Cheese in Cream Syrup)

For the rasagoolla
1 1/4 cup milk powder
2 tablespoons oil
1 tablespoon curds
1 teaspoon baking powder
1 teaspoon flour (maida)
1/2 egg

For the ras (syrup)
1 1/4 cup milk powder
    or 1 litre/1 quart milk
3/4 cup sugar
5 cardamoms
a few drops rose essence

Method
1. Mix all the ingredients for the rasagoolla (in the order given) very lightly to form a soft dough. Shape into balls, flatten slightly, and set aside.
2. Simmer the ingredients for the syrup until the sugar has dissolved.
3. Immerse the balls in the boiling syrup, cover and cook for 15 minutes on a slow fire. Cool.
4. Serve chilled.

Ras Malai (Eggless)
(Indian Cream Cheese in Cream Syrup)

For the rasagoollas (20)
1 litre/1 quart milk
juice of 1 lemon
1 cup sugar
4 cups water
2 teaspoons flour (maida)
a pinch of baking powder
1/4 teaspoon cardamom powder

For the ras (syrup)
1.5 litres/1.6 quarts milk
1 cup sugar
a few drops rose essence
1/2 teaspoon cardamom powder

For the garnish
1 tablespoon slivered almonds

Method for the rasagoollas
1. Bring the milk to a boil. Gradually add the lemon juice until it starts to curdle. Add 2-3 drops more of lemon juice and allow to boil once more. When the whey separates, turn off the heat and allow the paneer that has formed to settle for 15 minutes.
2. When sufficiently cool, strain the whey. Tie the resultant paneer block in a thin muslin cloth and hang for 3-4 hours until there is no trace of water left.
3. Transfer the paneer onto a plate. Add the sifted flour, baking powder, cardamom powder and a pinch of sugar. Knead gently for 10 minutes using the palms of your hands. Make 20 balls and set aside.

4. Boil the sugar with 2 cups of water until a syrup is obtained. Strain the syrup, place back on fire and add 1 more cup of water. When it starts to boil, add the rasagoollas and allow to boil. After 2-3 minutes, sprinkle half a cup of water on the boiling rasagoollas, and repeat the process after a minute. When the rasagoollas are sufficiently puffed (after 8-10 minutes of boiling), turn off the heat and let them remain in the syrup until required.

Method for the ras (syrup)

Boil the milk with sugar until it thickens. Add the rose essence and the cardamom powder, and mix well.

Method for the Ras Malai

1. When the rasagoollas are sufficiently cool, remove them from the syrup. Gently squeeze to remove the excess syrup and drop them in the thickened milk. Allow them to soak well.
2. Garnish with slivered almonds and refrigerate until ready to serve.

Vinegar Mangoes

Refer to Vinegar Mangoes in Part 6, Pickles and Chutneys.

—— *Menu* 5 ——

Cauliflower Pulav with Whey   **Serve with**
Shahi Dal   Pumpkin Raita
Paneer or Egg Korma   Stuffed Cabbage Rolls
Bhagara Baigan   Sweet-Hot Mango Chutney
Palak Puris   **Dessert**
                               Custard Souffle or
                               Apricot or Guava Stew
                               with Custard

Cauliflower Pulav with Whey

If you are making paneer korma use the whey obtained while making paneer for the pulav. If you are making egg korma use sour cream instead.

Ingredients

2 cups rice
3/4 cup ghee
1 large cauliflower
2 large onions
4 green chillies, slit
3 cloves garlic
1 teaspoon ginger, chopped
a handful of fresh coriander
1 cup sour cream or 4 cups whey

2 large cardamoms
4 cloves
2 cinnamon sticks
1 teaspoon whole shahjeera
   (black cumin)
1/2 teaspoon chilly powder
1/2 teaspoon pepper powder
1/2 teaspoon garam masala
salt to taste

Garnish

1 small cucumber
2 small carrots
3 small tomatoes
a few roasted almonds

Method

1. Wash the rice and drain on a cloth or paper towel. Cut the cauliflower into small florets, wash in warm water and set aside. Slice the onions and chop the coriander leaves.
2. Heat half of the ghee in a pressure cooker, fry the sliced onions until crisp and remove from cooker. To the same ghee, add the cauliflower and fry, sprinkling a little salt and pepper. Remove and set aside.

3. Pour the rest of the ghee into the cooker, add the whole spices, and stir fry. When done, add the chopped ginger, garlic and chillies. Fry until the garlic turns light brown in colour.

4. Add the rice and fry for a few minutes, while adding the powdered spices. Add the cauliflower sprigs, half of the fried onions and salt. If you are using whey, add 4 cups of whey, half of the chopped coriander, and cook covered without using the weight on medium heat until done. If you are using sour cream, beat the cream to a smooth consistency and add water to make 4 cups in all.

To serve

Wash and cut the cucumber and tomatoes into thin slices. Grate the carrots fine. Keep all these separately. Transfer the pulav on to a large serving plate, keeping the rice in the centre, and smoothening out the sides. Arrange the tomatoes and cucumber slices alternately all around the rice. Garnish with the fried onions, grated carrots, chopped coriander and the almonds. Serve hot.

Shahi Dal

Ingredients

1 cup tuvar or masoor dal
1/2 teaspoon turmeric powder
3 tablespoons ghee
1 large onion, chopped
1.3 cm/0.5 inch piece ginger, chopped
3 tomatoes, chopped
2 garlic cloves
3 green chillies, slit
2 tablespoons ground coconut
  or 1/2 cup thick coconut milk

Seasoning

2 bay leaves
3 cloves
3 cardamoms
3 cinnamon sticks
1/2 teaspoon chilly powder
1/2 teaspoon pepper powder
salt to taste

Method

1. Wash and boil the dal with turmeric, and set aside.

2. Fry the bay leaves, cloves, cardamoms and cinnamon in ghee. When done, add the ginger, garlic and green chillies and fry. Add the onions and continue to fry until they are browned. Add the tomatoes and fry until they turn soft. Now add the chilly and pepper powders, and fry for half a minute. Add the dal and salt (and a little water if too thick), and cook for a few minutes.

3. When the dal is sufficiently done, add the coconut milk or ground coconut, and cook for another minute or two. Remove from fire and serve very hot.

Paneer or Egg Korma

Ingredients
2 litres/2.1 quarts milk
2 cups shelled peas
6 tablespoons ghee
1 large onion
1 tablespoon chopped coriander
2 green chillies
6 cashew nuts, broken
1 cup light cream
juice of 2 lemons
4 cloves
2 1.3 cm/0.5 inch cinnamon sticks
4 cardamoms
1/2 teaspoon garam masala powder
1/2 teaspoon chilly powder
salt to taste

For the paneer korma
2 tablespoons flour
a generous pinch of saffron soaked in 1 cup of warm milk

Grind to a fine paste
1 large onion
2 green chillies
3 garlic cloves
2.5 cm/1 inch piece ginger
2 tablespoons grated coconut
2 teaspoons khus khus
6 cashew nuts
a handful fresh coriander

For the egg korma
6 eggs
a pinch of turmeric powder
salt to taste
1 medium onion
2 green chillies
2 tablespoons coriander

Method
1. Make the paneer as follows: boil the milk and while still on the fire, add some lemon juice gradually until the milk starts to curdle. Boil for another minute and remove from fire. When cool, strain through a muslin cloth. Keep the whey aside for the pulav. Take out the paneer, knead into a smooth dough, wrap it in a cloth, place a heavy flat weight on top and leave it for an hour. When the paneer block has flattened out, remove the weight and cut the paneer into cubes.
   350 gm/12 oz. of paneer may be purchased if you do not have the time to make it. Ricotta cheese is a suitable substitute.
2. Roll the paneer cubes in dry flour. Deep fry and soak in the saffron milk.
3. Chop the onions, cut the green chillies into 2-3 pieces each, and boil the peas. Heat the ghee in a kadai (wok), and add the nuts. Fry to a golden colour and remove. Add the cloves, cinnamon, cardamoms, chillies and the chopped onions, and fry until the onions are brown. Add the chilly and some of the garam masala powder, and fry for another couple of minutes.
4. Add the ground paste and fry until the ghee separates. Add the boiled peas, 2 cups of water and cook until a gravy is formed. Now add the paneer cubes along with the milk in which it was soaked. Also add some of the chopped coriander, and simmer for three minutes.

To serve

Beat the cream lightly. Pour the korma into a bowl and cream on top. Garnish with the rest of the garam masala and chopped coriander. Serve hot.

Egg Korma

The ingredients and method are the same as above, except that the paneer preparation is omitted.

To make the egg cubes

Beat the eggs, and add a pinch of salt and turmeric. Mince the onion, chillies and coriander leaves, and mix these with the eggs. Pour the mixture into a pan and steam cook until the eggs are cooked. Remove from fire, cool, and cut into cubes. Add this to the korma when the gravy is ready.

Bhagara Baigan

(A Spicy Eggplant Preparation)

Ingredients

8 small brinjals (round variety)
2 onions, chopped
3 chopped tomatoes (optional)
3 green chillies, slit
5 garlic cloves
3/4 cup oil
2 sprigs curry leaves
1/2 teaspoon turmeric
1 lemon-sized ball tamarind
salt to taste

For the masala

1 1/2 teaspoons poppy seeds
2 teaspoons sesame seeds
2 tablespoons coriander seeds
1 teaspoon cumin seeds
4 dried red chillies
3 garlic cloves
2 onions, chopped
3 tablespoons grated coconut
4 tablespoons chopped coriander

Method

1. Dry roast the poppy and sesame seeds in a kadai (wok), and remove. Add 2 teaspoons of oil, and fry the coriander seeds, cumin seeds and red chillies. Remove. Fry the chopped onion and garlic. Combine all the fried ingredients along with the coconut, half of the fresh coriander and salt, and grind to a fine paste.

2. Boil the tamarind in water for a few minutes, and squeeze to extract the pulp. Set aside. Wash and slit the brinjals into eights without allowing them to break. If the brinjals are too small, cut into fours instead. Fill the brinjals with some of the ground paste. If any ground masala is left over, set aside.

3. Heat half of the oil, add the stuffed brinjals, and fry on low heat, occasionally turning them over. When brinjals are fried, remove carefully, and set aside.
4. Pour the rest of the oil, add the curry leaves, slit chillies and garlic, and fry until the garlic is browned. Now add the onions and continue frying until they are done. If you are using tomatoes, add them at this stage and fry till they turn soft. Add any ground masala left over, and fry along with the turmeric powder.
5. Add the tamarind extract, 1 1/2 cups of water, a little salt, and cook for a few more minutes. Now add the fried brinjals, and cook for another minute. Take care to see that the brinjals do not break. Transfer the curry to a serving bowl, garnish with chopped coriander, and serve hot.

Palak Puris
(Spinach Puris)

Ingredients

2 cups wheat flour
1 cup flour (maida)
salt to taste
oil for frying

1 large bundle spinach
a handful of fenugreek leaves
3 green chillies
1.3 cm/0.5 inch piece ginger
2 cloves garlic
1/2 teaspoon aniseed

Method

1. Wash, chop and boil the spinach and fenugreek leaves. Cool. Grind to a paste along with the green chillies, ginger, garlic, aniseed and salt.
2. Mix the maida and wheat flour, and add the ground spinach, 3-4 teaspoons of oil and a little water to form a smooth dough. Cover the dough.
3. Divide the dough into lemon-sized balls, and roll out into slightly thick rounds. Deep fry, turning once to ensure that both sides are browned.

Pumpkin Raita

Ingredients

250 gm/9 oz. red pumpkin
2 green chillies, minced
1 1/2 cups curds (yoghurt)

1 teaspoon fresh mustard powder
2 teaspoons chopped coriander
salt to taste

Method

1. Grate the pumpkin and boil with just enough water and salt until soft. Cool and mash. Add the minced chillies.

2. Beat the curds and add the mustard powder, half the chopped coriander and mix with the pumpkin. Pour into a serving bowl and sprinkle the rest of the coriander on top. Serve chilled.

Stuffed Cabbage Rolls

Ingredients
12 large cabbage leaves
1 1/2 cups boiled mashed potatoes
1/2 cup boiled peas
1/2 teaspoon chilly powder
1/2 teaspoon garam masala powder
1 cup bread crumbs
oil for frying
salt to taste

Chop fine
1 large onion
3 green chillies
1.3 cm/0.5 inch piece ginger
2 teaspoons mint leaves
2 teaspoons fresh coriander

For the batter
4 tablespoons flour
1/4 teaspoon pepper
1/4 teaspoon salt
1/4 teaspoon chilly powder
1 cup water

Method
1. Boil the water with some salt. Immerse the cabbage leaves two at a time, cover, and cook for five minutes. Drain, remove and set aside. Blanch all the leaves thus.
2. Heat 2 tablespoons of oil. Add the chopped ingredients (except for the mint and coriander) and fry until they are done. Add the mashed potatoes and peas and fry for one minute. Add the chilly powder, garam masala, salt, chopped coriander and mint leaves, and mix well. Remove from fire and cool. Divide the dough into equal portions, one per cabbage leaf.
3. Remove the hard core of each leaf carefully, and spread it on a flat surface. Put some of the stuffing on one edge and roll carefully, turning in the edges gently.
4. Prepare the batter by mixing all the ingredients with water, and beat to a smooth paste. Dip each roll in this, roll in the bread crumbs and shallow fry, carefully turning it over when one side is done.

To serve
Arrange the fried rolls side by side on a plate. Garnish with chopped mint. Serve hot with tomato ketchup.

Custard Souffle

Ingredients

1 packet red jelly (jello) crystals
3 large eggs
4 cups milk
4 tablespoons custard powder
3 tablespoons sugar
2 1/2 cups water

For the icing

white of one egg
1 - 1 1/2 cups icing sugar
1 large fluted mould,
rinsed in cold water

Method

1. Dilute the jelly crystals in 1 cup of warm water. Mix thoroughly so that the jelly is smooth and the crystals have dissolved. Remove 2-3 tablespoons of this liquid and pour into the wetted mould, and leave in a refrigerator to set. To the rest of the jelly liquid, add 1 1/2 cups of water, mix, and cool.
2. Separate the egg whites. Mix the yolks with half a cup of cold milk and the custard powder.
3. Boil the rest of the milk with the sugar and cook until the milk thickens. Remove from fire and carefully add the egg-custard powder mixture, stirring vigorously so that no lumps are formed. Put back on fire and cook on low heat until the custard is thick and of a coating consistency. Remove from fire and allow to cool.
4. Mix together the custard and jelly, beating all the while. Beat two of the eggs whites stiff and blend into this mixture very lightly. Now pour this mixture into the mould on top of the set jelly, cover with lid, and put back in the refrigerator to set.

To serve

Unmould the jelly by loosening the edges with a sharp knife and carefully transfer to a serving plate by inverting the mould.

Icing

Beat 1 egg white stiff by gradually adding icing sugar until the white stands in peaks. Pipe this carefully onto the souffle with a piping nozzle and serve immediately.

Apricot or Guava Stew with Custard

Ingredients

8 ripe guavas
6 tablespoons sugar
4 cloves
2 large cardamoms
1 small cinnamon stick

For the custard

4 cups milk
3 tablespoons custard powder
3 tablespoons sugar
a few drops vanilla essence

For the apricot stew, use 400 gm (14 oz.) dried apricots. The rest is the same as above.

Method

1. Cut the guavas into two halves. Carefully scoop out the seeds and wash thoroughly. Put the fruit in a saucepan and add enough water to cover it. Add the sugar and spices, cover and cook till the guavas turn soft. Do not overcook the fruit.
2. Remove the fruit carefully and set aside to cool.
3. Boil the sugar water further until a thick syrup is formed. Remove the spices and allow the syrup to cool.
4. Prepare the custard as follows: boil the milk on a slow fire, adding sugar till it dissolves. Mix the custard powder to a smooth paste with some cold water. Add this to the boiling milk and keep stirring until the custard thickens. Add the essence, remove from fire, and allow to cool.

To serve

Carefully transfer the fruit on to a serving bowl, and pour the syrup. Pour the custard into a smaller bowl, and serve separately.

Apricot Stew

Wash and soak the apricots in water covering the fruit. Soak for at least an hour before cooking. The rest is the same as above. Before serving, remove the seeds by lightly pressing the fruit with a spoon.

---- *Menu* 6 ----

Puris	**Serve with**
Potato Curry (Aloo Palya)	Dahi Vadas
Chitranna	Cucumber Kosamalli
Vegetable Sagu	Capsicum Chilly Gojju
Milagu (Pepper) Rasam	
Curd (Yoghurt) Rice	**Dessert**
	Badam Kheer

Puris

Ingredients

2 1/2 cups wheat flour   oil for frying
1/2 cup flour (maida)   salt to taste
3 teaspoons oil to mix

Method

1. Mix the maida, wheat flour, oil and salt with some water to form a stiff dough. Roll into small puris on a floured board, and deep fry to a golden colour, turning over once. Serve immediately.

Potato Curry

Ingredients

1 kg/2.2 lb potatoes
250 gm/9 oz. onions
6 green chillies
2.5 cm/1 inch piece ginger
2 sprigs curry leaves
a handful fresh coriander
4 tablespoons oil
2 tablespoons besan (gram flour)
salt to taste
juice of 1 lemon

For the seasoning

1 teaspoon mustard seeds
1 1/2 teaspoons black gram dal
1 1/2 teaspoons Bengal gram dal
1/2 teaspoon turmeric powder
1/2 teaspoon chilly powder

Method

1. Boil and peel the potatoes. Break into small pieces.

2. Cut the onions into small pieces. Chop the green chillies, ginger and coriander leaves. Set aside.
3. Heat the oil and add the mustard. When done, add both the dals and fry until they turn golden in colour. Add the onions, chillies, ginger, curry leaves, chilly powder and turmeric. Fry until the onions are brown.
4. Add the potatoes, salt and chopped coriander, and mix thoroughly. Fry for another minute or two.
5. Mix the gram flour with 3/4 cup of water, add to the curry, and simmer for a couple of minutes. Remove from fire and add the lemon juice. Mix well.

Note

If a dry curry is preferred, omit the last step. Instead, add the lemon juice to the curry along with some coriander.

Chitranna

(Seasoned Rice)

Ingredients

1 1/2 cups rice
1/2 cup groundnuts (peanuts)
1 cup grated coconut
4 green chillies, slit
1/4 teaspoon turmeric powder
4 tablespoons oil
juice of 1 lemon
salt to taste

For the masala powder

1 1/2 tablespoon sesame seeds
1 tablespoon Bengal gram dal
1 tablespoon black gram dal
1/2 teaspoon pepper

For the seasoning

1/2 teaspoon cumin seeds
1 teaspoon mustard seeds
2 sprigs curry leaves

Method

1. Cook the rice so that each grain is separate. Cool on a plate, sprinkling some oil.
2. In 2 teaspoons of oil, fry the groundnuts on a low fire until browned. Remove and set aside.
3. Heat 1 teaspoon of oil and fry the ingredients for the masala powder until the dal turns golden. Remove, powder and set aside.
4. Heat the rest of the oil. Add the seasonings and when done, add the green chillies and turmeric powder. Add the coconut and fry on a low fire until light brown. Add the salt and fry for a minute. Remove.
5. Pour this mixture onto the rice. Add the masala powders, groundnuts and lime juice, and mix thoroughly using only the tips of your fingers. Transfer onto a serving plate and serve immediately.

Vegetable Sagu

(Mixed Vegetable Stew)

Ingredients

1 small cauliflower
3 medium potatoes
2 carrots
1 cup shelled peas
a handful of beans
1 large onion, chopped
2 tomatoes, chopped
1/2 teaspoon turmeric powder
a handful of coriander leaves
3 tablespoons oil
salt to taste

For the masala

3 teaspoons coriander seeds
1 teaspoon cumin seeds
1 teaspoon poppy seeds
1 tablespoon roasted gram dal or
1 tablespoon roasted channa dal
1 dried red chilly
2 cloves
1.3 cm/0.5 inch cinnamon stick
1 small onion, chopped
2 green chillies
1.3 cm/0.5 inch piece ginger
3 tablespoons grated coconut
1 tablespoon chopped coriander

Seasoning

2 sprigs curry leaves
1 teaspoon mustard seeds

Method

1. Fry the first seven ingredients for the masala in 2 teaspoons of ghee in a kadai (wok) until they are done. Remove from the kadai, add 2 more teaspoons of ghee, and fry the rest of the ingredients for the masala until the coconut and onion turn light brown. Grind all the fried ingredients together to a paste. Set aside.
2. Wash, scrape and cut the vegetables into small pieces. Steam cook with some salt and turmeric powder.
3. Heat the oil, and add the mustard and curry leaves. When done, add the chopped onions and fry until the onions are browned. Add the tomatoes and fry until they turn soft.
4. Add the vegetables and fry for a few minutes. Now add the ground paste, chopped coriander, and simmer for some time.

Note

Alternatively, do not cook the vegetables in Step 2. Instead, add them in Step 3, and cook them here instead. This process requires an additional three tablespoons of oil, but enhances the flavour.

Milagu (Pepper) Rasam

Ingredients
  2 lemon-sized balls tamarind
  salt to taste

Seasoning
  2 teaspoons ghee
  a pinch of asafoetida
  2 sprigs curry leaves

**Fry in 4 teaspoons oil
and grind to a paste**
  2 teaspoons pepper
  2 teaspoons cumin seeds
  2 teaspoons coriander seeds
  2 tablespoons tuvar dal
  2 dried red chillies (optional)

Method

1. Boil the tamarind in water, and squeeze to extract the pulp. Add the salt, 4 cups of water, and boil for a few minutes.
2. Mix the ground paste with 8 cups of water. Add to the boiling water from Step 1, and boil further until the quantity is reduced by a third.
3. Season the asafoetida and curry leaves in ghee, and add to the rasam. Serve very hot as an appetizer.

Curd (Yoghurt) Rice

Ingredients
  1 cup rice
  2-3 cups curds (yoghurt)
  1/2 cup milk
  1 teaspoon chopped ginger
  salt to taste

For the seasoning
  3 teaspoons sesame seed oil
  1 teaspoon mustard seeds
  2 green chillies, chopped
  1 teaspoon black gram
  1 sprig curry leaves

Method
  Follow the recipe from Menu 5 in Part 1.

Dahi Vadas

(Lentil Fritters in Seasoned Yoghurt)

Ingredients

2 cups black gram dal	3 cups curds (yoghurt)
2 sprigs curry leaves	1 cup milk
6 green chillies	
1 small piece ginger	**Seasoning**
salt to taste	3 teaspoons oil
oil for frying	1 teaspoon mustard seeds
chopped coriander (for garnish)	2 sprigs curry leaves

Method

1. Soak the dal for 3-4 hours in sufficient water.
2. Drain all the water, and grind to a smooth paste with the salt, chillies, ginger and curry leaves.
3. Beat the curds with milk. Add some salt. Season the mustard seeds and curry leaves in hot oil and mix.
4. Pat the batter into rounds, and deep fry to golden in batches of ten. Soak in the seasoned curds (from Step 3) until the next batch is ready. Remove the soaked vadas, and repeat the process until all the vadas are fried and soaked. Pour the remaining curds over the vadas, and transfer to a serving vessel. Garnish with chopped coriander. Serve chilled. (Makes 40).

Cucumber Kosamalli

(Seasoned Cucumber Salad)

Ingredients

For the seasoning

1 large cucumber	2 teaspoons oil
1/2 cup moong dal	1/2 teaspoon mustard seeds
1 1/2 tablespoons grated coconut	2 green chillies
juice of 1 lemon	2 sprigs curry leaves
a handful of coriander leaves	a pinch of asafoetida (optional)
salt to taste	

Method

1. Wash and soak the dal for an hour. Strain and set aside. Peel and chop the cucumber. Chop the coriander leaves Cut each chilly into two or three pieces.
2. Mix the soaked dal, cucumber, coriander, coconut and salt to-gether. Add the lemon juice.

3. Season the mustard in oil, and when done, add the asafoetida, green chillies and curry leaves. Mix in the ingredients from Step 2, transfer to a bowl and chill before serving.

Capsicum Chilly Gojju

(A Spicy Chutney with Green Peppers and Chillies)

Ingredients

250 gm/9 oz. capsicum (green peppers)
25 gm/1 oz. green chillies
1 lemon-sized piece of jaggery
1 lemon-sized ball of tamarind
4 tablespoons oil
1 teaspoon turmeric
salt to taste

For the seasoning

1 teaspoon mustard seeds
1/2 teaspoon fenugreek seeds
1/4 teaspoon asafoetida
2 sprigs curry leaves

Method

1. Cut each chilly into two or three pieces. Cut the capsicum into pieces of the desired size. Boil the tamarind in water, and squeeze to extract the pulp.
2. Heat the oil. Add the mustard, fenugreek and asafoetida, and when done, add the curry leaves and green chillies, and fry for a minute or two.
3. Now add the capsicum and turmeric powder, and fry for another minute. Add the tamarind pulp, jaggery, salt, and 1 1/2 cups of water, and cook on low heat until a thick consistency is formed.

Badam Kheer
(Almond Pudding)

Ingredients

1.5 litres/1.6 quarts milk
1 1/4 cup sugar
3/4 cup almonds
1 tablespoon long-grained rice
a few drops badam (almond) essence
a pinch of saffron
1 cup water (to grind)

Method

1. Soak the almonds in hot water. Wash and soak the rice separately for thirty minutes. Skin the almonds, strain the rice, and grind them together to a very smooth paste. Add 1 cup of water, mix and set aside.

2. Boil the milk along with the sugar until the latter has dissolved, and the milk reduces in quantity by half. Add the ground paste and saffron, and continue to boil, constantly stirring until the kheer is quite thick. Remove from fire and add the essence. Serve hot or chilled in cups.

```
┌─────────────────────────────────────────────┐
│            ── Menu 7 ──                       │
│  Tomato Rice              Serve with          │
│  Chutney Raita            Boiled Vegetable Salad │
│  Potato Cheese Balls      Dal-Vegetable or Egg Kabab │
│  in Spinach Gravy         Brinjal (Eggplant) Pickle │
│  Bread or Chapatis                            │
│                           Dessert             │
│                           Jelly-Cake Fiesta   │
└─────────────────────────────────────────────┘
```

Tomato Rice

Ingredients

2 cups rice
1 large onion
500 gm/1.1 lb tomatoes
3 green chillies
1 cup shelled peas
1/2 teaspoon turmeric
a handful of fresh coriander
1 cup ghee
a few raisins
a few cashew nuts
salt to taste

Grind to paste

5 garlic cloves
2.5 cm/1 inch piece ginger
3 green chillies
1 small onion
a handful of fresh coriander

Seasoning

3 cloves
3 cardamoms
2 small cinnamon sticks
1 teaspoon shahjeera (black cumin)
2 bay leaves

Method

1. Wash the rice, and allow to dry on a cloth. Slice the onions, slit the chillies and chop the coriander leaves. Set aside separately.

2. Boil the tomatoes. When cool, press through a sieve and extract the juice. Add enough water to make 4 cups.

3. Melt half of the ghee in a pressure cooker, and fry the raisins and cashew nuts. Remove and set aside. Fry the sliced onions until crisp, remove from the cooker, and set aside.

4. Add the rest of ghee, and fry the seasonings. When done, add the slit chillies and fry for a minute or two. Then add the ground paste along with the turmeric and fry on low heat until the ghee separates. Add the rice and fry for one or two minutes.

5. Now add the tomato juice, peas, half the fried onions and salt. Cook covered without using the weight.

To serve

Mix half of the nuts, raisins and some of the chopped coriander. Transfer the rice on to a serving plate and smoothen out the surface. Sprinkle the rest of the nuts, coriander and the fried onions. Serve hot.

Potato Cheese Balls in Spinach Gravy

For the koftas

5 medium potatoes (500 gm/1.1 lb)
2 medium onions
4 green chillies
a handful of fresh coriander
150 gm/5 oz. cheese
2 tablespoons light cream
4 tablespoons bread crumbs
2 tablespoons maida (flour)
1 1/2 cups oil
salt to taste

For the gravy

a handful of fenugreek leaves
2 large bundles spinach
1 large onion
2.5 cm/1 inch piece ginger
3 cloves garlic
2 green chillies

Seasoning

1 teaspoon cumin seeds
1/2 teaspoon garam masala
1 onion, chopped

Method

1. Mince the onions, green chillies and coriander leaves. Grate the cheese.
2. Wash and chop the spinach and fenugreek leaves. Cook with salt and sufficient water. When cool, grind along with the onions, ginger, chillies and garlic to a soft puree.
3. Boil and peel the potatoes. While still hot, mash. Add the minced ingredients, grated cheese, some salt and mix to a smooth dough. Make small balls of the dough and set aside. Make a thin paste of the maida with some water.
4. Dip the potato balls in the maida paste and coat with bread crumbs. Deep fry to a golden brown and set aside.
5. In the same oil, saute the cumin seeds and when done, add the chopped onions and fry until they are browned. Add the spinach puree and fry for a few more minutes. Then add about 2 cups of water, and cook on low heat till a gravy is formed.

To serve

Transfer the potato balls on to a wide bowl and pour the hot spinach gravy. Pour beaten cream and sprinkle garam masala. (If desired, paneer can be substituted for cheese.)

Chutney Raita

Ingredients
1 small cucumber
1 medium onion
2 cups curds (yoghurt)
salt to taste

Grind to paste
a handful of fresh coriander
a few leaves mint
1 small onion
2 garlic cloves
1/2 teaspoon cumin seeds
2 green chillies

Method
1. Beat the curds. Add the salt and ground paste, and mix well.
2. Chop the onion and cucumber into small pieces. Add to the curds, mix and serve chilled.

Dal-Vegetable Kabab

Ingredients
1 cup green gram dal
1 cup shelled peas
1 cup cauliflower florets
1 potato, chopped
2 slices of bread
1 cup flour
1 cup bread crumbs
oil for frying

Seasoning
1 large onion
2.5 cm/1 inch piece ginger
5 green chillies
1 tablespoon fresh coriander
1 tablespoon mint
1 teaspoon chilly powder
1 teaspoon garam masala
salt to taste

Method
1. Soak the dal in water for three to four hours. Drain the water and grind to a smooth paste along with the ginger, green chillies, onion and salt.
2. Cook the vegetables with some salt and just enough water. Cool and grind to a paste.
3. Heat 3 tablespoons of oil, and add both pastes, the chilly and garam masala powders, and fry on low heat until dry. Remove from fire. Cool, add the chopped coriander and mint leaves, and mix well.
4. Soak the bread in water. Squeeze dry, crumble, and add to mixture. Form kababs by taking pieces of the mixture, and making circular or oval shapes.
5. Mix the flour with a pinch of salt and sufficient water to form a thin paste. Dip the kabab in this, roll in bread crumbs and deep fry to a golden brown. Serve hot.

Egg Kabab

Ingredients
4 eggs
1 additional egg (for frying)

Method
1. Hard boil the eggs, peel, and set aside.
2. Follow the method for vegetable kababs through Step 4.
3. Take a large piece of dough, and work into a cup. Carefully place an egg inside the cup such that the egg is fully covered. Prepare all the eggs thus.
4. Beat one egg. Dip the kabab in it, then roll in bread crumbs and deep fry to a golden brown.
5. Just before serving, cut each kabab into two halves lengthwise. Serve with tomato ketchup.

Boiled Vegetable Salad

Ingredients
2 medium potatoes
1 beet root (optional)
2 medium carrots
a few florets cauliflower
2 medium tomatoes
1/2 cup shelled peas
a few leaves cabbage
25 gm/1 oz. cheese (optional)

Seasonings
juice of 1 lemon
1 tablespoon white vinegar
1 teaspoon pepper
1 teaspoon mustard powder
salt to taste
1 teaspoon sugar
3-4 tablespoons olive oil (optional)
a sprinkling of parsley and dill weed

Method
1. Cook the potatoes, carrots and peas with some salt and water. Cook the cauliflower and beets separately. Cut the potatoes, beets and carrots into thick rounds.
2. Cut the tomatoes into slices. Cut the cabbage into strips.
3. Mix the lemon juice, vinegar, pepper, salt, mustard, herbs, sugar and oil. Shake well, and refrigerate until ready to serve.

To serve
Arrange the vegetables on a salad plate in different layers, with a tomato flower in the centre. Sprinkle the peas and cheese, and leave in a refrigerator to chill. Just before serving, pour the seasonings and serve immediately.

Jelly-Cake Fiesta

Ingredients

2 egg sponge cake *(see next page)*
1 packet jelly (jello) crystals
4 tablespoons custard powder
3 cups milk
1/2 teaspoon instant coffee
6 cherries (for garnish)

3 cookies (biscuits)
2 tablespoons chopped nuts and
raisins

Method

1. Prepare the jelly using the directions on the packet. Cool and allow to set in a refrigerator.
2. Crumble the cake into fine crumbs and set aside.
3. Beat the jelly along with half of the cake crumbs. Add one teaspoon of the chopped nuts and raisins, and mix well. Place in a deep serving bowl, and leave in a refrigerator to set.
4. Boil 2 1/2 cups of milk with sugar. Mix the custard powder with the rest of the milk, and add to the boiling milk after the sugar has dissolved. Stir continuously until a thick custard is formed. Cool, mix in the rest of the cake crumbs and the chopped nuts.
5. When the jelly-cake layer has set, remove from the refrigerator and pour the custard cake over this. Put back in the refrigerator to allow the custard to thicken.
6. Just before serving, cover the cake custard layer with crushed biscuits. Garnish with the instant coffee powder and chopped cherries.

Note

If you do not wish to use eggs, omit the cake part of the recipe. Instead, mix the jelly with some chopped fruit and nuts. Pour in a transparent bowl, and leave in the refrigerator to set. Prepare the custard as mentioned, and cool. Add some fruits and nuts, and mix well. Pour this onto the jelly layer after it has set, and leave the bowl in the refrigerator for the custard to set.

Sponge Cake

Ingredients

1 1/2 cups flour

1 cup sugar

1/2 cup butter or margarine

1 teaspoon baking powder

3/4 cup milk

1 teaspoon vanilla essence

2 eggs

Method

1. Grease a cake tin with butter.
2. Sift the flour and baking powder, and set aside.
3. Beat the sugar and butter to a cream. Beat the eggs separately.
4. Add the eggs gradually to the creamed mixture, beating as you go along. If the mixture curdles, add a pinch of sifted flour.
5. Add portions of the milk and flour alternately, beating all the while. Add the essence and mix. Pour the batter into the tin and bake at 190°C (375°F) for 20 to 25 minutes, or until the top is lightly browned.
6. Remove the cake from the tin by loosening the sides. Cool.

Chapatis

Refer to Part 3, Menu 1.

—— *Menu 8* ——

Cabbage Soup	**Serve with**
Carrot Cups	Lentil Rissoles (Dal Cutlets)
Three layered Macaroni or	Cucumber Mould (salad)
Potato-Egg Casserole (optional)	**Dessert**
	Steamed Date Pudding or
	Baked Date Loaf (eggless)

Cabbage Soup

Ingredients

6 cups cabbage, chopped

2 medium potatoes, grated

1.3 cm/0.5 inch piece ginger, minced

1 cup peas, boiled

3 tablespoons butter

2 cups milk or 1 cup cream

pepper and salt to taste

Method

1. Melt the butter in a saucepan. Add the minced ginger and grated potato, and fry for a minute or two. Add the cabbage and fry until soft. Add 4 cups of water, salt and cook in a pressure cooker. Cool.
2. Pass the soup through a liquidiser. If it is too thick, add some water. Set aside until required.

To serve

Before serving, heat the soup. Heat the milk separately and mix with the soup. Add the boiled peas, pepper and some more salt if necessary. Serve piping hot. If you are using cream, pour the soup into bowls, and add a dollop of cream into each one. Serve with carrot cups.

Carrot Cups

Ingredients

12 slices bread
1 1/2 tablespoons cornflour
3 tablespoons butter or vanaspati
250 gm/9 oz. carrots
1/2 cup shelled peas
1 potato
1 capsicum (green pepper)
1 medium onion
a handful of onion leaves (scallions)
2 green chillies

1/2 teaspoon pepper
1/2 teaspoon chilly powder
a pinch ajinomoto (optional)
3 tablespoons oil
1/2 cup tomato ketchup
salt to taste
12 cup moulds

Method for the cups

1. Trim the crusts of the bread. Grease the moulds well. Butter only one side of each slice. Lightly moisten a slice and press into the mould. Prepare all the cups thus.

2. Arrange the cups on a baking sheet and bake in a hot oven (200°C) for 10 minutes or until crisp. Remove from the oven and set aside until needed.

To make the stuffing

1. Mince the green chillies, onion leaves and onions. Chop the capsicum, potato and carrots.

2. Heat the oil, and add the minced ingredients. Fry until the onions turn transparent. Now add the chilly and pepper powders, salt, ajinomoto (optional) and the chopped vegetables, and fry for a few minutes. Sprinkle a little water, cover and cook.

3. Mix the cornflour with some water to a smooth paste and add the tomato ketchup. Pour the mixture into the cooked vegetables and simmer on low heat until almost all the water has evaporated. Remove from fire.

To serve

Remove the cups from the moulds. Fill each one with the above mixture and serve immediately. If desired, a little grated cheese can be sprinkled on top of each cup.

Three layered Macaroni

Ingredients

300 gm/11 oz. macaroni
2 kg/4.4 lb tomatoes
2 large onions, chopped
2 large bundles spinach
200 gm/7 oz. grated cheese
1 tablespoon tomato sauce
1 teaspoon chilly sauce (optional)
1 teaspoon chilly powder
1 teaspoon pepper powder
2 green chillies, minced
1 teaspoon sugar
salt to taste

For the white sauce

3 cups milk
9 tablespoons butter
3 level tablespoons flour
1/2 cup bread crumbs
a large oven-proof dish

Method

1. Boil the macaroni as per the instructions on the packet. Set aside. Grate the cheese and set aside.
2. Chop 4-5 cups of spinach so as to yield 2 cups of puree.
3. Boil the tomatoes briskly. Cool, peel the skins, and pass through a sieve or a liquidiser. Strain, take out the puree, and set aside.
4. Melt 1 1/2 tablespoons of butter, and add half of the chopped onions. Fry to a pinkish colour, and add the tomato puree, salt, sugar and chilly powder. Cook until thick, remove from fire, and cool. Add the tomato sauce, a quarter of the cheese, and set aside.
5. Melt 1 1/2 tablespoons of butter. Add the minced chillies and fry along with the rest of the onions until the onions turn pink. Add the chopped spinach, and fry a few minutes. Add salt, cover and cook on low heat. When done, remove, cool, and grind to a puree. Add 1/2 teaspoon pepper, chilly sauce and a quarter of the cheese.
6. Melt 3 tablespoons of butter on low heat, add the flour, and fry to a light brown. Remove from fire and add some of the milk, gradually making sure that no lumps are formed. Add the rest of the milk, place on fire and cook stirring constantly until the mixture attains a custard-like consistency. Remove from heat and add 1/4 teaspoon pepper, salt and a quarter of the cheese.
7. Grease a large pie-dish and set the layers thus: cover the bottom of the dish with a third of the cooked macaroni. Sprinkle some salt, pepper, a little cheese and a few blobs of butter. Spread the tomato puree evenly on this. Next spread a second layer of macaroni. Sprinkle salt, pepper, cheese and butter. Spread the spinach puree on this layer. Finally, spread the rest of the macaroni, and sprinkle

some salt and pepper. Pour the white sauce ensuring that it spreads evenly. Sprinkle the rest of the cheese and a layer of bread crumbs. Add a few blobs of butter.

8. Bake at 200°C (400°F) for 20-30 minutes or until the top is browned.

Lentil Rissoles (Dal Cutlets)

Ingredients

250 gm/9 oz. gram dal (channa dal)
2 medium onions, chopped
2 garlic cloves
3 green chillies
1/2 teaspoon chilly powder
1/2 teaspoon pepper
1/2 teaspoon garam masala

1 tablespoon flour
2 tablespoons chopped coriander
1/2 cup bread crumbs
2 tablespoons butter or vanaspati
oil for frying
salt to taste

Method

1. Boil the dal in a pressure cooker until soft. Drain the water and grind to a paste with garlic and chillies. Heat 2 tablespoons of butter, add the chopped onions and fry until the onions turn pink. Add the chilly and pepper powders, 1 1/2 tablespoons of flour, and fry for a minute or two.

2. Add the ground dal and continue stirring until the mixture is dry. Add the chopped coriander, mix thoroughly, remove from heat and cool.

3. Take a small lump of the mixture and make cutlets of a cylindrical shape, 7.5 cm (3 inches) long and 2.5 cm (1 inch) thick (diameter). Set aside.

4. Make a thin paste of the rest of the flour and water. Dip the cutlets first in this and then in the bread crumbs. Deep fry to a golden colour.

Potato-Egg Casserole

Ingredients

1 kg/2.2 lb potatoes
4 large onions
4 green chillies
2.5 cm/1 inch piece ginger
4 garlic cloves
4 eggs

1/2 teaspoon chilly powder
1/2 teaspoon pepper
4 tablespoons butter or ghee
1 tablespoon chopped coriander
salt to taste

Method

1. Grind the ginger, garlic and green chillies to a paste. Slice the onions.

2. Boil, peel and slice the potatoes thick.
3. Melt the butter and fry the onions to a light brown. Add the ground paste and continue to fry adding the chilly and pepper powders. Fry until the ghee comes to the surface.
4. Add the potatoes and salt, and stir carefully adding half of the chopped coriander.
5. Grease a flat oven-proof dish. Transfer the potato mixture to it, smoothen the surface, and sprinkle the rest of the chopped coriander.
6. Beat the whites of the eggs stiff. Add the yolks and blend with the whites, along with a little salt and pepper, and pour over the potatoes. Bake at 200°C (400°F) for 20-25 minutes until the eggs set. Serve very hot.

Note

If eggs are not desired, omit Step 6.

Cucumber Mould

Ingredients

1 large cucumber	2 tablespoons powdered gelatine
2 sliced tomatoes	2 tablespoons sugar
1 small carrot, grated fine	1/2 teaspoon salt
1/2 teaspoon chopped mint	1/2 teaspoon pepper
2 tablespoons lemon juice	a pinch of green colour
1 1/2 cups boiling water	a fluted mould

Method

1. Wash and prepare the vegetables as specified. Grate half the cucumber and slice the other half. Refrigerate until required.
2. Mix the gelatine, sugar, salt and boiling water. Stir until they dissolve, then cool, and add one tablespoon of lemon juice, mint, grated cucumber and colour. Pour this into a fluted mould (which has been rinsed in cold water) and set in a refrigerator.

To serve

Unmould the jelly on to a salad plate. Surround the sides with cucumber and tomato slices. Garnish with the grated carrots. Add pinches of salt, pepper and sugar to the remaining lemon juice, and pour over the vegetables.

Note

Finely shredded cabbage may be added to the salad, if desired.

Steamed Date Pudding

Ingredients
5 slices bread
2 eggs
1/2 cup milk
500 gm/1.1 lb dates
1/2 teaspoon baking powder
1/2 cup bread crumbs
4 tablespoons butter or vanaspati
1/3 cup flour
1/2 cup sugar
a pinch of nutmeg

For the caramel
1 cup sugar

For the custard
500 ml/1 pint milk
2 tablespoons custard powder
2 tablespoons sugar

To bake
a large pudding mould

Method
1. Make the caramel syrup as follows: melt the sugar in a saucepan on low heat until all of it has dissolved. Raise the heat until the sugar starts to turn dark brown. Remove from heat, add 1/2 cup of water and mix thoroughly. Put back on the flame and cook on low heat until the mixture attains a thick honey consistency. Set aside to cool.
2. Stone and chop the dates. Grate the nutmeg and sift the flour and baking powder. Remove the crust from the bread and soak in water for a few minutes. Squeeze out all the water, crumble, and set aside.
3. Cream the butter and sugar adding the eggs one at a time, beating all the while until a smooth mixture is obtained. Add the bread crumbs, chopped dates, caramel syrup, flour, nutmeg and milk. Mix thoroughly.
4. Cover the mould with a thick brown paper or a doubled aluminium foil. Cut this an extra 2 inches all around. Grease the mould and paper generously, and set aside.
5. When the mixture is ready, pour it into the mould. Cover the mould with the brown paper and tie it down with a piece of string. Steam bake for 30-40 minutes. When done, a needle passed through should come out clean.
6. To prepare the custard, refer to the recipe for Guava Stew in Part 3, Menu 5.

To serve
Unmould the pudding on to a serving bowl. Serve the custard separately. (This can be served either hot or cold.)

Baked Date Loaf (Eggless)

Ingredients
250 gm/9 oz. chopped dates
2 1/4 cup flour
2 1/2 teaspoons cooking soda
1 cup vegetable oil
1 cup sugar
6 cups water
1/4 teaspoon salt
1 teaspoon mixture of ground cloves, cinnamon and nutmeg
a loaf tin

To serve
custard or whipped cream

Method
1. Sift together the flour and soda, and set aside.
2. Pour the water and oil into a saucepan. Add the salt, sugar, spices and the chopped dates. Cook this mixture. Let it simmer for five minutes before you remove it from the fire. (It should be of a semi-solid consistency.) Cool.
3. Gradually add the flour to the cooled mixture until it blends completely to form a smooth batter. If the batter is too thick, add 1/2 - 1 cup of water and mix well to a smooth dropping consistency.
4. Pour the batter into an ungreased tin and bake at 150°C (300°F) for 30-45 minutes or until it is done. (A needle passed through should come out clean.)

To serve
Unmould the loaf onto a plate, cut into thick slices and serve either with custard or whipped cream.

—— *Menu* 9 ——

Tomato Cream Soup	**Serve with**
Cheese Croutons	Mexican Salad
Cottage Cheese Casserole	Spaghetti Rolls
Baked Savoury Omelette (optional)	**Dessert**
	Apple Walnut Loaf served
	with Cream or Crumble
	Top Apple Pie

Tomato Cream Soup

Ingredients

1 kg/2.2 lb tomatoes	2 tablespoons butter
1 onion	1 tablespoon cornflour
1 potato	1 cup milk
1 medium carrot	2 teaspoons sugar
1/2 teaspoon cloves or powdered nutmeg	1 cup heavy cream to serve
salt and pepper to taste	

Method

1. Wash the vegetables. Cut the tomatoes and chop the onions. Grate the carrot and potato.
2. Fry the onions in butter to a pinkish colour. Then add the grated vegetables and fry for a few minutes. Add the tomatoes and fry for a minute or two. Add the salt, sugar and a little water, and cook in a pressure cooker. Cool. Pass through a liquidiser, then strain the resultant puree to discard the uncooked skin and tomato seeds. Set aside.
3. Make a smooth paste of the cornflour with milk. Bring the soup to a boil, add the cornflour paste and spice, and stir for a while. Add pepper and salt if necessary.

To serve

Add a large dollop of cream to each portion along with a few cheese croutons, and serve immediately.

Cheese Croutons

Ingredients

8 slices of bread

1 cup grated cheese

1 teaspoon of mixed mint and coriander leaves

butter

pepper and salt to taste

Method

1. Trim the edges of each slice, and butter generously. Cut each slice into four pieces and sprinkle the grated cheese, herbs and a little pepper and salt.
2. Place the croutons on a greased baking sheet and grill in an oven at 200°C (400°F) for 15-20 minutes.

Cottage Cheese Casserole

Ingredients

20 slices bread

2 capsicums (green peppers)

2 onions

1 medium carrot

1 medium potato

3 large tomatoes

3 green chillies

a handful of coriander leaves

4 tablespoons tomato sauce or tomato ketchup

1 1/2 cups paneer

whey (to cook vegetables
    and soak bread slices)

6 tablespoons oil or vanaspati

1/2 teaspoon chilly powder

1/2 teaspoon pepper powder

salt to taste

Method

1. Grease a rectangular or oval casserole (pie-dish).
2. Remove the crusts from the bread, and soak each slice in whey. Line the dish with sufficient slices to cover the entire bottom. Set aside. (If you are purchasing paneer, soak the slices in 1 cup of milk.)
3. Chop all the vegetables and coriander very fine.
4. Heat the oil. Add the chopped chillies first, then the onions, and fry until the onions turn pink. Now add the capsicums and continue to fry until they turn soft. Add the tomatoes and fry further until they are cooked.
5. Add the rest of the chopped vegetables and fry a few minutes. Sprinkle some water or whey, add salt, and simmer covered for a few minutes.
6. When the vegetables are done, add the crumbled paneer, chopped coriander, chilly and pepper powders, and cook until the vegetables are almost dry. Add the tomato sauce and mix thoroughly.
7. Pour this vegetable mixture over the bread slices.

8. Crumble 4 slices of bread after removing the crust to very fine crumbs. Sprinkle these on top of the vegetable mixture. Cover the crumbs with blobs of butter and bake at 190°C (375°F) for 30-45 minutes until the top is browned.

To make the paneer

Ingredients
2 litres/2.1 quarts milk (should yield 1 1/2 cups of paneer)
1 lemon

Method
1. Boil the milk and while it is still on the fire, add some lemon juice gradually until the milk starts to curdle. Boil for another minute and remove from fire. When cool, strain through a muslin cloth. Tie the paneer in a muslin cloth and press to remove the excess liquid. Keep both the paneer and whey aside until required. Crumble the paneer before adding it to the vegetables.

Spaghetti Rolls

Ingredients

100 gm/4 oz. spaghetti	3/4 cup flour
2 potatoes	3/4 cup milk
2 medium onions	3 tablespoons oil
4 green chillies	oil for frying
1/2 cup shelled peas	1/2 cup bread crumbs
1 tablespoon fresh coriander	salt to taste
2.5 cm/1 inch piece ginger	
1/2 teaspoon chilly powder	**For the paste**
1/2 teaspoon pepper powder	1/2 cup flour
1/2 teaspoon garam masala powder	1 cup water

Method
1. Add the spaghetti to boiling water to which 1 teaspoon of oil and some salt has been added. When cooked, drain the water and set aside.
2. Peel and cut the potatoes into cubes. Add the peas and cook in just enough water with some salt. When done, remove from fire, mash a bit, and set aside.
3. Chop the onions, green chillies, ginger and coriander leaves. Fry the chopped ingredients except the coriander in 3 tablespoons of oil until the onions are slightly browned. Add the pepper, chilly and garam masala powders, and fry for a few more minutes.

4. Add the flour and continue to fry on low heat until the flour is slightly browned. Remove from fire, and add the milk gradually ensuring that no lumps are formed. Put back on fire, and stir until the mixture thickens. Remove from fire and allow to cool.
5. To this, add the potato-peas mixture, spaghetti and chopped coriander, and mix thoroughly. Add some more salt if necessary.
6. Make elongated rolls of the above mixture, dusting with flour if necessary. Set aside.
7. Mix the water and flour to make a thin paste. Dip the rolls in this, roll in bread crumbs and deep fry until golden. Serve hot with chilly sauce.

Baked (Savoury) Omelette

Ingredients
6 eggs
4 tablespoons gram flour
3 tablespoons ghee or vanaspati
1/2 teaspoon chilly powder
1/2 teaspoon pepper powder
salt to taste

Grind to paste
4 green chillies
2 garlic cloves
1.3 cm/0.5 inch piece ginger
a pinch of cumin seeds
a handful of coriander leaves

Method
1. Separate the egg yolks from the whites.
2. Beat the yolks to a creamy texture whilst gradually adding gram flour, chilly powder, pepper and salt. Set aside. Beat the whites stiff.
3. Fry the ground paste in ghee. Remove from fire and allow to cool.
4. To this add the yolk-gram flour mixture and blend thoroughly. Add the egg whites, and fold into the omelette carefully.
5. Pour this mixture into a greased pie dish, and bake in a moderate oven (190°C/ 375°F) for 30 minutes or until the eggs set. Serve hot.

Mexican Salad

Ingredients
1 small cucumber
1/2 small cabbage
2 medium carrots
3 tomatoes
3 slices pineapple
    or 1 medium apple
2 oranges

For the dressing
4 tablespoons white vinegar
3 tablespoons olive oil
1/2 teaspoon pepper powder
1/2 teaspoon mustard powder
1/2 teaspoon chilly powder
2 teaspoons sugar
salt to taste

Method

1. Mix together the ingredients for the dressing and chill.
2. Wash and cut the vegetables as follows: slice the tomatoes, and cut the cucumber into small pieces. Grate the carrots, shred the cabbage, and chop the pineapple or apple into small pieces. Peel the oranges, cut into small pieces, and remove the seeds.
3. In a large salad plate, first arrange the tomato slices all around. Then mix together the rest of the vegetables and fruits and pile in the centre of the plate. Pour the dressing, and serve immediately.

Apple Walnut Loaf

Ingredients

4 eggs
1 1/2 cup sugar
2 cups walnuts, grated fine
1 large apple, grated
6 slices bread

2 teaspoons refined oil
1 teaspoon powdered cinnamon
1 cup heavy cream to serve
a greased loaf tin

Method

1. Remove the crusts from the bread slices, and crumble them to fine crumbs.
2. Break the eggs, separating the white from the yolk. Beat the whites stiff and set aside.
3. Beat the yolks with sugar until thick and creamy. Add the bread crumbs, grated walnuts, grated apple and cinnamon powder. Mix thoroughly.
4. Fold in the egg whites gradually and lightly. Pour the batter into a greased loaf tin and bake in a moderate oven (190°C/375°F) for 25-30 minutes or until done. Remove from oven.
5. Loosen the edges when cooled and transfer loaf onto a serving plate.

To serve

Cut the loaf into thick slices. Beat the cream to a smooth consistency very lightly. Top each slice with a dollop of cream and serve. Makes 4 large slices.

Crumble Top Apple Pie (Eggless)

For the pastry
- 2 cups flour
- 1/2 teaspoon salt
- 2/3 cup margarine
- 5 tablespoons chilled water

For the filling
- 4 tart apples
- 1/2 cup sugar
- 1 teaspoon powdered cinnamon
- 1/4 teaspoon powdered nutmeg

For the crumble top
- 1/2 cup margarine
- 1/2 cup sugar
- 3/4 cup flour

To serve
- whipped cream

Method

Pastry

1. Sift the flour and salt together. Set aside.
2. Mix the margarine with the flour lightly, using only the tips of your fingers. This must be done quickly before the margarine melts.
3. Gradually add the chilled water and work into a smooth dough. Chill.
4. Roll out the dough 1 inch wider than the diameter of the pan. Carefully transfer the dough into the pan. Prick the base with a fork and flute the overhanging dough on the rim of the pan.

Filling

1. Cut the apples into 1.3 cm (0.5 inch) thick slices. Cover the pastry with this, beginning on one side with each slice overlapping the other until the entire pastry is covered.
2. Mix together the sugar, nutmeg and cinnamon. Lightly sprinkle this over the apple slices.

Crumble Top

1. Mix the crumble top ingredients together until the mixture has the appearance of fine bread crumbs. Spread a layer of this mixture over the apple slices.
2. Bake the pie at 230°C (450°F) for about 20-25 minutes. Then reduce the heat and bake further until the edges are golden in colour and the apples are tender.
3. Serve warm with whipped cream.

---- *Menu 10* ----

Sweet Corn Soup	**Serve with**
Vegetable Fried Rice or	Chillies in Vinegar
Egg Fried Rice	Chilly Sauce
Sweet and Sour Carrots	Egg Fuyong with Hot Sauce or
Cauliflower Manchurian	Green Chilly Sauce or
	Vegetable Cakes with
	Tomato Sauce
	Dessert
	Eight Treasure Pudding or
	Fresh Fruits

Sweet Corn Soup

Ingredients

8 fresh corn cobs   1 teaspoon soya sauce
3 tablespoons cornflour   1 teaspoon ajinomoto (optional)
2 tablespoons sugar   salt to taste

Method

1. Grate the corn. Add eight cups of water and pressure cook. till the corn is soft and boiled.

2. Mix the cornflour to a paste with cold water. Bring the soup (from Step 1) to a boil and add the paste, sugar, salt and ajinomoto (optional). Cook for a few more minutes and then add soya sauce. Mix well.

3. This recipe serves 8.

To serve

Serve very hot with chillies in vinegar or green chilly sauce.

Vegetable Fried Rice

Ingredients

2 cups long grain rice
2 small carrots
2 medium capsicums
2 medium onions or 4 spring onions
1 cup shelled peas
a handful of French beans
1/4 small cabbage
1/2 small cauliflower
2 green chillies
a few onion leaves (scallions)

6 tablespoons oil
4 tablespoons soya sauce
2 tablespoons vinegar
2 tablespoons tomato sauce
1 teaspoon chilly sauce
1/2 teaspoon ajinomoto (optional)
1/2 teaspoon chilly powder (optional)
1/2 teaspoon pepper powder
salt to taste

For the Egg Rice

4 eggs

To garnish

12-15 roasted almonds

Method

1. Clean, wash and cook the rice with 1 teaspoon of oil, some salt and 6 cups (or more) of boiling water such that every grain is separate and the rice is not overcooked. Drain the excess water, if any, sprinkle some oil, and set aside to cool. For best results, use an automatic rice cooker.

2. Chop the onions and scallions. Cut the beans and carrots into small pieces, the cabbage and capsicum into strips, and the cauliflower into florets. Mince the green chillies fine. Keep the vegetables separate.

3. Steam cook the beans, peas and carrots. Alternately, cook them in just enough water until they are tender but not overcooked. Drain excess water, and set aside.

4. Heat the oil and fry the chillies, chopped onions and onion leaves until the onions turn pink. Stir in first the capsicum, next the cauliflower florets, and lastly the cabbage. Cook on a high flame for 3-5 minutes, or until the vegetables turn soft, stirring all the while. When done, add the cooked carrots, beans and peas, and mix well.

5. Now add the ajinomoto (if desired), chilly powder, pepper, and salt. Stir well. Add in the soya sauce, vinegar, and the tomato and chilly sauces. Mix these well with the vegetables.

6. Add the rice gradually, mixing it with the vegetables, and stir fry for another 2-3 minutes.

Egg Fried Rice

Method

1. Break the eggs into a bowl. Beat thoroughly with a pinch of salt and pepper. Set aside.
2. Follow the method in the previous recipe up to Step 5. When the vegetables and seasonings are added, reduce the heat and pour the eggs into it. Stir until the eggs are well blended. Cover the vessel for a minute or so. When the eggs are cooked, add the rice slowly, mixing it well into the vegetable-egg mixture. Cook for another couple of minutes.

To serve

Transfer to a rice plate and smoothen the surface. Garnish with slivered roasted almonds. (Blanch and skin the almonds, cut into slivers, and deep fry.)

Sweet and Sour Carrots

Ingredients

5 medium carrots (500 gm/1.1 lb)	4 tablespoons cornflour
2 medium onions or 4 spring onions	3 cups water
3 capsicums (250 gm/9 oz.)	3 tablespoons sugar
4 tablespoons oil	1 teaspoon chilly powder
1 cup vinegar	1 teaspoon pepper
2 tablespoons tomato sauce	1/2 teaspoon ajinomoto (optional)
salt to taste	

Method

1. Wash and scrape the carrots. Boil 4 cups of water to which 1/2 teaspoon salt has been added. Add the carrots and cook for 3-5 minutes or until slightly soft. Remove from fire, drain the water, cool and cut into rounds.
2. Peel and cut the onions into thick slices. If spring onions are used, cut into fours. Cut the capsicums into strips. Set aside.
3. Heat the oil. Fry the onions for 1-2 minutes on high heat until they turn pink. Add the capsicums and fry until they are soft. Add the carrots, salt, pepper, ajinomoto (optional), and stir for another couple of minutes.
4. Mix the cornflour with a little water to a smooth paste. Add the chilly powder, tomato sauce, vinegar, sugar and water, and boil for a while. Pour this into the vegetables, and allow to cook for another 3-5 minutes until quite thick. Add a little water if the mixture is too thick.

Cauliflower Manchurian

Ingredients
2 medium cauliflowers

For the marinade
4 tablespoons soya sauce
1/2 teaspoon pepper
1 teaspoon garlic, minced
1/2 teaspoon ginger, minced
salt to taste
a pinch of ajinomoto (optional)

For the batter
1 onion, minced fine
1 cup flour
1/2 cup cornflour
1 pinch of baking powder
a pinch of salt
1 1/2 cups water
oil for frying

For the sauce
1/2 cup tomato sauce
1/2 teaspoon chilly sauce

Method
1. Break the cauliflower into florets. Wash thoroughly, drain and set aside.
2. Mix together all the ingredients for the marinade. Soak the florets in this for about 15-20 minutes.
3. Mix all the batter ingredients except the onion to a smooth paste.
4. Fry the onions to a dark brown. Remove from the oil, cool, and add to batter. Mix well.
5. Remove the florets, 4-5 at a time, from the marinade. Shake the excess liquid, dip in the batter, and deep fry to a dark brown. Drain on absorbent kitchen paper before serving.

To make the sauce
After frying the cauliflower, pour the marinade ingredients into a saucepan, and add the tomato and chilly sauces. Beat for a few minutes, pour into a small sauce bowl and serve with the cauliflower.

Egg Fuyong

Ingredients
4 eggs
1 small onion or 3 spring onions
1 small carrot
1 capsicum (green pepper)
1/2 cup green beans
1/8 small cabbage
1/8 cauliflower
5 cm/2 inches piece celery stalk
1/2 teaspoon pepper
1 teaspoon soya sauce
1 teaspoon chilly sauce
a pinch of sugar
3 tablespoons oil
salt to taste
oil for frying
1/2 teaspoon ajinomoto (optional)

Method

1. Wash and chop the vegetables fine. Mince the onions and celery.
2. Heat 3 tablespoons of oil, and add the onions. Fry for a minute or two, and stir in the rest of the vegetables. Add the salt, pepper, sugar and ajinomoto (optional). Mix well. Cook for another 2-3 minutes, remove from fire, and cool.
3. Beat the eggs and add the soya and chilly sauces, and a little more salt if necessary. Pour this mixture on to the vegetables and mix well. Divide the mixture into 8 portions.
4. Cook each portion in a frying pan with oil, turning it over to ensure that both sides get done.

To serve

Arrange these little omelettes in a flat plate. Garnish with chopped celery and serve with hot sauce.

Vegetable Cakes

Ingredients

4 medium potatoes (500 gm/1.1 lb)
1/4 cabbage
1 small carrot
1 small capsicum (green pepper)
a handful of green beans
1 medium onion
1/2 cauliflower
1/2 teaspoon ginger, chopped

3 teaspoons soya sauce
1 teaspoon tomato sauce
1 cup bread crumbs
1 teaspoon pepper
1/2 teaspoon ajinomoto (optional)
oil for frying
salt to taste

To serve

tomato ketchup
1 tablespoon celery, chopped

For the batter

1/2 cup flour
1 cup water
a pinch of salt

Method

1. Wash and chop the vegetables. Boil and mash the potatoes.
2. Heat 3 tablespoons of oil, and fry the onions. Add the ginger, the other vegetables except for the potatoes, and stir fry for 2-3 minutes. Add the salt, ajinomoto (optional), sprinkle some water, cover the vessel and cook on medium heat until the vegetables are tender. Do not overcook the vegetables.
3. Remove the vegetables from the fire. Add the mashed potatoes, soya and tomato sauces, and some more salt if necessary. Mix well. Divide the mixture into 8 equal portions, make small balls and flatten them into cakes.

4. Mix the batter ingredients together to a smooth consistency.
5. Dip the cakes in batter, then roll in bread crumbs, and deep fry until golden.

To serve

Arrange the cakes on a serving plate. Top each one with 1/2 teaspoon tomato ketchup and a pinch of chopped celery.

Eight Treasure Pudding

Ingredients

1 1/2 cups cooked rice

1 cup sugar

3 tablespoons heavy cream

a few drops almond essence

6 glacé cherries

6 walnuts

6 whole almonds

6 sultanas

6 pitted dates

3 tablespoons crystallised lemon, finely chopped

3 tablespoons orange peel

1 tablespoon crystallised ginger, finely chopped

For the sauce (optional)

4 tablespoons sugar

2 tablespoons cornflour

8 tablespoons water

Method

1. Mix the cooked rice, sugar and cream. Place on low heat and stir constantly until the sugar has blended well with the rice. Remove from heat, add the essence and set aside.
2. Dice and chop the ingredients on the right hand side. Grease a 9-inch pudding bowl, and arrange all these in a pattern at the bottom.
3. Pour the cooked rice on to the dry fruits, taking care not to disturb the arranged pattern.
4. Cover the bowl with a foil cut to a size one inch larger than the bowl. Steam cook the pudding in a pressure cooker for 25-30 minutes or until it is done. Cook on medium heat without using the weight.

To prepare the sauce

Mix together the sugar, water and cornflour. Place this on low heat and stir until the mixture thickens. Remove from heat and pour into a bowl. Unmould the pudding in a glass dish and serve while still hot with the above sauce.

Sauces

Chillies in Vinegar

Ingredients

1 1/2 cups brown vinegar

15-20 green chillies

1 teaspoon salt

2 teaspoons sugar

Method

1. Chop the green chillies very fine.
2. Mix all the ingredients together in a bowl, stirring well with a wooden spoon. Pour into a glass jar, cover and set aside at least 4 hours before use.

Hot Sauce

Ingredients

1 cup vinegar

2 tablespoons sugar

2 cups water

1/2 teaspoon ajinomoto (optional)

2 teaspoons pepper

3 tablespoons cornflour

1 teaspoon red chilly powder

salt to taste

Method

1. Mix all the ingredients in a sauce pan. Place on a slow fire and cook stirring constantly until the mixture thickens.
2. Simmer for a couple of minutes, remove from heat and pour the sauce into a bowl.

Green Chilly Sauce

Ingredients

25 green chillies

10 garlic cloves

1 1/2 cups vinegar

2 tablespoons sugar

1/2 tablespoon soya sauce

salt to taste

Method

1. Peel the garlic and chop it along with the chillies. Grind both to a fine paste in half of the vinegar along with sugar and salt.
2. Add the soya sauce and the rest of the vinegar to the ground paste. Mix well and pour into a bowl.

Red Chilly Sauce

Ingredients

20 dried red chillies
12 garlic cloves
1 1/2 cups vinegar

1-2 tablespoons sugar
a pinch red colour (optional)
salt to taste

Method

1. Peel and chop the garlic. Break the red chillies into pieces. Grind both to a smooth paste in half of the vinegar.
2. To this add the rest of the vinegar, salt, sugar and the colour (optional). Mix well and pour into a bowl.

Tomato Sauce

Ingredients

500 gm/1.1 lb tomatoes
4 garlic cloves
1 medium onion
2 tablespoons sugar
2 drops of orange colour (optional)
salt to taste

Spices

3 cloves
3 cardamoms
2.5 cm/1 inch cinnamon stick
1/2 teaspoon cumin seeds
1/2 teaspoon pepper
1/2 cup vinegar

Method

1. Wash and chop the tomatoes. Mince the onion and garlic.
2. Mix the spices together and tie in a muslin bag.
3. To the chopped tomatoes add the minced garlic, onion and the spice bag, and cook until the tomatoes are done.
4. Cool and squeeze all the liquid from the bag. Pass this pulp through a sieve.
5. Add the sugar, salt and vinegar to the liquid from Step 4, and bring the mixture to a boil. Reduce the heat and simmer for some more time stirring constantly. Remove from heat and add the colour.

These sauces can be prepared in advance if necessary.

SOMETHING NICE FOR TEA

SOMETHING NICE FOR TEA

Menu 1

Sweet
Apple Upside-down Cake
Raisin Cookies
Golden Delight (Mango Halwa)
Badam Pedas

Savoury
Ribbon Sandwiches
Aloo Bonda with Coconut Chutney
Vegetable Vermicelli
Chilly Biscuits

Menu 2

Sweet
Chocolate Nut Layer Cake
Coconut Jam Fingers
Almond Carrot Halwa
Besan Burfi

Savoury
Vegetable Samosas-Imli Chutney
Cheese Rolls in Tomato Sauce
Khandvi
Butter Biscuits

Menu 3

Sweet
Banana Loaf
Ginger Biscuits
Tricolour Halwa
Sweet Puffs

Savoury
Peas or Peanut Masala with Bread
Rava Vadas with Curry Leaf Chutney
Dhokla
Cheese Pompoms or Cheese Puris

Menu 4

Sweet
Fruit Cake
Chocolate Brownies
Potato Halwa
Date-Walnut Squares

Savoury
Vegetable Loaf
Moong Dal Pakodas with Sweet-
    Sour Chutney
Egg or Cheese Toast
Mattri

SOMETHING NICE FOR TEA

Menu 5

Sweet
Marble Cake
Butterscotch Squares
Bread Halwa
Currant Buns

Savoury
Channa Batura
Aloo Tikki with Chilly Chutney
Peas Pastry
Jeera Sticks

Menu 6

Sweet
Strawberry and Cherry Cake
Peanut Cookies
Badshah Halwa
Carrot Delight

Savoury
Mutter Kachodi
Philouries
Aloo Poha
All served with Sweet-Hot Chutney
Cheese-nut Squares

Menu 7

Sweet
Chocolate Cake
Doughnuts
Shahi Tukra
Carrot-Coconut Burfi

Savoury
Mini Pizza
Vegetable Cutlets with Ketchup
or Vegetable Bhajjias
Potato Cheeselings or
Potato Puffs (with eggs)

Menu 8

Sweet
Eggless Cake
Jam Biscuits
Semia Kesari
Badshah (Balushahi)

Savoury
Khara Bath (Vegetable Uppuma)
or Aval Dosai with Onion Chutney
Masala Vada with Onion Chutney
Omha Biscuits or Omhapudi

---- *Menu 1* ----

Sweet	Savoury
Apple Upside-down Cake	Ribbon Sandwiches
Raisin Cookies	Aloo Bonda with
Golden Delight (Mango Halwa)	Coconut Chutney
Badam Pedas	Vegetable Vermicelli
	Chilly Biscuits

Apple Upside-down Cake

For the cake

1 1/2 cups flour	2 teaspoons ginger juice
1/2 cup sugar	1 teaspoon lemon juice
1/2 cup butter or margarine (pressed)	3/4 cup milk
1 1/2 teaspoons baking powder	1/4 teaspoon cinnamon powder
3 eggs	1/4 teaspoon salt

For the topping

1 large/2 small tart apples
4 tablespoons brown sugar
3 tablespoons butter or margarine

Method

1. Grease a round cake tin thoroughly.
2. Mix together the brown sugar and butter, and spread it in a layer over the bottom of the tin covering it fully.
3. Peel, core and cut the apples into 0.6 cm (0.25 inch) slices and spread them in a circle evenly covering the sugar-butter mixture completely.
4. Sift the flour, baking powder, salt and cinnamon.
5. Beat the eggs thoroughly with a whisk.
6. Beat the sugar and butter until creamy, and add the eggs a little at a time whilst continuing to beat the mixture.
7. Gradually add first the flour mixture, then the lemon and ginger juices, and finally the milk until the resultant batter is of a spreading consistency.
8. Spread the batter carefully over the apple layer covering it completely. Bake at 190°C (375°F) for 25-30 minutes or until done. Remove the cake from the oven.

To serve
    While still warm, loosen the edges of the cake. Invert the cake carefully on to a serving plate, so that the apple layer is on top.

Raisin Cookies

Ingredients
    1/2 cup butter or margarine   1/2 cup raisins
    1/2 cup sugar   1/2 chopped walnuts
    1 egg   1/2 cup grated coconut
    1 cup flour   1/2 teaspoon vanilla essence
    a pinch of salt

Method
1. Cream the butter and sugar until light. Add the egg and continue beating until well blended.
2. Sift the flour with salt, and add the creamed mixture along with the raisins, essence, walnut and coconut. Mix thoroughly.
3. Grease a baking tray. Place teaspoonfuls of the mixture on it, and bake at 175°C (350°F) for 10-12 minutes or until golden brown on top.

    This recipe makes three dozen cookies.

Golden Delight (Mango Halwa)

Ingredients
    3 medium mangoes   1/2 cup water
    1 tablespoon cashew nuts, chopped fine   4 cups milk
    a pinch of saffron   2 cups sugar
    1 cup ghee (clarified butter)

Method
1. Skin and cut the mangoes into pieces. Steam until pulpy and cool. Remove any strands from the pulp.
2. Boil the milk until it is reduced to 1 cup. Cool.
3. Mix the cooled milk and mango pulp. Add the saffron mixed with a little warm milk.

4. Boil the water and sugar until the syrup is of a one-thread consistency. Do not overcook the syrup.

5. Add the mango milk mixture and stir on low heat until it starts to thicken. At this time, add the ghee a little at a time until the mixture starts to leave the sides of the vessel. Remove from fire, and mix in half of the nuts.

6. Grease a round bowl and pour the halwa into this. Sprinkle the rest of the chopped nuts on top. Serve chilled.

Badam Pedas

(Almond Fudge)

Ingredients

1 cup whole milk powder	3 cups sugar
2 cups milk	a few drops almond essence
1/2 cup almonds	a large pinch of saffron
3/4 cup ghee	1/4 cup warm milk

Method

1. Blanch and skin the almonds. Grind to a very fine paste using 3/4 cup milk while grinding. Soak the saffron in 1/4 cup warm milk, mix thoroughly with the ground paste, and set aside.

2. Warm 1 cup of milk. Add the milk powder gradually to form a smooth paste. Add this to the ground almond paste and mix well.

3. Boil the sugar with 1 cup of water briskly until it dissolves. Strain, put back on fire and boil further until a thick syrup of a one-thread consistency is obtained. Remove from fire and add the milk-almond mixture. Beat thoroughly.

4. Put back on fire and cook on moderate heat, gradually adding the ghee until the mixture starts to thicken and solidify. Keep stirring during this process. Add the almond essence. Remove from fire, spread on a greased plate, and cool.

5. Take small pieces of this semi-solid mixture, and roll them into balls. Then smoothen the balls, and flatten them into peda shapes. Alternately, press into sandesh moulds.

Ribbon Sandwiches

Ingredients

1 large sandwich loaf
1 cup butter
1 cup grated cheese
1 carrot
1 beet
2 teaspoons pepper
2 teaspoons lemon juice
salt to taste

For the chutney

a handful of mint leaves
a handful of coriander leaves
1 small onion
1.3 cm/0.5 inch piece ginger
2 green chillies
1/2 teaspoon garam masala powder
salt to taste

Method

1. Grate the carrot, beet and cheese. Do not mix.
2. Beat the butter with the pepper and some of the salt. Divide into 4 portions.
3. Grind the chutney ingredients to a smooth paste. Add the lemon juice and set aside.
4. Mix one portion each of seasoned butter with grated carrot, grated beet and ground chutney. Keep each of these separate.
5. Cut the loaf into very thin slices (if unsliced).
6. Take 4 slices at a time. Spread the butter-chutney on the first slice and sprinkle some cheese. On the second slice, spread the butter-beet mixture. On the third slice, spread the butter-carrot mixture. On the fourth slice, sprinkle the cheese.
7. Form sandwiches with the four layers from above.
8. Remove the crusts, and then cut the layered sandwiches into 3 portions. Arrange in rows on a plate.

Aloo Bonda

Ingredients

1 kg/2.2 lb potatoes
250 gm/9 oz. onions
5 green chillies
1.3 cm/0.5 inch piece ginger
a handful of coriander leaves
1 teaspoon lemon juice
salt to taste
oil for frying

Seasoning

4 tablespoons oil
1/2 teaspoon mustard seeds
1/2 teaspoon turmeric powder
1 teaspoon chilly powder
2 sprigs curry leaves

For the batter

1 1/2 cups gram flour (besan)
1/2 cup rice flour
2 teaspoons hot oil for mixing
a pinch of baking soda (optional)

1/2 teaspoon chilly powder
1/2 teaspoon turmeric powder
salt to taste

Method

1. Boil, peel and break the potatoes into small pieces. Set aside.
2. Chop the onion, ginger, green chillies and coriander leaves.
3. Heat the oil and add the mustard seeds. When done, add the chopped ingredients except for the coriander. Fry until the onions are browned, adding the turmeric and chilly powders.
4. Stir in the potatoes, salt, and the coriander. Remove from fire, cool, and add the lemon juice.
5. Divide the potato mixture into balls and set aside.

Batter

1. Mix all the ingredients together in a large bowl, and gradually add 1 cup of water. Beat thoroughly to make the batter light.
2. Gradually add an additional 1 to 1 1/2 cups of water, and mix thoroughly until the batter is of a coating consistency. Dip the potato balls in this and deep fry. Serve hot with coconut chutney.

Vegetable Vermicelli

Ingredients

200 gm/7 oz. vermicelli
1 large potato
1 large onion
1 medium capsicum (green pepper)
1/2 small cauliflower
3/4 cup shelled peas
4 green chillies
2.5 cm/1 inch piece ginger
1 tablespoon chopped coriander
2 tablespoons ghee
5 cashew nuts, broken (optional)
salt to taste

Seasonings

4 tablespoons oil
1 teaspoon mustard
2 teaspoons Bengal gram dal
2 teaspoons black gram
2 sprigs curry leaves
juice of one lemon

To serve

grated coconut (optional)

Method

1. Break the vermicelli into small pieces. Heat the ghee and fry the cashew nuts until golden. Remove and set aside. Now fry the vermicelli to a light brown. Set aside.
2. Chop the onion and ginger. Cut the chillies into 2-3 pieces each. Set aside.
3. Cut the potato into small cubes. Break the cauliflower into small florets. Cut the capsicum into small pieces.
4. Heat the oil and add the seasonings. When done, add the chopped ingredients, except for the coriander. Fry until the onions are browned.
5. Stir in first the capsicum, then the potato and cauliflower. Fry for 3 minutes. Add salt, peas, 4 cups of water and cook until vegetables are tender.
6. Add the vermicelli, some of the chopped coriander and some more water if necessary. Cook until the vermicelli is done and quite dry. There should be no traces of water.
7. Remove from heat and add the lemon juice and half the nuts.

To serve

Transfer the vermicelli to a large bowl. Garnish with the rest of the chopped coriander, the nuts and, if desired, a tablespoon of grated coconut. Serve hot with coconut chutney.

Coconut Chutney

Ingredients

1 grated coconut
a large bunch of coriander leaves
5 green chillies
salt to taste
1 cup curds (yoghurt)
3 tablespoons roasted gram dal

Seasoning

2 teaspoons oil
1/2 teaspoon mustard seeds
1 teaspoon black gram dal
2 sprigs curry leaves

Method

1. Grind the coconut, coriander, green chilly, gram dal and salt to a smooth paste. Beat the curds smooth, and mix in the ground paste.
2. Season the ingredients given in oil. Pour over chutney and mix.

Chilly Biscuits

Ingredients	Chop very fine
2 cups flour	4 green chillies
1/2 cup pressed butter/margarine	2.5 cm/1 inch piece ginger
1/2 teaspoon baking powder	2 sprigs curry leaves
1/2 teaspoon pepper powder	a handful chopped coriander
1/2 teaspoon chilly powder	1 small onion (optional)
a pinch of sugar	
curds (yoghurt) to mix	
salt to taste	

Method

1. Sift the flour, salt and baking powder.
2. Rub the butter into the flour very lightly using only the tips of your fingers so that the mixture resembles bread crumbs.
3. Add the pepper, chilly powder and sugar to the chopped ingredients. Mix this with the flour and knead to a soft dough adding sufficient curds. Knead until the dough is smooth. Cover and set aside for 10-15 minutes.
4. Flatten the dough into a sheet 0.6 cm/0.25 inch thick. Cut out small circles using a biscuit cutter. Pierce the biscuits with a fork or pin.
5. Grease and dust (with flour) a baking sheet. Place the biscuits on the sheet and bake at 190°C (375°F) for 15-20 minutes or until done.

---- *Menu 2* ----

Sweet	Savoury
Chocolate Nut Layer Cake	Vegetable Samosas-Imli
Coconut Jam Fingers	Chutney
Almond Carrot Halwa	Cheese Rolls in Tomato Sauce
Besan Burfi	Khandvi
	Butter Biscuits

Chocolate Nut Layer Cake

Ingredients
3 cups flour
2 1/4 cup sugar
1 teaspoon baking powder
1/4 teaspoon salt
1 teaspoon vanilla
1 cup milk
3/4 cup oil or 1 cup margarine
2 eggs
1 tablespoon grated chocolate (for the garnish)

Chocolate nut filling
2 tablespoons cocoa
2 cups icing sugar
a handful of walnuts
1/2 teaspoon vanilla essence
4 tablespoons water
6 tablespoons fresh cream
1 tablespoon butter

Method
1. Sift the flour, baking powder and salt twice.
2. To the sugar, add 1/2 cup water and boil on a slow fire until the sugar has dissolved. Now boil briskly until a thick syrup is obtained. Set aside to cool.
3. Break the eggs, separating the white from the yolk. Beat the whites stiff with an egg beater, gradually adding the remaining sugar. Beat until light and fluffy and the mixture starts standing in peaks. Keep aside.
4. In a large mixing bowl, put the sifted ingredients, cooled sugar syrup, milk, oil and essence. Beat this mixture slowly at first, then briskly (150-200 strokes) until the mixture is well blended. Add the egg yolks one at a time beating all the while until the mixture is light.
5. Gradually stir the whites into the batter, and mix gently.
6. Grease a 22 cm (9 inches) diameter round tin with oil. Line it with greased brown paper. Pour the batter into the tin and bake at 190°C (375°F) for 25-30 minutes and the top is nicely browned. A skewer passed through the cake should come out clean.
7. Remove the cake from the tin and cool. When sufficiently cool, cut horizontally into equal halves and set aside.

To prepare the chocolate nut

1. Put the icing sugar, cocoa and 3 tablespoons of water in a saucepan. Melt over gentle heat stirring all the while until the sugar dissolves. Add the butter and stir until the mixture is well blended. Add 1 tablespoon of water if the mixture is too thick. Add the vanilla essence and beat the mixture to a smooth consistency. Cool.
2. Set aside 6 walnuts. Grate the rest of the nuts, add to the cooled cocoa, and mix well.
3. Beat the cream lightly. Spread half of it on the bottom half of the cake, and spoon out half of the chocolate walnut mixture.
4. Place the second half of the cake on the first, pressing lightly so that the two are sandwiched together.
5. Spread the rest of the cream on the top layer, then the chocolate nut mixture and smoothen out the surface if necessary. Sprinkle the grated chocolate.
6. Chop the walnuts kept aside into quarters and halves. Press the halves on the top layer and the quarters on the sides. Chill the cake slightly so that the icing is set before serving.

Coconut Jam Fingers

Ingredients

1 cup flour
1/2 cup butter or margarine
1 cup sugar
1 teaspoon baking powder
2 eggs
1/4 teaspoon salt

3/4 cup desiccated coconut
3 tablespoons strawberry jam
milk to mix
a few drops almond essence
20 cm/8 inches square cake tin

Method

1. Cut the brown paper to the size of the tin and line the bottom. Grease the tin and paper thoroughly and set aside.
2. Sift the flour, baking powder and salt. Keep separate.
3. Beat the eggs with a whisk and set aside.
4. Beat the butter and sugar until creamy. Gradually add the eggs and continue to beat.
5. Fold in the flour lightly along with 1/2 cup desiccated coconut, adding a little milk to make the batter smooth. Add the almond essence and mix thoroughly.
6. Pour the batter into the tin and bake in a moderate oven (190°C/375°F) for 20-30 minutes.

7. While still warm, remove the cake carefully from tin and place on a wooden plank. Melt the jam, and spread this over the cake fully. Sprinkle 1/4 cup desiccated coconut on the jam layer. (If desired, finely chopped almonds may also be sprinkled at this time.)
8. When cool, cut into 2.5 cm by 7.5 cm (1 inch x 3 inch) finger lengths.

Almond Carrot Halwa

Ingredients

500 gm/1.1 lb carrots
4 cups milk
1 cup almonds
1/2 cup ghee

2 cups sugar
4 cardamoms, powdered
a few drops almond essence
a pinch of saffron

Method

1. Grate the carrots and boil in just enough water. Cool. Blanch and skin the almonds. Keeping a few aside, grind the rest with the cooked carrots.
2. To the ground paste add the milk, sugar, saffron and half of the ghee. Cook in a heavy-bottomed vessel on a slow fire stirring constantly until the mixture starts to leave the sides of the vessel. Add the rest of the ghee until the mixture forms one mass. Remove from fire.
3. Add the essence and cardamom powder, and mix thoroughly. Chop the almonds and set aside. Mix in half of it.
4. Grease a glass bowl with some ghee and transfer the halwa on to it. Smoothen out the surface, and garnish with the rest of the almonds. Serve hot.

Besan Burfi

(A Yellow Chickpea Flour Milk Confection)

Ingredients

2 cups grated coconut
1 cup besan (gram flour)
3 cups sugar
3 tablespoons ghee
a few cashew nuts, broken
4 cardamoms, powdered
a pinch of saffron

Method

1. Heat 1 tablespoon of ghee. Add the cashew nuts and fry until golden. Remove the cashew nuts. To the same ghee gradually add the besan, stirring gently. Fry on low heat until golden brown. Remove and set aside.
2. Heat 1 cup of water and add the sugar. Boil on low heat until the sugar dissolves. Increase the heat and boil briskly until a thick syrup is obtained.
3. Add the coconut and fried besan. Stir until the mixture solidifies and starts to leave the sides of the vessel.
4. Add the rest of the ghee and saffron. Mix well and allow to cook for a couple of minutes.
5. Remove from fire, and add the nuts and cardamom powder. Mix well. Pour onto a greased plate and while still warm cut into squares.

This recipe makes 20.

Vegetable Samosas

Ingredients
1 1/2 cups flour (maida)
1/2 cup wheat flour
4 tablespoons vegetable shortening/vanaspati
4 tablespoons oil
1 teaspoon chilly powder
1/4 teaspoon turmeric powder
1/2 teaspoon garam masala
oil for frying
salt to taste

Filling
2 medium potatoes
1/2 small cauliflower
3/4 cup shelled peas
1 carrot (optional)
a handful of beans
1/2 inch piece ginger
4 green chillies
a handful of fresh coriander
1 large onion

Method

1. Add the salt and vanaspati to the flour and wheat flour and mix lightly so that the mixture resembles bread crumbs. Add water gradually and mix to obtain a stiff dough. Cover and set aside.

For the filling

1. Peel and cut the potatoes into small cubes. Chop the beans, carrots and cauliflower into fine pieces. Steam cook the vegetables along with peas, a little salt and very little water. Do not overcook.
2. Chop the chillies, ginger, onions and coriander. Heat the oil, and add the chopped ingredients (except coriander). Fry until the onions are browned along with turmeric and chilly powder.

3. Add the steamed vegetables and stir until the water evaporates. Add the garam masala powder, coriander and some more salt if necessary. Mix thoroughly and allow to cool.

Note

As an alternative to steam cooking the vegetables, you may fry them and cook covered with a little water.

To make the samosas

1. Divide the dough into small round balls, and roll them into puris using a rolling-pin on an oiled flour board. If you are making cone-shaped samosas, use larger balls.
2. Placing 2 teaspoonsful of filling on one half of a puri, fold the other half over so that the edges meet. Stick the edges to-gether with water. The samosas made thus are half-moon shaped. If you wish to make conical samosas, follow the directions below:

   Cut the puri into two equal halves. Form a cone with each semicircle by joining the edges and sealing with a little water. Place some filling in the cone, and seal the top by pressing the edges using a little water. Ensure that the samosas are properly sealed to prevent the filling from spilling while frying. Make all samosas thus.
3. Deep fry the samosas in hot oil and serve hot.

Note

If dried peas are to be used, soak them overnight, and cook in a pressure cooker. For this recipe, use only peas and potatoes.

Imli Chutney
(Tamarind Chutney)

Ingredients

1 cup tamarind
a small piece of jaggery
2 teaspoons cumin seeds
salt to taste

a small bunch of coriander leaves
a small bunch of mint leaves
8 green chillies

Method

1. Boil the tamarind in water, and knead to extract thick pulp.
2. Grind the coriander, mint and green chillies to a paste.
3. Add the ground paste, salt and jaggery to the tamarind pulp and boil until thick in consistency.
4. Dry roast the cumin seeds. Powder and add to chutney.

Cheese Rolls in Tomato Sauce

For the chutney

a large bundle of mint	1/2 teaspoon cumin seeds
a handful of coriander leaves	a few peppercorns
5 green chillies	a generous pinch of garam masala
2.5 cm/1 inch piece ginger	1 cup grated cheese
1 small onion	1 large loaf of bread
3 cloves garlic	juice of 1 lemon
salt to taste	

For the sauce

1.5 kg/3.3 lb tomatoes	2 teaspoons sugar
300 gm/10 oz. onions	1 1/2 tablespoons oil
2 teaspoons red chilly powder	

Method

1. Grind all the chutney ingredients (except the cheese, bread and lemon) to a fine paste. Add the lemon juice and cheese. Mix well and set aside.
2. Trim the edges of a slice of bread and dip in water for 30 seconds. Press gently with both palms to remove excess water. Spread the chutney-cheese mixture on the slice, and make a roll by pressing the edges to-gether. Process all rolls thus and set aside.
3. Deep fry the rolls and arrange on a serving plate.

For the sauce

1. Boil the tomatoes in 2 cups of water. Cool, peel skin, and pass through a liquidiser. Strain the resulting pulp. Add some water if too thick.
2. Chop the onions fine, and fry in hot oil to a pink colour. Add the tomato puree, chilly powder, sugar and salt. Boil for 5-8 minutes and remove from heat.

To serve

Pour the tomato sauce on the rolls and serve. If desired, garnish with grated cheese.

Khandvi
(Gram Flour Rolls)

Ingredients

1 cup besan (gram flour)	2 green chillies, finely chopped
1 cup curds (yoghurt)	1 tablespoon chopped coriander
2 cups water	1 tablespoon coconut gratings
4 teaspoons oil	1/4 teaspoon turmeric powder
salt to taste	1/2 teaspoon mustard

Method

1. Mix the gram flour, curds, water, turmeric powder and salt. Beat the mixture to form a smooth paste, making sure there are no lumps.
2. Cook the mixture, stirring constantly. When it starts to thicken, add a teaspoon of oil and continue to cook until a small portion when spread on a plate does not stick to your fingers.
3. Remove from fire and spread on a stainless steel plate (or marble slab) at once. When it cools, roll up quickly and cut roll into 1-inch circles. Alternately, cut long strips of the spread mixture and then roll each strip.

To serve

Arrange the rolls on a plate. Season the mustard and minced chillies in the rest of the oil and pour over the rolls. Garnish with the chopped coriander and grated coconut.

Butter Biscuits

Ingredients

2 cups flour (maida)	1/4 teaspoon baking powder
3/4 cup margarine	salt to taste
1 teaspoon sugar	2 tablespoons milk

Method

1. Mix the margarine with salt and sugar.
2. Sift the flour with baking powder. Add the margarine and enough milk to knead to a smooth dough.
3. Roll the dough into a rectangle. Cut into small rounds using a biscuit cutter. Prick biscuits with a fork.
4. Bake at 175°C (350°F) for 30 minutes.

This recipe makes 3 dozen biscuits.

—— *Menu 3* ——

Sweet	**Savoury**
Banana Loaf	Peas or Peanut Masala
Ginger Biscuits	with Bread
Tricolour Halwa	Rava Vadas with
Sweet Puffs	Curry Leaf Chutney
	Dhokla
	Cheese Pompoms or
	Cheese Puris

Banana Loaf

Ingredients

1 1/2 cups flour (maida)	2 ripe bananas
3/4 cup sugar	1/2 cup margarine
1 teaspoon soda	a pinch of salt
1 teaspoon baking powder	1 egg
1 teaspoon vanilla essence	a little milk
2 tablespoons raisins	
1 tablespoon currants	

Method

1. Sift the flour, soda, baking powder and salt twice.
2. Beat the sugar and margarine to a cream.
3. Beat the egg and gradually fold into the creamed mixture.
4. Mash the bananas well and add to the mixture.
5. Fold in the flour lightly, adding milk if necessary, to make it of a dropping consistency.
6. Add the raisins, currants and essence. Mix well.
7. Grease a loaf tin thoroughly. Pour the mixture into it and bake at 190°C (375°F) for 35-45 minutes or until done.
8. When cool, remove loaf from the tin, cut into slices and serve.

Ginger Biscuits

Ingredients

2 cups flour (maida)

1/2 cup semolina (sooji)

1/2 cup jaggery syrup

1/2 cup sugar

1/2 tablespoon ginger powder

or 1 tablespoon ginger juice

3/4 cup vegetable shortening/
    vanaspati, melted

1/2 teaspoon baking powder

1/2 teaspoon baking soda

a pinch of salt

juice of 1 lemon

Method

1. Sift together the maida, sooji, salt, baking powder and soda.
2. Mix together the jaggery syrup, ginger juice/powder, lemon juice, sugar and melted vanaspati. Beat the mixture thoroughly.
3. To this add the sifted ingredients and mix to form a smooth dough.
4. Divide the dough into lemon-sized pieces. Pat into rounds, and pierce each biscuit with a fork or pin.
5. Dust a greased tray with flour. Place the biscuits on it and bake at 175°C (350°F) for 15 minutes or until done. Makes 20.

Note

To make the jaggery syrup, boil together 1 cup of water with 1 cup of powdered jaggery. When dissolved, strain the syrup, put back on fire, and boil until a honey-like consistency is obtained.

Tricolour Halwa

Ingredients

1 vegetable marrow

or 1/2 bottle gourd

2 large carrots

2 large potatoes

2 1/4 cups grated coconut

6 cups milk

3 cups sugar

6 cardamoms

1 cup ghee

4 tablespoons cashew nuts

4 tablespoons raisins

2 drops green colour

2 drops yellow colour

Method

1. Wash, peel and grate each of the vegetables separately. Wash the potato gratings in a little cold water and squeeze dry. Boil this in some water. Boil the carrot and marrow separately in water. When cooked, mash the pulp and set aside.
2. Powder the cardamom. Chop the cashew nuts and fry them in one tablespoon of ghee along with the raisins. Set aside.
3. Divide the sugar, milk, ghee, cardamom and coconut into 3 equal parts. Divide the dry fruits into 4 portions. Set both aside.
4. Place the potato gratings and one portion of sugar, milk and coconut in a flat heavy-bottomed vessel and cook until the mixture starts to thicken, stirring constantly. Now add a third of the ghee gradually. When done, the mixture will start to leave the sides of the vessel. Add a third of the cardamom powder and a fourth of the fried nuts and raisins. Mix well. Pour the mixture on to a well-greased transparent dish. Smoothen the surface and set aside.
5. Repeat the above process with the carrot pulp, adding yellow colour. When done, put this over the potato layer and set aside.
6. Repeat this process once again with the marrow pulp and green colour. Put this over the carrot layer.
7. Garnish with the rest of the nuts and raisins. Serve hot.

Sweet Puffs

Ingredients

2 cups flour
1/2 teaspoon salt
4 tablespoons vegetable shortening/vanaspati
ghee or vanaspati for frying

For the filling

2 cups grated copra
1 cup sugar
3 tablespoons raisins
2 tablespoons cashew nuts,
    chopped
1/2 teaspoon cardamom powder
3 teaspoons poppy seeds

Method

1. Mix the salt, flour and vanaspati with very little water to form a stiff dough. Cover and leave for 30 minutes.
2. Mix together all the ingredients for the filling.
3. Divide the dough into lemon-sized balls and roll into puris. Place one tablespoon of the stuffing in one half and fold the other half over so that the ends meet. Press the edges together with wet fingers to seal.
4. Deep fry the puffs in hot ghee to golden.

Since these puffs keep, they may be made in advance.

Peas or Peanut Masala with Bread

Ingredients

a large loaf of bread
butter for frying
2 large potatoes
2 large onions
2 1/2 cups dehydrated peas
or 2 1/2 cups peanuts, shelled
a handful of coriander leaves
4 green chillies, slit
8 tablespoons oil
3 bay leaves
salt to taste
1 large lemon

Grind to a fine paste

3 tablespoons grated coconut
2 tablespoons coriander powder
1/2 tablespoon cumin powder
1 tablespoon poppy seeds
1 teaspoon chilly powder
1 teaspoon garam masala
1/2 teaspoon turmeric powder
2.5 cm/1 inch piece ginger
4 garlic cloves
a few coriander leaves

Method

1. Peel and cut the potatoes into cubes. Wash and set aside.
2. Mince the onions and chop the coriander fine.
3. Heat some of the oil in a kadai (wok) and fry the potatoes to a golden colour. Remove from oil and set aside. Boil the peas or peanuts and set aside.
4. Pour the rest of the oil into the kadai. Add the bay leaves and slit chillies, and fry for a minute. Add the minced onions, fry until brown and then add the ground paste. Continue to fry until the oil surfaces.
5. Add the peas (or peanuts), salt and some of the chopped coriander. Cook for a few minutes until the gravy is well blended.
6. Remove from heat, and add the fried potatoes and lemon juice. Pour into a bowl and garnish with the rest of the chopped coriander.

To serve

Cut the bread into slices, butter both sides and shallow fry in butter until golden. Place the fried slices on a plate and serve with the above curry.

Rava Vadas

Ingredients

2 cups rava (semolina)
5 green chillies
2.5 cm/1 inch piece ginger
a little fresh coriander
salt to taste
oil for frying

For the seasoning

1 teaspoon mustard seeds
2 teaspoons Bengal gram dal
2 teaspoons black gram dal
2 tablespoons oil
2 sprigs curry leaves

Method

1. Chop the green chilies, ginger and coriander.
2. Heat the oil and add the seasonings. Fry. When done, add the chopped ingredients. Fry for 1-2 minutes. Add 2 cups of water, salt and the chopped coriander. Bring the water to a boil.
3. When the water is boiling, gradually add the rava and cook on low heat until all the water is absorbed. Remove from fire, transfer on to a plate and cool.
4. When cool, divide the mixture into small balls and flatten into vadas (patties).
5. Deep fry the vadas in hot oil and serve hot with chutney.

This recipe makes 30.

Curry Leaf Chutney

Ingredients

12 green chillies
2.5 cm/1 inch piece ginger
1 tablespoon Bengal gram dal
2 teaspoons sesame seeds
1 teaspoon mustard seeds

1 lemon-sized ball tamarind
1 1/2 tablespoons oil
salt to taste
1 tablespoon grated coconut
4-5 cups picked curry leaves

Method

1. Chop the green chillies and ginger. Clean and wash the curry leaves.
2. Roast the sesame seeds in a kadai (wok) and remove. Add the oil and fry the mustard. When done, add the dal and fry to a golden colour. Remove. Add the chopped chillies and ginger and fry, adding curry leaves.
3. Grind the roasted and fried ingredients together, adding salt, coconut and tamarind. Add some water, mix and serve.

Note

You can substitute coriander leaves for curry leaves.

Dhokla

Ingredients

1 1/2 cups channa dal
4 tablespoons curds (yoghurt)
6 green chillies, chopped
1.3 cm/0.5 inch piece ginger, chopped
2 tablespoons grated coconut
a little coriander, chopped
salt to taste

Seasonings

4 tablespoons oil
1/2 teaspoon baking soda
1/2 teaspoon mustard seeds
1/4 teaspoon turmeric powder
1/2 tablespoon sugar

Method

1. Soak the dal for 4-6 hours and grind coarse.
2. Add the curds and baking soda. Cover and set aside for a few hours.
3. When sufficiently fermented, add the chillies, ginger, a little coconut, some of the coriander, turmeric, salt, sugar and 2 tablespoons of oil. Mix the batter thoroughly.
4. Pour the batter on to a greased plate and steam cook for 25-30 minutes. When done, cool and cut the steamed mixture into squares. Place on a large serving-plate.
5. Heat the rest of the oil and add the mustard. When done, pour this over the dhoklas. Sprinkle the rest of the coconut and coriander.

Cheese Pompoms (With Eggs)

Ingredients

1 heaped cup flour (maida)
1 cup grated cheese
1 cup water
1 cup butter
2 eggs
oil for frying

Seasonings

1 teaspoon chopped green chillies
2 teaspoons chopped coriander
1/2 teaspoon chilly powder
1/2 teaspoon pepper
salt to taste

Method

1. Combine the water and butter in a saucepan. Place on fire and stir on a very slow flame until well blended.
2. Remove from fire and gradually add the flour ensuring that there are no lumps in the mixture. Mix thoroughly, put back on fire and cook until the mixture starts to leave the sides of the pan.

3. Remove from heat and cool. Beat the eggs, and add them one at a time to the mixture. Mix thoroughly. Add the cheese and seasonings, and beat the batter to a very smooth consistency.
4. Divide the mixture into small balls using floured hands and fry in hot oil until golden.

Cheese Puris

Ingredients

1 cup semolina (cream of wheat)
1/2 cup flour
1/2 cup vegetable shortening/vanaspati
1/2 cup curds (yoghurt)
salt to taste
oil for frying

For the filling

1 cup grated cheese
6 green chillies, minced
2 tablespoons chopped coriander
a pinch of salt
3/4 teaspoon pepper

Method

1. Mix the vanaspati, curds, salt, semolina and flour in a large mixing bowl to form a smooth dough. If the dough seems stiff, add some water and a little curds. Knead for 10 minutes, cover, and set aside for an hour.
2. Take a small ball of dough and work into a cup. Using a little oil, put in 2-3 teaspoons of the filling, and close the cup. Roll into puris as thin as possible. Pierce with a fork.
3. Deep fry the puris in hot oil, pressing them down so they do not puff up. Fry until golden brown. Serve hot with chutney.

This recipe makes 15-20 puris.

```
———— Menu 4 ————
```

Sweet
Fruit Cake
Chocolate Brownies
Potato Halwa
Date-Walnut Squares

Savoury
Vegetable Loaf
Moong Dal Pakodas with
Sweet-Sour Chutney
Egg or Cheese Toast
Mattri

Fruit Cake

Ingredients

1 cup butter
1 cup sugar
2 cups flour
a pinch of salt
1 teaspoon vanilla essence
1 teaspoon instant coffee
1 teaspoon mixed spices
4 tablespoons caramel syrup
2 teaspoons rum
2 teaspoons lemon juice
2 tablespoons milk
1/2 teaspoon lemon rind, grated
1/2 teaspoon orange rind, grated
1/2 teaspoon baking powder

3 eggs
2 cups sultanas, raisins,
    cherries, sliced ginger,
    mixed peel, currants
    mixed together
1 1/2 cups chopped walnuts,
    almonds and cashew
    nuts mixed together
1/4 cup jam
a few whole walnuts, almonds
    and cashew nuts
jam for glacé (optional)

Method

1. Clean and chop the dry fruits and nuts. Mix the lemon juice, rind of lemon and orange, rum and spices. Soak the dry fruits and nuts in this for a few hours or overnight if possible to improve the flavour of the cake.
2. Sift the flour, baking powder, salt and instant coffee.
3. Beat the butter and sugar until light and fluffy.
4. Beat the eggs thoroughly with vanilla. Add this gradually to the creamed mixture, and beat for 5 minutes.
5. Fold in the flour and dry fruits lightly, adding the caramel syrup, jam, nuts and sufficient milk to form batter of a dropping consistency.
6. Grease a cake tin well and line with greaseproof paper. Pour the mixture into this and bake at 150°C (300°F) for 90 minutes. Warm the jam and spread it on the cake (optional).

Caramel Syrup

Put 4 tablespoons of sugar in a saucepan and melt over gentle heat. When all the sugar has dissolved, raise the heat and allow the sugar to burn until a dark brown colour is obtained. Remove from heat. Add 1/2 cup water. Mix, put back on fire and boil slowly until a thick honey-like syrup is formed.

Chocolate Brownies

Ingredients
1 cup sugar
2/3 cup butter
1 cup sifted flour
4 tablespoons cocoa
1/2 teaspoon vanilla essence
2 eggs

a pinch of baking powder
1/4 teaspoon salt
1 tablespoon powdered sugar
1/2 cup walnuts, chopped
a few halved walnuts

Method
1. Grease an eight-inch square tin and line it with greased brown paper. Set aside. Sift the flour, baking powder and salt.
2. Beat the eggs and sugar until light and fluffy.
3. Put the cocoa and butter in a small bowl and place this over a larger bowl of boiling water. Beat the mixture to a smooth paste. Remove from heat and very gradually add the egg sugar mixture.
4. Fold in the flour lightly, and add the essence and chopped nuts. Mix well and pour the batter into the greased tin.
5. Bake at 190°C (375°F) for 20-30 minutes. When done, remove from tin, and cool on a wooden plank.
6. Cut the cake into 3.75 cm (1.5 inch) squares. Dust the top with powdered sugar, and press a halved walnut into each piece.

Potato Halwa

Ingredients
1.5 litres (1.6 quarts) milk
6 medium potatoes
1 1/2 cups sugar (or more to taste)
1 cup ghee

a few drops almond essence
a pinch of saffron (optional)
a handful of chopped nuts
5 cardamoms, powdered

Method

1. Wash and grate the potatoes. Soak in cold water for a few minutes. Squeeze out all the water and set aside.
2. Boil the milk, add the potato gratings and cook on medium heat until they are done. Add the sugar and stir until the sugar dissolves and the mixture starts to thicken. Add the saffron mixed with 1 teaspoon of milk.
3. Gradually add the ghee a little at a time and cook on low heat until the halwa starts to leave the sides of the vessel. Add the cardamom, essence, some of the nuts, and remove from fire.
4. Transfer the halwa onto a bowl and smoothen the surface. Garnish with the rest of the nuts.

Date-Walnut Squares

Ingredients

2 cups flour
1/2 cup powdered sugar
1 cup margarine or vanaspati
a few halved walnuts
1/2 teaspoon baking soda
a baking tray

For the filling

1/2 cup chopped walnuts
1/2 cup grated coconut
3/4 cup chopped dates
3 tablespoons water
1/2 teaspoon vanilla essence

Method

1. To prepare the filling, mix all its ingredients together in a saucepan. Stir over slow heat until a smooth mixture is obtained. If necessary, add a little more water. Set aside.
2. Cut 2 brown paper sheets to the size of the tray. Set aside.
3. Sift the flour and baking soda together.
4. Cream the sugar and margarine to a smooth paste. Now add the flour and make a very soft dough of a rolling consistency. Add a little milk if necessary.
5. Divide the dough into two portions and roll one portion on the brown sheet. Carefully transfer it to the baking tray. Peel off the sheet and spread the filling evenly all over the pastry.
6. Roll out a second portion on the second sheet, and place this carefully on top of the filling. Peel off the sheet and press the sides together.
7. Cut the dough into 3.75 cm (1.5 inch) squares. Press a walnut half on each square. Bake at 190°C (375°F) for 15-20 minutes.

Vegetable Loaf

Ingredients

1 kg/2.2 lb potatoes
2 medium carrots
1 cup peas, shelled
1/2 small cauliflower
a handful of tender French beans
1 large onions
3 green chillies
2.5 cm/1 inch piece ginger
2 tablespoons coriander, chopped

1/2 teaspoon garam masala
1/2 teaspoon pepper powder
1/2 teaspoon chilly powder
salt to taste
2 cups dried bread crumbs
2 loaf tins
2 tablespoons butter
4 tablespoons vegetable shortening/ vanaspati
tomato ketchup (to serve)

Method

1. Boil, peel and while still warm, mash the potatoes adding some salt, half of the chilly, pepper powders, butter and chopped coriander. Mix thoroughly and set aside.
2. Wash and chop the other vegetables. Boil in water with the salt and peas. When cooked, mash. Chop the onions, ginger and green chillies.
3. Heat the vanaspati, and add the chopped ingredients (except coriander). Fry until the onions are browned. Add the cooked vegetables, masala powders, and the rest of the chopped coriander. Mix well and fry for a while until all the water has evaporated.
4. Grease each loaf tin with some vanaspati. Sprinkle a third of the crumbs over the base of each tin. Divide the potato dough and the vegetables into two portions. For each portion, spread half of the potato dough over this. Top this with the vegetable layer. Spread evenly. Cover this layer with the second half of the potato dough, then sprinkle the rest of the crumbs very lightly.
5. Smoothen the surface, spread some butter or melted vanaspati, and bake in a moderate oven (190°C/375°F) for 20-30 minutes until the top is nicely browned.

To serve

Remove the loaf carefully from tin and cut into thick slices. Serve hot with tomato ketchup.

Moong Dal Pakodas
Served with sweet and sour chutney

For the pakodas

2 cups green gram dal
6 green chillies
2.5 cm/1 inch piece ginger
2 sprigs curry leaves
a small pinch of asafoetida
1 tablespoon coriander, chopped
1 onion, chopped (optional)
oil for frying
1 cup curds (yoghurt)
salt to taste

For the chutney

50 gm tamarind
3 tablespoons jaggery
1/2 cup grated coconut
2 teaspoons sesame seeds
1 1/2 tablespoons peanuts
2 teaspoons cumin seeds
2 teaspoons red chilly powder
1/2 teaspoon garam masala
1 tablespoon coriander, chopped
salt to taste

To make the chutney

1. Dry roast the cumin seeds. Powder and set aside.
2. Roast the sesame seeds, peanuts and grated coconut. Grind to a paste.
3. Boil the tamarind in some water and squeeze to extract the pulp.
4. To this tamarind pulp, add the ground paste, 1 1/2 teaspoons chilly powder, jaggery and salt. Cook for a few minutes.
5. When the chutney is thick, add the garam masala powder, half of the chopped coriander, and a little water if needed. Boil for 2-3 minutes. Remove from heat and set aside.

To make the pakodas

1. Soak the dal for a few hours. Remove all the water and grind to a paste adding the chillies, ginger, curry leaves, asafoetida and salt. Do not add water while grinding unless it is absolutely necessary.
2. Add the chopped coriander and mix well. If desired, a finely chopped onion can be added.
3. Deep fry spoonfuls of the mixture in heated oil to make the pakodas.

To serve

Transfer the pakodas on to a deep plate and pour the chutney into this. Beat the yoghurt and pour this over the chutney. Garnish with powdered cumin seeds, a little chilly powder and some chopped coriander.

Egg or Cheese Toast

Ingredients
a large loaf of bread
butter
tomato ketchup
chilly sauce

For the egg toast
4 eggs
1 large onion
4 green chillies
a handful of coriander
3 tablespoons vegetable shortening/vanaspati
salt and pepper to taste
a pinch of turmeric powder
a baking tray

For the cheese toast
2 cups grated cheese
2 tablespoons cream
4 teaspoons flour
1 large onion, minced
4 green chillies, minced
a handful of minced coriander
3 tablespoons vegetable shortening/vanaspati
1 cup milk
salt and pepper to taste

Method
1. With a large biscuit cutter cut out circles from the slices of bread. Butter generously on one side only.
2. Grease a baking tray, place the bread rounds on this and bake in an oven at 225°C/ 400°F for 15-20 minutes or until crisp. Set aside until required.

Egg Toast

1. Mince the onions, green chillies and coriander. Beat the eggs with a pinch of turmeric and set aside.
2. Heat the vanaspati, add the chillies and onions, and fry until the onions are browned. Add the eggs, salt and pepper. Stir until the eggs are cooked. Add the coriander, mix, and remove from heat.
3. Spread a tablespoon of the mixture on each slice, and put a dab of tomato ketchup. Serve immediately.

Cheese Toast

1. Heat the vanaspati. Add the minced ingredients except the coriander, and fry until the onions are pinkish in colour.
2. Add the flour and fry on low heat until lightly browned. Remove from fire, and add milk gradually. Then put back on fire and cook until a thick sauce is formed.

3. Remove from heat and add the grated cheese, cream, minced coriander, salt, and pepper. Mix well and set aside.
4. Spread a table spoon of this mixture on the toast, top with some chilly sauce and serve immediately.

Mattri

(Savoury Biscuit)

Ingredients

1 cup flour

1 cup semolina

1/2 cup vegetable shortening/vanaspati

2 teaspoons ajwain or cumin seeds

oil for frying

1 teaspoon pepper

salt to taste

milk to mix

warm water to mix

Method

1. Mix together the flour, semolina, salt, pepper, ajwain and vanaspati. Mix in the flour lightly to obtain a bread-crumb consistency.
2. Add the milk and warm water, and mix to a stiff dough. Knead the dough for 15 to 20 minutes, cover, and set aside for another twenty minutes.
3. Roll into thick puris. Prick with a fork and deep fry until golden. Serve with sweet/sour chutney.

—— ⨍Menu 5 ——

Sweet
Marble Cake
Butterscotch Squares
Bread Halwa
Currant Buns

Savoury
Channa Batura
Aloo Tikki with Chilly
Chutney
Peas Pastry
Jeera Sticks

Marble Cake

Ingredients

3 cups flour (maida)
1 1/2 cups sugar
1 cup margarine or vanaspati
4 eggs
1 cup milk to mix
1 tablespoon powdered sugar

1 teaspoon lemon rind
1 teaspoon lemon juice
1/4 teaspoon salt
2 teaspoons baking powder
a few drops green colour
a few drops pink colour

Method

1. Sift the flour, baking powder and salt twice.
2. Cream the fat and sugar until light and fluffy. Add the lemon juice and lemon rind.
3. Add the eggs one at a time and beat lightly until the mixture is well blended.
4. Add the flour to the creamed mixture. If the batter is too thick, add a little milk until the mixture is of a dropping consistency. Add the essence and stir.
5. Divide the mixture into 3 portions. Colour one portion pink and another green by adding a couple of drops of the colour either neat or mixed with a little milk.
6. Grease a round tin and line with greased brown paper. Place a large serving spoon of the plain batter in the tin followed by a spoon of the pink batter, and then a spoon of green batter. Repeat this process until all the batters are used up. Shake the tin lightly so that the batter spreads evenly.
7. Bake at 175°C/350°F for 45 minutes. When done, test the cake by passing a skewer through it. (It should come out clean.)
8. Remove the cake from the tin and while still warm, dust the top with the powdered sugar. Alternately add a layer of lemon icing.

For the Icing

Ingredients

224 gm/8 oz. icing sugar
a few drops lemon juice
1 1/2 tablespoons warm water
a few drops lemon essence
a few drops yellow colour

Method

Put the icing sugar and lemon juice in a saucepan. Add the water gradually and mix to form a coating consistency. Add the colour and essence. Place the saucepan on low heat and stir just once. Remove from fire and pour over the cake in a layer. Allow the icing to run on the sides. If any icing remains, cover the sides using a palette-knife dipped in hot water.

Butterscotch Squares

Ingredients

1 cup flour	1/2 teaspoon salt
1/2 cup butter or margarine	1/2 teaspoon vanilla essence
2 cups pressed brown sugar	1 cup walnuts, chopped
2 teaspoons baking powder	a few halved walnuts
2 eggs	1/2 cup milk to mix
a square tin	

Method

1. Sift the baking powder, flour and salt.
2. Melt the butter in a saucepan over very gentle heat. When melted, remove from heat, add the sugar and mix until well blended. Cool the mixture.
3. Break the eggs into the same saucepan one at a time stirring all the while. When both the eggs have been added, beat the mixture vigorously until the sugar has dissolved completely and the batter is smooth.
4. Gradually add the flour to the mixture. When all the flour has been added, stir in the essence and the nuts. If the batter is thick, add the milk gradually until the batter is of a dropping consistency.
5. Grease a square tin and pour the mixture into this. Bake in a moderate oven (190°C/375°F) for 30 minutes. When done, cut the cake into squares while still warm. Press a halved walnut into each square.

Bread Halwa

Ingredients

1 small loaf bread
1 1/2 cups sugar
2 cups milk
1/2 cup cream (optional)
1 cup ghee
1/2 cup water

1 tablespoon cashew nuts, chopped
1 tablespoon raisins
1/2 teaspoon nutmeg, grated
4 cardamoms, powdered
a pinch of saffron soaked in milk

Method

1. Remove the crusts from the slices and cut into cubes.
2. Heat half of the ghee and fry the cashew nuts to a golden brown. Next fry the raisins and set aside.
3. Fry the bread cubes until crisp and golden. Remove.
4. Into the same vessel pour the water and sugar, and boil to make a thick syrup. (While making the syrup add 1-2 tablespoons of milk. When a thick scum forms at the top, remove it and strain the syrup to make it clear. Put back on fire.)
5. Now add the bread cubes and cook until they turn soft. Mash them a bit and gradually add the milk along with the saffron. Cook further stirring constantly until all the milk has been absorbed.
6. Gradually add the rest of the ghee and stir the mixture until it starts to leave the sides of the vessel.
7. Remove from fire. Add the cream, cardamom powder or grated nutmeg and half of the cashew nuts and raisins. Mix thoroughly.

To serve

Transfer the halwa into a serving bowl and smoothen the surface. Sprinkle the rest of the nuts on top. Serve hot.

Currant Buns

Ingredients

2 cups flour
1/4 teaspoon salt
2 tablespoons butter
1 teaspoon sugar
1 1/2 teaspoons fresh yeast
or

For the filling

1/2 cup currants
1/2 cup raisins
1/2 teaspoon cinnamon powder
1 1/2 tablespoons butter
a little sugar

1 teaspoon dry yeast
4 tablespoons milk
4 tablespoons water

Method

1. Add the sugar to a warm milk-water mixture and stir until it dissolves. Add the yeast and set aside until it ferments. Grease and dust a baking tray.
2. Sift the flour and salt into a bowl. Add the yeast and work the flour into a pliable, soft dough. Remove the dough from the bowl, and knead on a floured board for about 10 minutes. Put the dough into a greased bowl, cover with a wet cloth and set aside to 'prove'. The dough will double in size.
3. Turn the dough again on to a floured board, and roll into a rectangular shape. To make the filling, melt the butter and spread on the dough 1.3 cm (0.5 inch) short of the edges. Mix together the raisins, currants, sugar and cinnamon and spread on melted butter.
4. Roll the rectangle from the narrow end, and trim the ends of roll. Cut the roll into 6-8 pieces.
5. Brush the pieces with melted butter, place the rolls on tray with the cut sides up, spacing them evenly. Place the tray in a warm place for 12-15 minutes for the dough to 'prove'.
6. Sprinkle some sugar on the top of each bun and bake in a hot oven at 220°C/425°F for 15 minutes. Reduce the heat and bake for another 15 minutes. Cool on a wire tray.

Channa Batura

(Spicy White Chickpeas with Yoghurt Puris)

Ingredients for channa

2 cups white chick peas (kabuli channa)
3 large onions
1 large piece ginger
4 garlic cloves
4 green chillies, slit
2 tablespoons chopped coriander
1/2 cup tamarind
or 4 medium tomatoes
5 tablespoons oil
3 bay leaves
a pinch of baking soda
salt to taste

Grind to paste

4 tablespoons coriander seeds
1 tablespoon cumin seeds
4 dried red chillies
1 small piece turmeric
5 cloves
3 large cardamoms
2 2.5 cm/1 inch cinnamon sticks

Or use powdered

3 tablespoons coriander powder
3 teaspoons chilly powder
1 teaspoon turmeric powder
1 teaspoon garam masala
1 tablespoon cumin powder

Method

1. Soak the channa overnight in water with a pinch of baking soda. On the next day, wash thoroughly and cook in a pressure cooker until soft.
2. Grind 2 onions, ginger and garlic to a paste. Slice the remaining onion and chop the tomatoes. Grind the dry ingredients separately or use them in powder form as specified.
3. Heat the oil, and add the bay leaves and the slit chillies. Fry for a minute or two, and add the onion paste. Fry until the onions are nicely browned. Add the other masalas (paste or powder) and fry until they are done.
4. If you are using tamarind, extract the pulp and add it to the cooked masala. Alternately, stir in the chopped tomatoes and fry until they are soft.
5. Add the cooked channa, salt, and some water. Simmer for 15-20 minutes or until the gravy is thick. Add half of the chopped coriander and mix.

To serve

Pour the channa into a bowl and sprinkle the coriander. Garnish with slices of onion and serve hot.

Batura ingredients

3 1/2 cups flour (maida)
1/2 cup wheat flour (white)
1/4 cup milk
1/4 cup water
1/2 teaspoon fresh or 1 teaspoon dry yeast
or
1/2 teaspoon each of soda and baking powder
salt to taste

2 tablespoons vegetable shortening/vanaspati
1/2 cup curds (yoghurt)
a pinch of sugar
vegetable shortening/vanaspati/oil for frying

Method

1. Sift the maida, wheat flour and salt.
2. Dissolve a pinch of sugar in warm milk and water. Add either the yeast or the soda and baking powder dissolved in warm water. Set aside for 15-20 minutes.
3. Add the vanaspati, curds, and the yeast or soda mixture to the sifted flour and make a soft dough. Cover and keep aside for at least 8 hours before making the baturas.
4. Divide the dough into lemon-sized balls and roll into thick puris. Shallow or deep fry to golden brown. Serve immediately with channa.

Aloo Tikki

Ingredients

2.2 lb/1 kg potatoes

2 medium onions

6 green chillies

a small bunch of coriander leaves

a few mint leaves

oil or vanaspati for frying

3 slices of bread

salt to taste

1 tablespoon cumin powder

1 tablespoon coriander powder

1 teaspoon chilly powder

a pinch garam masala

1/2 teaspoon pomegranate seeds

or 1 teaspoon lemon juice

1 cup bread crumbs

Method

1. Boil, peel and mash the potatoes while still warm.
2. Mince the chillies, onions, coriander and mint.
3. Soak the bread in water, squeeze dry, and add to the potatoes.
4. Add the minced ingredients (from Step 2), masala powders, salt and lemon juice. Mix thoroughly.
5. Take small rounds of potato dough and flatten on the palm of your hands. Then roll in the bread crumbs and shallow fry. Serve immediately with the chutney.

Chilly Chutney

Ingredients

2 handfuls roasted peanuts

2 handfuls coriander leaves

8 green chillies

a handful of mint leaves (optional)

salt to taste

a pinch of sugar

juice of 1 lemon

Method

1. Mix the peanuts, coriander leaves, mint leaves, salt and green chillies. Grind.
2. Add the lemon juice and sugar, and mix well.

Peas Pastry

Ingredients

2 cups flour	1 teaspoon chilly powder
1 cup margarine or vanaspati	1 teaspoon pepper
1 teaspoon baking powder	1 tablespoon chopped coriander
1 cup grated cheese	salt to taste
1 cup boiled peas	milk to mix dough
1 tablespoon butter	

Method

1. Mash the boiled peas. Add half of the chilly and pepper powders, salt, chopped coriander, and the butter. Mix and set aside.
2. Sift the flour and baking powder. Add the rest of the chilly and pepper powders, and margarine. Mix the flour lightly. Add the cheese and sufficient milk to form a soft dough. Cover and set aside for sometime.
3. Roll the dough 0.6 cm/0.25 inch thick. Cut out 5 cm/2 inch circles, place on a greased tray, and bake at 245°C/475°F for 10-12 minutes.
4. When done (the biscuits will be golden), remove from the oven and while still warm, split the biscuit in the centre, and fill with some of the peas mixture. Alternately, the biscuits may be served piping hot with a spoonful of the peas mixture piled in the centre and dotted with a blob of tomato ketchup.

Jeera Sticks

(Cumin Biscuits)

Ingredients

1/2 cup semolina	1 1/2 teaspoons cumin seeds
1 1/2 cups flour	1 teaspoon pepper powder
2 tablespoons vegetable shortening/vanaspati	salt to taste
1 tablespoon curds (yoghurt)	oil for frying

Method

1. In a mixing bowl, mix the vanaspati, curds, cumin seeds, pepper and salt until the mixture becomes fluffy.
2. Add the semolina and flour, and knead to a soft dough. Add a little water if necessary to make dough of a rolling consistency. Set aside for an hour.
3. Take a quarter of the dough at a time, and roll out into a rectangular piece 0.6 cm/0.25 inch thick. With a sharp knife, cut 2.5 cm/1 inch x 5 cm/2 inch strips. Deep fry in hot oil to a golden brown.

---- *Menu 6* ----

Sweet
Strawberry and Cherry Cake
Peanut Cookies
Badshah Halwa
Carrot Delight

Savoury
Mutter Kachodi
Philouries
Aloo Poha
All served with Sweet-Hot
Chutney
Cheese-nut Squares

Strawberry and Cherry Cake

Ingredients

2 cups flour (maida).
2 teaspoons baking powder
1 cup powdered sugar
1 cup butter or margarine
3 eggs
1/2 cup milk
1 teaspoon strawberry essence
3 drops of cochineal (pink)
15 crystallised cherries
a pinch of salt

For the frosting (optional)

2 - 2 1/2 cups sugar, powdered
    and sifted
white of 1 large egg
2 1/2 - 3 teaspoons water
1/4 teaspoon strawberry essence
1 1/2 teaspoons lemon juice

Method

1. Sift together at least twice the flour, baking powder and salt. Set aside 2 teaspoons separately.
2. Beat the eggs until light and frothy. Cream the butter and sugar lightly.
3. Add the beaten eggs to the creamed mixture beating all the while. Beat for a few more minutes.
4. Carefully fold in the flour adding some more milk if necessary. Mix the cochineal with 1 teaspoon milk. Add this to the batter along with the essence. Add enough milk to make the batter of a dropping consistency.
5. Setting aside 3 cherries, cut the rest into eights. Roll in 1 teaspoon of flour (that was kept aside), and add the cut cherries to the batter. Stir well.
6. Grease a round tin approximately 18-20 cm/7-8 inches in diameter. Line the bottom of the tin with greased brown paper.
7. Pour the batter into the tin. Cut 3 cherries lengthwise into quarters. Roll in 1 teaspoon of flour. Keeping 1 piece in the centre, place the rest carefully all along the border on the top of the batter.

8. Bake at 190°C/375°F in an oven for 30-40 minutes until the top is lightly browned.
9. Remove carefully and cool on wire tray.

Note

If you are icing the cake omit putting cherries on top of the batter.

Method for the frosting

1. When the cake has cooled to room temperature, place it in the centre of a cake plate. Brush away any loose crumbs.
2. Keep a large vessel a third full of hot water ready at hand. Place this vessel on a slow flame.
3. Put all the ingredients except the essence in a mixing bowl. Mix gently using a stainless steel spoon or spatula. Allow the bowl to stand on top of the hot water without touching it. (This is the double boiler.)
4. First stir gently, then vigorously until the mixture stands in peaks.
5. Remove from fire and continue to beat until the icing has reached a spreading consistency. Add the essence and beat for a few more minutes. If you desire a pink topping, add one drop of cochineal now.
6. When the icing is ready, put a large heap of it in the centre of the cake. Allow it to spread on its own gradually. Now put spoonfuls of the icing all over the cake, so that the top is entirely covered. Dip a knife in hot water and smoothen out the surface. Using the knife, ice the sides as well. This step must be executed quickly since the icing sets rapidly.
7. When the icing is just about to set, put in a full cherry in the centre. Cut the rest (3) into eights and arrange all along the border on top of cake and the sides as well.
8. Alternately decorate the top with fresh, frozen or tinned strawberries.

Peanut Cookies

Ingredients

2 cups flour (maida)	1/2 teaspoon baking powder
1 cup butter	a pinch of salt
1 cup sugar	1 egg
1 cup peanuts	a few drops of vanilla essence

Method
1. Sift the flour, baking powder and salt. Powder the peanuts.
2. Cream the butter and sugar lightly.
3. Beat the egg along with the vanilla and add to the creamed mixture.
4. Add the flour and half the peanut powder along with a little milk.
5. Make small balls from the mixture, and roll in the remaining peanut powder. Place on a greased tray.
6. Bake at 175°C/350°F for 20 minutes or until golden. Makes 3 dozen.

Badshah Halwa
(A Lentil-based Pudding)

Ingredients

1 cup moong dal	5 cardamoms, powdered
2 cups + 1 cup milk	1 tablespoon cashew nuts
1 1/2 cups sugar	1 tablespoon raisins
1 cup + 1 tablespoon ghee	a pinch of saffron soaked in milk

Method
1. Broil (dry roast) the dal on a slow fire, stirring all the while until it turns golden brown. Remove from heat, cool and soak in 2 cups of water. After a couple of hours, drain the water and add 1 cup of milk. Grind to a very fine paste.
2. To the ground paste, add 2 cups of milk, sugar and the saffron. Blend the mixture well.
3. Cook the mixture on a slow fire, stirring constantly, until it starts to thicken. Add the ghee gradually and continue to stir until the mixture starts to solidify and leave the sides of the vessel. Add the cardamom powder and mix well. Remove from fire and pour into a bowl.
4. In 1 tablespoon of ghee fry the raisins and chopped cashew nuts. Mix half into the halwa. Smoothen out the surface and garnish with the rest of the nuts and raisins. Serve hot.

Carrot Delight

Ingredients

1 cup grated carrots
1 cup grated coconut
1 cup powdered jaggery

6 powdered cardamoms
6 chopped cashew nuts
oil or ghee for frying

For the batter

1/4 cup rice
1/4 cup black gram dal
1/2 teaspoon salt

To make the stuffing

1. Bring half a cup of water to a boil. Add the jaggery and cook until a thick syrup is formed.
2. Add the coconut and carrot gratings and continue to stir until all the water has evaporated.
3. Add the powdered cardamom and cashew nuts, and mix. Allow to cool.
4. Make marble-sized balls of the mixture and set aside.
5. To make the batter, soak the rice and dal together for 2-3 hours. Grind to a very smooth paste with very little water. Add 1/2 teaspoon salt and mix.
6. Heat the ghee or oil. Dip the carrot balls in batter to coat fully. Fry to golden brown. Makes 20.

Mutter Kachodi

(Pastry with a Spicy Peas Filling)

Ingredients

2 cups flour
2 tablespoons vegetable shortening/vanaspati
1/2 teaspoon salt
oil or vanaspati for frying

Filling

2 cups peas, shelled
2.5 cm/1 inch piece ginger
5 green chillies
2 tablespoons vegetable shortening/ vanaspati
1 teaspoon cumin seeds
salt to taste

Method

1. Sift the flour with salt. Add the vanaspati and mix lightly until the flour is crumbly. Add some warm water and make a very stiff dough. Cover the dough

and set aside.

2. Boil the peas with some salt and grind to a paste with the green chillies, ginger and cumin seeds.

3. Heat 2 tablespoons of oil and fry the pea paste until quite dry. Remove from heat and set aside.

4. Take a small portion of the dough and work it into a cup. (Dip your fingers in oil while doing so.) Put 2-3 teaspoonsful of the stuffing into the cup. Close the cup, flatten on a floured board and roll lightly into a thick puri. Roll carefully to prevent the filling from spilling out of the puri.

5. Deep fry the puris to golden brown. Drain on an absorbent kitchen towel, and serve piping hot with hot and sweet chutney. Makes 20.

Hot Chutney

Ingredients

a small bunch of coriander leaves

a small bunch of mint leaves

6 green chillies

1 lemon

salt to taste

1 teaspoon cumin seeds

a small pinch of asafoetida

1 teaspoon chilly powder

1 teaspoon amchoor (dehydrated
    mango powder)

Method

1. Dry roast the cumin seeds and asafoetida. Powder and set aside.

2. Grind the coriander leaves, mint, green chillies and salt with some water to a smooth paste.

3. To the ground paste, add the chilly powder, amchoor, roasted and powdered ingredients and lemon juice. Mix well.

Sweet Chutney

Ingredients

1 cup tamarind

1 cup jaggery

1/2 cup stoned dates

2 tablespoons red chilly powder

1 teaspoon coriander seeds

1 teaspoon aniseed

1 teaspoon cumin seeds

salt to taste

Method

1. Soak the dates in water. Soak the tamarind separately.
2. Dry roast the coriander seeds, cumin seeds and aniseeds. Powder and set aside.
3. Squeeze the tamarind gently in a little boiling water to extract the pulp. Grind this with the dates, jaggery, salt and chilly powder. Add sufficient water to make it of the desired consistency. Add the powdered ingredients and mix well.

Philouries
(Gram Flour Fritters)

Ingredients

2 cups gram flour (besan)
1 large onion
3 green chillies
3 cloves garlic
2 tablespoons curds (yoghurt)
oil for frying
a pinch of baking soda

Grind together to paste

1 1/2 teaspoons cumin seeds
1/2 teaspoon turmeric powder
2 dried red chillies
salt to taste

Method

1. Mince the onion, green chillies and garlic.
2. In a mixing bowl add 1 tablespoon of oil, besan, soda and some water. Beat for 3-5 minutes or until frothy.
3. Add the ground paste, minced ingredients, and curds. Mix thoroughly. Add some more water if necessary.
4. Fry spoonfuls of the batter in heated oil until golden brown.
5. Serve with both hot and sweet chutney.

Note

A tablespoon of chopped coriander may be added to the batter.

Aloo Poha

(A Tasty Snack with Potatoes and Beaten Rice)

Ingredients

2 cups beaten rice (heavier variety)
(chivda or poha)
1 large onion
2 medium potatoes
5 green chillies
2.5 cm/1 inch piece ginger
3/4 cup peas, shelled

3 tablespoons oil
1 teaspoon mustard seeds
1/2 teaspoon turmeric
2 sprigs curry leaves
a small bunch of coriander leaves
2 tablespoons coconut, grated
salt to taste

Method

1. Peel and cut the potatoes into cubes. Boil with just enough water and some salt. Set aside. Boil the peas and set aside.
2. Soak the poha in water. Wash and squeeze dry.
3. Chop the onion, chillies, ginger and coriander.
4. Heat the oil. Add the mustard and when done, add the onions, green chillies, ginger, and curry leaves. Fry until the onions are browned adding the turmeric powder. When done, add the boiled potatoes and peas. Fry until all the water has evaporated.
5. Add the poha, salt, half the coriander and coconut. Add the lemon juice and mix well.
6. Transfer the poha on to a rice plate. Garnish with the rest of the coconut and coriander. Serve hot.

Cheese-nut Squares

Ingredients

4 cups flour
1 cup pressed margarine
1 1/2 cups grated cheese
2 tablespoons milk
6 cashew nuts

1 teaspoon baking powder
1 teaspoon chilly powder
1 teaspoon mustard powder
1 teaspoon pepper powder
1 teaspoon table salt

Method

1. Grease a baking tray and sprinkle a little flour all over. Cut two brown papers to the size of the tray, grease and set aside.
2. Mix the chilly, mustard and pepper powders with the cheese.
3. Sift the flour with salt and baking powder.
4. To the flour, add the margarine and mix lightly to crumbs. Do not rub hard.
5. When all the flour and margarine has been mixed, add the milk gradually, a little at a time to form a soft dough. Divide the dough into two equal portions.
6. Place the brown paper on a wooden board and using very little flour roll one portion of the dough to about 0.3 cm/0.125 inch thick on this paper.
7. Transfer the dough carefully on to the baking tray by keeping the dough on the tray and the brown paper on the top. Peel off the paper.
8. Sprinkle the cheese over the dough within 1.3 cm/0.5 inch of the edges.
9. Roll out the remaining dough also on brown paper and carefully transfer this onto the tray on top of the cheese layer, covering it fully. Peel off the brown paper.
10. Press the edges lightly and using a sharp knife mark 2.5 cm (1 inch) or 5 cm (2 inch) squares as desired.
11. Slit the cashew nuts into halves or quarters. Press halves onto the 2-inch squares and quarters onto the one-inch squares.
12. Bake at 190°C/375°F for 20 minutes or until slightly browned.

This recipe makes 1-2 dozen depending upon the size.

```
—— Menu 7 ——
```

Sweet
Chocolate Cake
Doughnuts
Shahi Tukra
Carrot-Coconut Burfi

Savoury
Mini Pizza
Vegetable Cutlets with
Ketchup
or Vegetable Bhajjias
Potato Cheeselings or
Potato Puffs (with eggs)

Chocolate Cake

Ingredients

1 1/2 cups flour
1 1/4 cup sugar
1/2 cup cocoa
1 cup butter or margarine
2 tablespoons milk to mix
a pinch of salt

4 eggs
2 teaspoons baking powder
1 teaspoon vanilla essence
1 tablespoon icing sugar (optional)
8 halved walnuts
1/2 cup chopped walnuts

Method

1. Sift the flour, cocoa and baking powder 2 or 3 times.
2. Beat the butter and sugar to cream. Add the eggs, one at a time, and continue to beat while the eggs are being added. Beat for some more time till thoroughly blended.
3. Add the flour and milk alternately till the batter is of a dropping consistency. Add the essence.
4. Add the chopped nuts to the batter. Mix, pour the batter into a cake tin and bake at 190˚C/375˚F for 30 minutes or until the cake is done.
5. When the cake is still warm, press the walnut halves on the top and sides. When cool, sprinkle the icing sugar.

Doughnuts

Ingredients	**Powder together**
2 cups flour (maida)	0.6 cm/0.25 inch piece cinnamon
1/2 cup vegetable shortening/vanaspati	5 cloves
1/2 cup sugar	a pinch of nutmeg
1 egg	1 cup powdered sugar
2 teaspoons baking powder	
milk to mix	
oil for frying	
1/2 teaspoon vanilla essence	

Method

1. Sift the flour and baking powder a couple of times so that the baking powder is well mixed with the flour.
2. To the flour add the vanaspati and mix lightly (with the tips of your fingers only) so that the mixture resembles bread crumbs.
3. Beat the egg lightly. Add the sugar and mix until it dissolves. Add the essence and stir this into the flour along with the milk to form a soft dough.
4. Knead the dough on a cold surface (e.g. a marble slab) for a while.
5. Roll out the dough lightly, dusting with flour if necessary.
6. Using a doughnut cutter cut out 1.3 cm/0.5 inch thick circles.
7. Fry in hot oil until golden brown and drain on absorbent kitchen towels.
8. While still warm roll them in the sugar-cinnamon mixture.

Note

If you do not have a doughnut cutter, make a large circle with a cutter or a sharp lid. Make a smaller hole in the centre with a bottle can. Makes 3 dozen small doughnuts.

Shahi Tukra

(Royal Toast)

Ingredients

15 slices of bread	3 cardamoms
2 litres/2.1 quarts milk	1 tablespoon almonds
1 cup ghee	1 tablespoon cashew nuts
1 cup sugar	1 tablespoon raisins
a generous pinch of saffron	a few drops kewra or rose essence

Method
1. Chop the nuts and fry them along with the raisins in 1 tablespoon of ghee. Set aside. Powder the cardamom and keep separate.
2. Setting aside 2 cups of milk, boil the rest until it is reduced to a fourth of the original quantity. Add the powdered cardamom to the boiled milk.
3. Deep fry the bread slices one or two at a time in ghee until golden and crisp.
4. Soak the fried slices in the milk that was set aside for a few minutes. Ensure that the bread does not become too soft. Remove and place on a plate.
5. Boil 1/2 cup water with sugar and saffron until a thick syrup is obtained. Remove from fire. Add the essence, thickened milk and beat thoroughly to get a uniform mixture. If the mixture is too watery, put back on fire and cook until it thickens.
6. Cover the bread slices with thickened milk. Garnish with the fried nuts and raisins. Serve warm.

Carrot-Coconut Burfi

Ingredients

1 cup grated coconut	2 cups milk
2 cups grated carrot	5 cardamoms, powdered
2 cups sugar	2 tablespoons chopped nuts
3 tablespoons ghee	

Method
1. Boil the grated coconut and carrot together in milk until the carrots are tender and the milk is reduced in quantity by half.
2. Add the sugar and continue to boil until the mixture thickens.
3. Add the ghee a little at a time until the mixture starts to leave the sides of the vessel. Add the powdered cardamom and any desired essence. Mix thoroughly, pour on a greased plate and cut into squares. Alternatively, divide the mixture into small balls and pat each ball into a flat thick circle. Press a few nuts in the centre of each burfi.

Mini Pizza

Ingredients

3 cups flour
3 teaspoons fresh yeast
or 1 1/2 teaspoons dry yeast
1/2 cup warm water
1/2 cup warm milk
2 teaspoons sugar
1/2 cup margarine/vanaspati
salt to taste
1 large baking tray

For the filling

2 large onions
3 medium capsicums
(green peppers)
5 tomatoes
1 1/2 cups cheese
2 cloves garlic, optional
2 green chillies
1 teaspoon chilly powder
2 tablespoons tomato sauce
3 tablespoons oil
salt and pepper to taste

Method

1. Mix the water and milk, and stir in the sugar until it dissolves. Add the yeast and set aside to ferment.
2. Sift the flour and salt in a large bowl. Add the fat and mix it in lightly till the mixture resembles bread crumbs.
3. Add the yeast mixture to the flour and knead to a smooth, pliable dough adding some more milk or water if necessary.
4. Grease a bowl with the oil and put the dough inside. Cover with a wet cloth and keep in a warm place until it doubles in size.

For the filling

1. Chop the onions, garlic, chillies, capsicums and tomatoes. Keep the vegetables separately.
2. Heat the oil. Add the chopped onions and garlic and fry until the onions turn pink. Add the chillies and capsicums and continue to fry until the capsicums turn soft. Add the tomatoes and keep frying until they are done.
3. Mix in the tomato sauce, salt, pepper and chilly powder, and half of the cheese. Set aside.

To make the pizza

1. Take small portions of the dough and pat or roll into circles, 3 inches in diameter.
2. Grease and dust the baking tray. Place the pizzas in the tray, ensuring that they are separated by at least an inch. Prick the base in several places with a fork.
3. Spread a heaped tablespoonful of filling on each pizza and smoothen the surface. Sprinkle some cheese.
4. Bake at 205°C/400°F for 25-30 minutes.

Vegetable Cutlets

Ingredients

500 gm/1.1 lb potatoes
2 medium onions
1 cup peas, shelled
2 carrots
1 small cauliflower
4 green chillies
1.3 cm/0.5 inch piece ginger
a few coriander leaves
a few mint leaves (optional)

1 teaspoon chilly powder
1/2 teaspoon garam masala powder
1/2 teaspoon pepper
salt to taste
3 tablespoons oil
3 slices bread
1 1/2 cups flour (maida)
1 cup bread crumbs
oil for frying

Method

1. Boil the potatoes and carrots. While still warm, mash thoroughly without allowing lumps to form. Boil and mash the peas and cauliflower.
2. Chop the green chillies, ginger, onion, coriander and mint leaves.
3. Heat the oil and add the chopped ingredients except for the mint and coriander. Fry till the onions turn brown in colour. Add the chilly powder, garam masala and pepper powder, and fry for half a minute. Add the mashed ingredients and salt. Mix thoroughly.
4. Soak the bread slices in water for half a minute or so. Remove the crusts and add to the vegetable mixture from Step 3 along with the chopped mint and coriander leaves.
5. Mix the flour with sufficient water to make a paste.
6. Take large lemon-sized balls of the dough, and press them into oblong or round shapes. Dip in the flour paste, roll in the bread crumbs and shallow or deep fry. Serve sizzling hot with tomato ketchup.

Vegetable Bhajjias

(Deep-fried Vegetable Fritters)

Ingredients

One or more of the following vegetables, the weight totalling 500 gm/1.1 lb

potatoes
onions
capsicum (green peppers)
green bananas
brinjal (eggplant)

For the batter

1 1/2 cups besan (gram flour)	2 tablespoons hot oil (to mix)
1/2 cup rice flour	salt to taste
1/2 teaspoon turmeric powder	oil for frying
1 1/2 teaspoons chilly powder	a pinch of baking soda
1 teaspoon ajwain	a pinch of asafoetida
1 1/2 cups water	

Method

1. Wash and slice the vegetables into very thin slices. Soak them in water till they are needed.
2. Mix the besan, rice flour, oil, water and soda. Beat thoroughly till a frothy batter is obtained.
3. Add the chilly powder, turmeric powder, asafoetida, salt and ajwain to the batter.
4. Squeeze out the water from vegetables by pressing them with the palms of your hands. Leave on a plate.
5. Dip the vegetable slices in batter and deep fry to golden. Serve immediately.

Potato Cheeselings

Ingredients

1 large potato, boiled	1/2 cup vegetable shortening/
1 cup flour	vanaspati
1 cup grated cheese	1/2 teaspoon chilly powder
	salt and pepper to taste

Method

1. Grate the boiled potato. Add the flour, chilly powder, salt, pepper, cheese and vanaspati. Mix to a smooth dough and keep covered for 30 minutes.
2. On a floured board, spread the dough lightly using a floured rolling-pin into one large rectangle 0.3 cm/0.125 inch thick.
3. Cut strips 5 cm (2 inch) x 2.5 cm (1 inch) and arrange these on a greased and dusted baking tray, a little apart from each other.
4. Bake in an oven at 200°C/395°F for 20-30 minutes until the top is browned.

Potato Puffs

Ingredients
1 cup flour
2 tablespoons butter
2 cups boiled and mashed potatoes
2 eggs
1 cup water
oil for frying

Seasonings
2 teaspoons chopped herbs
a pinch of nutmeg
salt to taste
pepper to taste

Method
1. Boil the water along with the butter. Gradually add the flour and keep stirring so that no lumps are formed.
2. Remove from fire. Add the mashed potatoes, lightly beaten eggs and seasonings. Mix thoroughly.
3. Drop spoonsful of the batter in hot oil. Fry to a light golden colour and drain on absorbent kitchen paper. Serve hot.

—— *Menu 8* ——

Sweet
Eggless Cake
Jam Biscuits
Semia Kesari
Badshah (Balushahi)

Savoury
Khara Bath (Vegetable Uppuma)
or Aval Dosai with
Onion Chutney
Masala Vada with
Onion Chutney
Omha (Ajwain) Biscuits
or Omhapudi

Eggless Cake

Ingredients

250 gm/9 oz. flour
100 gm/3.5 oz. butter
1 tablespoon sugar
300 ml/0.6 pint sweetened condensed milk
1 tablespoon cocoa (optional)
2 tablespoons chopped nuts (optional)

1 cup water
1 teaspoon vanilla essence
1 teaspoon baking soda
2 teaspoons baking powder
a pinch of salt

Method

1. Sift the flour, cocoa, baking soda, baking powder and salt.
2. Melt the butter and pour into a large bowl. Add the condensed milk, water, vanilla and sugar. Using a wooden spoon, beat the mixture thoroughly till smooth.
3. Add the sifted ingredients, mix, and continue beating till well blended. Add the chopped nuts if desired.
4. Grease a round cake tin. Pour the batter into it and bake at 190°C/375°F for 30-40 minutes or until the cake is done.

Note

If you are using cocoa use an additional tablespoon of sugar.

Jam Biscuits

Ingredients

2 cups flour
1/2 cup margarine or vanaspati
a pinch of salt
1 cup jam
2 tablespoons ice-cold water (to mix)

Method

1. Sift the flour with salt in a mixing bowl.
2. Add the fat and lightly mix in the flour, using only the tips of your fingers. The mixture should resemble bread crumbs.
3. Add the water little by little and gradually work the flour into a smooth dough of rolling consistency. If the dough is too hard, add some more water. Cover and set aside in a cool place.
4. Taking a quarter of the dough at a time, roll into a 0.6 cm/0.25 inch thick circle. Using a pastry cutter dusted with flour, cut out circles and prick with a fork.
5. Grease a tray and dust it with flour. Place the biscuits on this and bake at 230°C/450°F for 12-15 minutes.
6. When the biscuits have cooled, take two at a time and put 1 teaspoon of jam on each biscuit, spreading it out evenly. Sandwich with the second biscuit.

Semia Kesari

(Vermicelli Pudding)

Ingredients

2 cups vermicelli (semia)
1 cup sugar
3/4 cup ghee
1 tablespoon cashew nuts
1 tablespoon raisins

a generous pinch of saffron
3/4 teaspoon powdered cardamom
3 cups water
3/4 cup khoya (optional)

Note

Khoya is thickened milk used in the preparation of sweets. It can be made by thickening the milk on a slow flame.

Method

1. Break the vermicelli into small pieces.
2. Heat 2 tablespoons of ghee in a thick-bottomed vessel. Fry the cashew nuts and raisins. Remove from vessel and set aside.
3. To the same ghee, add the vermicelli and fry on low heat till golden brown.
4. Boil the water, add the fried vermicelli and cook on low heat until the vermicelli is done. Add some more water while cooking, if necessary. If you are using khoya, add it at this stage and cook until it is well blended with the vermicelli.
5. Now add the sugar, saffron (soaked in a little water) and the rest of the ghee. Stir on low heat until the mixture starts to leave sides of vessel and the ghee separates.
6. Remove from fire. Add half of the nuts and raisins and all of the cardamom powder. Mix well.
7. Transfer the 'kesari' to a bowl. Smoothen the surface and garnish with the rest of the nuts and raisins.

Note

If you are using khoya, add an extra tablespoon of ghee to give the kesari a rich flavour and texture.

Badshah (Balushahi)

(Indian Baclava)

Ingredients

2 cups flour
2 cups sugar
1/2 cup ghee or vanaspati
1/4 cup curds (yoghurt)
1/4 cup milk
1 cup water
vegetable shortening/vanaspati for frying

1 teaspoon baking powder
a pinch of baking soda
a pinch of salt
a generous pinch of saffron
1/2 teaspoon cardamom powder

For the garnish

2 tablespoons desiccated coconut
1 drop pink colour
1 drop green colour

Method

1. Sift the flour with baking powder and soda. Put this on a plate, add the salt and curds, and mix well.

2. Add the vanaspati and gradually work the flour to a soft dough adding very little milk or water if necessary. Cover tightly and set aside.
3. Add the water to the sugar and bring to a boil. Add 2 tablespoons of milk and boil until the sugar is dissolved. Strain and boil further until a clear syrup is obtained.
4. Boil the syrup further until a one thread consistency is formed. Remove from fire. Add the cardamom powder and saffron (mixed with a teaspoon of milk). Keep the syrup warm.
5. Divide the dough into large lemon-sized pieces, pat into a round shape, and make a dent in the centre.
6. Heat the vanaspati and fry 4-5 badshahs at a time on very low heat. Stir continuously until they are golden in colour. If the badshahs have not been done fully (if you open one, the centre will still be uncooked), fry for some more time. Keep basting the oil while frying.
7. Put the fried badshahs in the sugar syrup and press down with a ladle. When the second lot is fried, remove the first lot from the syrup and arrange on a plate. When all have been fried and soaked in syrup, boil the left-over syrup and pour this over the badshahs.
8. While still warm, press a large pinch of coloured coconut (green and pink alternately) in the centre.

To colour the coconut

To 1 tablespoon of the desiccated coconut add a pinch of green colour mixed with a drop of water. Colour the other tablespoon pink. Allow to dry before use.

Khara Bath (Vegetable Uppuma)

(Cream of Wheat with Seasoned Vegetables)

Ingredients

1 1/2 cups semolina (cream of wheat)
3 tablespoons ghee
3 tablespoons oil
1/2 teaspoon turmeric powder
1 teaspoon garam masala (optional)
6 cashew nuts
juice of 1 large lemon
1 large onion
1 tomato
1 capsicum (green pepper)
6 green chillies
1.3 cm/0.5 inch piece ginger, chopped
a handful of coriander leaves
1 small potato
1 small carrot
a few florets cauliflower
1/2 cup green beans
1/2 cup peas, shelled
salt to taste

Seasoning

1 teaspoon mustard seeds
1 teaspoon gram dal
2 teaspoon black gram dal
3 sprigs curry leaves

For the garnish

2 tablespoons grated coconut
1 tablespoon chopped coriander

Method

1. In a large kadai (wok), heat 1 tablespoon ghee. Fry the cashew nuts to golden and remove. To the same ghee add the semolina, fry to light brown and remove.
2. Cut the vegetables into small pieces. Boil the capsicum, green beans, cauliflower, carrot and potato along with the peas, salt and very little water. Do not overcook. Set aside.
3. Heat the oil in a kadai (wok). Add the seasonings: first the mustard and when done, the gram dals. Fry till they turn golden brown. Add the chopped chillies, ginger, curry leaves and onions. Fry till the onions turn brown in colour.
4. Add the tomato, capsicum, turmeric and garam masala powder. Fry for a minute. Add the cooked vegetables and stir for a while.
5. Add 3 cups of boiling water, salt and the chopped coriander. Simmer for a few minutes.
6. Now add the fried semolina gradually, stirring while you add, so that no lumps are formed. Cover and allow to cook on a slow fire.

7. When all the water has been absorbed add the rest of the ghee and mix well. Remove from fire. Add the lemon juice, half of the grated coconut and cashew nuts. Mix thoroughly.
8. Transfer the uppuma on to a serving plate and garnish with rest of the coconut, cashew nuts and coriander leaves.

Aval Dosai

(Beaten Rice Pancakes)

Ingredients

3/4 cup aval (beaten rice)
1 1/2 cups rice
2 tablespoons curds (yoghurt)
salt to taste
oil for frying

Method

1. Soak the rice in water and the aval separately in curds. Set aside for two to three hours.
2. Drain the water from the rice and grind to a smooth paste. Add the aval and grind further. Add the salt and set aside to ferment for 8 hours.
3. Heat a skillet and rub in a tablespoonful of oil in it. Pour a ladleful of batter in a circle (not very thin) and using a spoon, put one to two teaspoons of oil all around. Cover with a lid and allow to cook on low heat. Cook only on one side. This recipe makes 20.

Onion Chutney

Ingredients

4 medium onions
8 dried red chillies
1 small piece of tamarind
1 teaspoon jaggery
salt to taste

Seasoning

3 tablespoons oil
1/2 teaspoon mustard
a large pinch of asafoetida
2 sprigs curry leaves
1/2 teaspoon turmeric powder

Method

1. Peel and cut the onions into thick slices.
2. Grind all the ingredients (on left) to a rough paste along with the onions.

3. Heat the oil and add the seasonings. Now add the ground mixture and fry on low
    heat until the oil comes to the surface.

Masala Vada

(Spicy Lentil Fritters)

Ingredients

2 cups gram dal (channa dal)

4 green chillies

4 dried red chillies

1.3 cm/0.5 inch piece ginger

5 sprigs curry leaves

2 medium onions

a small bunch of coriander leaves

a few leaves mint (optional)

salt to taste

oil for frying

Method

1. Soak the dal in water for 2-3 hours. Strain the water and grind to a rough paste
    along with the chillies, ginger, curry leaves and salt.
2. Chop the onions, coriander and mint. Add to the ground batter and mix well.
3. Heat the oil in a kadai (wok). Taking small lumps of the batter, flatten them on
    the palm of your hand or on a plastic sheet. Gently drop them in the oil and fry till
    golden brown turning over once or twice.

Note

If you like the vadas very crisp, fry once (half fry), set aside, and fry again when
required. Serve piping hot. Makes 40.

Omha Biscuits

(Ajwain/Carom Seed Biscuits)

Ingredients

2 cups flour (maida)

1 teaspoon dry yeast

or 2 teaspoons fresh yeast

1 teaspoon sugar

1/2 teaspoon salt

1/2 cup vegetable shortening/
   vanaspati

1 teaspoon omha (ajwain)

1 cup warm water

Method

1. Dissolve the sugar in warm water. Add the yeast and set aside.
2. Sift the flour and salt. Add the omha and vanaspati, and mix lightly until the mixture resembles bread crumbs.
3. Pour the yeast mixture into the flour and mix to form a smooth dough. Knead for at least 10-15 minutes.
4. Place the dough inside a greased bowl for a minimum of one hour.
5. Divide the dough into small balls, and pat them into flat circles 0.6 cm/0.25 inch thick.
6. Grease and dust a tray. Place the biscuits on the tray and pierce them with a fork.
7. Bake at 190°C/375°F for 15-20 minutes. Makes 20.

Omhapudi

(A Savoury Snack Made from Yellow Chick Pea Flour)

Ingredients

2 cups gram flour (besan)
1 cup rice flour
1 teaspoon omha (ajwain)
7 dried red chillies
salt to taste

2 tablespoons oil for mixing
oil for frying
a press or chakli mould

Method

1. Grind together the omha, red chillies and salt to a very fine paste.
2. Mix the two flours. Heat 2 tablespoons of oil, and add to the flours. Add the ground paste and enough water to make a soft pliable dough. Set aside for 15-20 minutes.
3. Heat the oil in a kadai (wok). Fill 3/4 of the mould with dough, hold it in the centre of the vessel, and press in a circulatory motion.
4. Fry one side, turn over carefully, and fry the other side as well, occasionally basting some oil onto it.
5. When done, the omhapudi will be golden brown in colour. Remove from oil. If stored in a tightly sealed container, it will last over a fortnight.

Note

If you do not have a mould, take a perforated ladle and hold it over the hot oil. Take a piece of dough and placing it over the ladle, press down with a small flat bowl (katori). Fry as before.

BREAKFAST IDEAS

BREAKFAST IDEAS

Menu 1

Rice or Rava Idlis
Urad Vadas

Onion Sambar
Coconut Chutney

Sweet
Gulab Jamun

Menu 2

Masala Dosa
Regular or Maida Dosa

Potato Curry
Coconut Chutney

Sweet
Rava Kesari

Menu 3

Gobi or Muli Parathas
Aloo Kababs
Curds/Yoghurt (optional)

Pudina Chutney
Mixed Vegetable Pickle

Sweet
Gaajar (Carrot) Halwa

Menu 4

Aloo Dum
Luchis

Pottal Bhajjia
Pineapple Chutney

Sweet
Rasapulipitha

BREAKFAST IDEAS

Menu 5

Egg or Paneer Scramble
Fried Tomato Slices
Spinach Cutlets

Bread
Butter
Mango Chutney
with Vinegar

Sweet
Coconut Pancakes
with or without eggs

Menu 6

Vegetable or Egg Florentine
or Vegetable Cheese
Florentine
Potato Croquettes
Fried Beet Root and Onion Slices

Bread Rolls
Butter
Tomato Chutney

Sweet
Banana Fritters or
Malpuras

Menu 7

Cheese Omelette
or Vegetarian Omelette
French Fries (optional)
Seasoned Baked Beans

Bread
Butter
Apple Chutney

Sweet
Orange Muffins
or Fruits of the Season

```
┌─────────────────────────────────────────────┐
│              ——— Menu 1 ———                   │
│                                               │
│   Rice or Rava Idlis   Onion Sambar    Sweet  │
│   Urad Vadas           Coconut Chutney Gulab Jamun │
└─────────────────────────────────────────────┘
```

Rice Idlis

Ingredients

    2 cups parboiled rice
    1 cup black gram dal
    1 teaspoon fenugreek seeds
    a little oil
    salt to taste

Method

1. Soak the rice separately. Soak the fenugreek seeds and dal to-gether for at least 5 hours. Grind the rice to a rough paste. Grind the dal to a very fine light paste. Mix the ground rice and dal together, add the salt and keep overnight to ferment. If the room temperature is not warm enough (at least 26°C/80°F), place the mixture in the oven with the light on.

2. The next morning, beat the batter a couple of times with a ladle. If it is too thick, add some water.

3. Grease the idli pans with oil, pour a ladleful of batter in each pan and pressure cook without the weight for 7-10 minutes. Serve hot with sambar and chutney.

Onion Sambar

Refer to Part 3, Menu 3.

Coconut Chutney

Refer to Part 3, Menu 3.

Rava Idlis

Ingredients

2 cups rava (cream of wheat)
3 cups curds (yoghurt)
2 tablespoons ghee
6 cashew nuts, broken
1/2 teaspoon baking soda
salt to taste
2 tablespoons grated coconut

Mince very fine

4 green chillies
2.5 cm/1 inch piece ginger
2 sprigs curry leaves
a small bunch of coriander

Seasoning

1 1/2 tablespoons oil
1/2 teaspoon mustard
1 teaspoon black gram dal
1 teaspoon Bengal gram dal

Method

1. Heat the ghee and fry the cashew nuts to a golden colour. Remove the cashew nuts. To the ghee add 1 tablespoon of oil, then the seasonings and fry. When done, add the minced ingredients except for the coriander leaves. Fry for a minute.
2. Add the rava and fry until golden in colour. Remove from fire and allow to cool on a plate.
3. Beat the curds along with half a cup of water. Add the salt, coriander leaves, grated coconut, baking soda, fried rava and cashew nuts. Mix the batter thoroughly.
4. Grease the idli pans with some oil. Check the batter, and if too thick, add some water so that the batter is of a pouring consistency. Pour a ladle into each pan and pressure cook for 8-10 minutes without using the weight until the idlis are done.

Urad Vadas

Ingredients

2 cups black gram dal
5 green chillies
1 small piece ginger

2 sprigs curry leaves
salt to taste
oil for frying

Method

1. Soak the dal for 2-3 hours. Drain the water and grind to a fine paste along with all the ingredients (except the oil). If desired, 1-1 1/2 tablespoons of chopped coriander may be added.

2. Heat the oil in a kadai (wok). Take a lemon-sized ball of batter, place on a small plastic sheet, and pat into a vada making a hole in the centre. Deep fry to a golden brown stirring occasionally. Repeat process until all the batter is used up. Serve immediately. (Makes 30).

Gulab Jamun
(Fried Milk-Flour Balls in Rose Syrup)

Ingredients

8 tablespoons whole milk powder
2 tablespoons flour
2 tablespoons ghee
a pinch of baking powder or soda
1/2 cup milk (to mix)

1 1/2 cups sugar
1 1/2 cups water
1/2 teaspoon cardamom powder
a few drops rose essence
ghee or vanaspati for frying

Method

1. Sift the flour and baking powder. Add the milk powder and ghee, and mix lightly until the mixture resembles bread crumbs. Add the milk gradually to form a soft spongy dough. Keep aside for 15-20 minutes.
2. Make a syrup of a one-thread consistency by mixing the sugar in water. Add the essence and keep warm. If the syrup gets thick, add some hot water, since the jamuns will not soak in thick syrup.
3. Take out small pieces of dough and flatten them into rolls or rounds on the palms of your hands. Fry on very low heat stirring continuously, till dark brown in colour. Place the jamuns in the syrup. After half of them have been fried and soaked in the syrup, transfer them to another bowl, and repeat the process with the second half. Continue till all the dough has been used up.
4. When all the jamuns have soaked in syrup and have been removed to a bowl, boil the remaining syrup with a little water, if too thick. Pour the hot syrup over the jamuns. Serve hot or cold. (Makes 20).

—— *Menu 2* ——

Masala Dosa	Potato Curry	**Sweet**
Regular or Maida Dosa	Coconut Chutney	Rava Kesari

Masala Dosa

For the dosa
2 cups parboiled rice
1 cup uncooked rice
1 cup black gram dal
1/2 teaspoon fenugreek seeds
salt to taste
ghee or butter
oil for frying

For the potato curry
500 gm/1.1 lb potatoes
2 medium onions
4 green chillies
2.5 cm/1 inch piece ginger
2 sprigs curry leaves
a handful of coriander leaves
juice of 1 lemon

For the chutney
1/2 coconut, grated
a pinch of asafoetida
2 teaspoons oil
1 1/2 tablespoons black gram dal
1 lemon-sized ball of tamarind
3 dried red chillies
salt to taste

Seasonings
3 tablespoons oil
1/2 teaspoon mustard
1 teaspoon gram dal
1 teaspoon black gram dal
1/2 teaspoon turmeric powder
1/2 teaspoon chilly powder

Method
For the dosa
1. Soak both the parboiled and uncooked rice together in water. Separately, soak the dal and fenugreek seeds together in water. After 3-4 hours, drain the water and grind both separately to a fine paste. Add the salt, some water if necessary, and mix both together thoroughly. Keep overnight to ferment.
2. On the next day, check the batter. If too thick, add some water and mix so that it is of a pouring consistency.
3. Heat a tava (skillet) and grease with some oil. Pour a ladleful of batter and spread as quickly as possible into a thin circle. Pour a little oil (1/2 teaspoon) all around and on the centre as well. Cook until the dosa is done, then turn over and cook the other side until it is crisp. Set the dosas aside.

Note
If parboiled rice is not available, soak 2 1/4 cups of uncooked rice.

For the potato curry
1. Boil, peel and break the potatoes into small pieces.
2. Chop the onion, green chillies, ginger, curry leaves and coriander fine.
3. Heat the oil. Season with the mustard and the gram dals. When done, add the chopped ingredients (except the coriander leaves), and the chilly and turmeric powders. When the onions are browned, add the potatoes and salt and mix thoroughly. Add the coriander leaves and lemon juice if desired. Mix well.

For the chutney
1. Heat the oil, and add the asafoetida, red chillies and then the dal. Fry till the dal turns brownish. Remove from fire. Grind this with coconut, salt and tamarind to a slightly rough paste. Add a little water to make the chutney of a spreading consistency.

To make the masala dosas
1. When required, reverse the dosa and place on a tava (skillet). Spread approximately a tablespoon of chutney evenly all over the dosa. Put 2 tablespoons of potato curry in the centre, fold the left a third over the centre, and then the right side over the left. Sprinkle a little ghee or butter. Roast for a minute or two. Remove from fire and serve immediately.
2. Alternately, stuff the dosa with potato curry only, and serve the chutney separately.

Maida Dosa

Ingredients

1 cup flour (maida)	1 teaspoon cumin seeds
1/2 cup semolina (rava)	2 green chillies, minced
1/2 cup rice flour	2 sprigs curry leaves
1/2 cup curds (yoghurt)	a pinch of asafoetida
2 cups water	salt to taste
oil for frying	

Method
1. Mix together the maida, rava, rice flour, salt and curds. Add the water and beat thoroughly. Set aside for 10-15 minutes.
2. Before preparing, add the minced chillies, curry leaves, cumin seeds, asafoetida, and some more water, if too thick.
3. Prepare the dosas in the usual way (see the method used for dosa above), but be quick to spread the flour on the tava, as the dosas get cooked rather quickly.

Makes 8 dosas.

Rava Kesari
(Semolina Pudding)

Ingredients

1 cups rava (semolina)
3/4 cups sugar
3/4 cup ghee
6 cardamoms

8 cashew nuts
1 tablespoon raisins
a generous pinch of saffron
2 cups water
1/4 cup milk

Method

1. Powder the cardamom. Break the cashew nuts into small pieces. Fry the nuts and raisins in 1 tablespoon of ghee in a kadai (wok) until the nuts turn brown. Soak saffron in 1/4 cup of warm milk. Set aside.
2. Pour 2 tablespoons of ghee in the kadai. Fry the rava on very low heat to a golden colour.
3. Add 2 to 2 1/2 cups of water gradually, ensuring that no lumps are formed. When the water has been added, allow to cook for a few minutes.
4. When cooked, add the sugar and continue to stir. Add the saffron mixed with a little warm milk.
5. Add the rest of the ghee in small quantities till all the ghee has been used up. Stir for some more time. Add 3/4 of the fried nuts and raisins as well as the cardamom powder and mix well.
6. Transfer the halwa onto a bowl and smoothen the surface. Garnish with the rest of the nuts and raisins. Serve hot.

—— *Menu 3* ——

Gobi or Muli Parathas	Pudina Chutney	**Sweet**
Aloo Kababs	Mixed Vegetable	Gaajar (Carrot)
Curds/Yoghurt	Pickle	Halwa
(optional)		

Gobi or Muli (Radish) Parathas

For the filling

1 medium cauliflower
   or
250 gm/9 oz. radish
4 green chillies
1 small piece ginger
a small bunch of coriander
1/2 teaspoon chilly powder
1/2 teaspoon turmeric powder
1/2 teaspoon garam masala powder
1 teaspoon dhania-jeera (coriander-cumin) powder

For the parathas

3 cups wheat flour
3 teaspoons ghee or vanaspati
salt to taste
ghee or oil for frying

Method

1. Mix the flour with 3 teaspoons of ghee, salt and some water, and knead to a soft dough. Cover and set aside.
2. Chop the green chillies, ginger and coriander leaves. Set aside.
3. Wash and grate the cauliflower or radish. If you use radish, add some salt, 1/2 teaspoon of turmeric powder, mix, and set aside.

For the cauliflower parathas

1. To the grated cauliflower add the salt, chopped ingredients and the powdered spices with the exception of the turmeric powder. Mix thoroughly.
2. Take a large lump of dough and with greased hands form a cup. Put some of the filling inside, close the cup and pat into a round. Very carefully roll out into a thick round on a floured board, dusting with flour.
3. Put the paratha on the tava (skillet) on medium heat and cook on both sides using ghee until it is browned. Serve very hot with pickle and chutney.

For the muli parathas

1. Squeeze out all the water from the grated radish. Heat 1 tablespoon of oil, add all the ingredients, and stir fry until the mixture is dry. Prepare as above.

An alternate method of preparing the stuffed parathas is as follows:

1. Roll out two chapatis slightly thicker than ordinary ones.
2. Spread the filling on one, 1 cm away from the edges.
3. Put the other chapati on top of the first, seal the edges by pinching the two chapatis together all around the edges with wet fingers. Cook as above.

Note

These parathas are usually served with curds (yoghurt) and/or pickles. The recipe for the mixed vegetable pickle is described in Part 6 (Pickles and Chutneys).

Aloo Kababs

Ingredients

4 medium potatoes
2 slices of bread
bread crumbs
oil for frying
1/4 cup flour (maida)

Seasonings

1 teaspoon coriander powder
1 teaspoon cumin powder
1/2 teaspoon garam masala
1/2 teaspoon chilly powder
salt to taste

Method

1. Boil, peel and mash the potatoes. Add the crumbled bread slices and all the seasonings. Mix to a dough.
2. Make rolls from small pieces of dough and set aside.
3. Mix the flour with 1/2 cup of water to a paste. Dip the rolls in this, roll in the bread crumbs and deep fry to a golden brown. Serve very hot with pudina chutney.

Pudina Chutney
(Mint Chutney)

Ingredients

a handful of mint leaves
1 medium onion
2 cloves garlic
2 green chillies
salt to taste

1 teaspoon cumin powder
1 teaspoon coriander powder
1 teaspoon garam masala powder
or 2 each of the following:
cloves, cinnamon sticks, cardamom

Method

1. Grind all the ingredients very fine.
2. Add some lemon juice, and mix well.
3. Optionally, mix in finely chopped onions, or a cup of curds (yoghurt) beaten well. Add chilly powder to taste.

Gaajar Halwa

Ingredients

300 gm/10 oz. carrots
5 cups milk
1 cup sugar
1/2 cup ghee

1 tablespoon cashew nuts
1 tablespoon raisins
1 tablespoon almonds
4 small cardamoms
a generous pinch of saffron

Method

1. Grate the carrots. Blanch the almonds, and chop them along with the cashew nuts. Powder the cardamoms. In 1 teaspoon of ghee, fry the cashew nuts and raisins. Set aside.
2. Cook the carrots in milk along with the saffron on a slow fire, stirring all the while till the carrots are done. Add a little more milk, if necessary, to cook the carrots.
3. Add the sugar and cook further till the halwa is quite thick and almost dry.
4. Now pour the ghee and fry the mixture till all the ghee has been absorbed and the halwa turns golden.
5. Remove from fire, and mix in the cardamom powder and half the nuts and raisins.
6. Transfer the halwa to a bowl, sprinkle the rest of the nuts and raisins, and serve hot.

```
 ┌────────────────────────────────────────────────┐
 │              —— Menu 4 ——                        │
 │   Aloo Dum      Pottal Bhajjia      Sweet        │
 │   Luchis        Pineapple Chutney   Rasapulipitha│
 └────────────────────────────────────────────────┘
```

Aloo Dum

Ingredients

500 gm/1.1 lb small (baby) potatoes

2 medium onions

2 medium tomatoes

1 teaspoon turmeric powder

1 teaspoon chilly powder (optional)

salt to taste

Seasoning

1 dried red chilly (optional)

1 teaspoon cumin seeds

3 bay leaves

1 tablespoon ghee

1/2 teaspoon garam masala (optional)

6 tablespoons vegetable/mustard oil

Grind to a paste

2 tablespoons coriander seeds

1/2 tablespoon cumin seeds

4 cloves garlic

1-2 dried red chillies

1/2 teaspoon pepper

2 cloves

2 cardamoms

1.3 cm/0.5 inch cinnamon stick

1.3 cm/0.5 inch piece ginger

Method

1. Wash, cook and peel the potatoes. Prick each one with a needle, taking care that they do not break in the process. Chop the onions and tomatoes.

2. Pour half the oil in a kadai (wok), and heat. When hot, add the potatoes, and fry carefully to a golden colour, turning occasionally. Sprinkle some salt, mix and set aside.

3. Pour the rest of the oil into the kadai. Add the bay leaves, cumin and the dried red chillies, broken into small pieces. When done, add the onions and fry to a golden brown.

4. Add the ground paste, turmeric and chilly powder. Continue to fry until the oil surfaces.

5. Add the chopped tomatoes and fry until they turn soft. Now add the water, salt and the fried potatoes. Simmer gently on low heat till the gravy is thick.

6. Before serving, heat 1 tablespoon of ghee, add 1/2 teaspoon garam masala powder and fry for half a minute. Pour into the aloo dum.

To get a typically Bengali flavour, use mustard oil.

Luchis

(Small Maida Puris, a Typically Eastern Dish)

Ingredients

2 cups flour (maida)
4 teaspoons oil
salt to taste
oil for frying

Method

1. Sift the flour and salt. Heat 4 teaspoons of oil, and add sufficient water to make a stiff dough.
2. Roll out very thin, small puris. Deep fry and serve immediately. (Makes 25.)

Pottal Bhajjia

(Shallow-fried Spiced Pottal)

Pottal is a longish vegetable, shaped somewhat like a gherkin.

Ingredients

250 gm/9 oz. pottal
1 teaspoon turmeric powder
salt to taste

1 teaspoon chilly powder (optional)
4 tablespoons oil for frying

Method

1. Scrape, wash and slit the pottal into finger-length pieces. Smear with the turmeric and salt and set aside,. When about to make, squeeze out the water, but retain it for cooking.
2. Heat the oil. Add the pottal pieces, and shallow fry on slow heat. Sprinkle the water kept aside and cook, turning all the while until it is crisp. If desired, 1 teaspoon of chilly powder may be added while frying. Drain on an absorbent kitchen towel.

Note

You can substitute brinjal (eggplant, round variety) for pottal. Wash the brinjal and cut into thick slices, but do not retain the water squeezed out. Smear the brinjal slices with besan (gram flour) with the chilly powder, turmeric and salt, and proceed as before. Shallow fry to crisp and golden.

Pineapple Chutney

Ingredients

1 small pineapple
1 teaspoon turmeric powder
1 teaspoon chilly powder
2 tablespoons sugar
1 teaspoon flour
3 teaspoons oil
salt to taste

Mix together (panchporan)

2 teaspoons aniseed
2 teaspoons onion seeds
2 teaspoons mustard seeds
2 teaspoons cumin seeds
1/2 teaspoon fenugreek seeds

Method

1. Clean, core and cut the pineapple into small thin pieces.
2. Heat the oil and add half the quantity of the panchporan. When done, add the pineapple pieces, turmeric, chilly powder, salt, sugar and 2 cups of water. Cook till the pineapple is done.
3. Mix the maida with some water to a paste, and add it to the chutney.
4. Fry the rest of the panchporan on a dry tava (skillet). Powder roughly and add to chutney.

Note

If pineapples are not available, use green mangoes and prepare in the same way.

Rasapulipitha

(Coconut-Semolina Balls in Thickened Milk)

Ingredients

4 cups milk

1 cup grated coconut

2 cups sugar

3 tablespoons semolina (cream of wheat)

4 cardamoms

4 cloves

a few drops rose essence

Method

1. Mix the grated coconut, semolina and half the sugar, and cook on a slow fire, stirring continuously until the mixture thickens. When the mixture is done, you should be able to make the balls.
2. Remove from fire. Add the powdered cardamoms and mix. Make marble-sized balls and chill.
3. Boil the milk adding the cloves and the rest of the sugar. Cook stirring constantly until the milk is thick. Remove from fire and discard the cloves. Add the essence and allow to cool.
4. Add the coconut balls to the cooled thickened milk. Chill for some time before serving.

--- Menu 5 ---

Egg or Paneer	Bread	**Sweet**
Scramble	Butter	Coconut Pancakes
Fried Tomato Slices	Mango Chutney	with or without
Spinach Cutlets	with Vinegar	eggs

Egg or Paneer Scramble

Ingredients

4 eggs

or 1 litre/1 quart milk and 1 lemon

1 medium onion

2 tomatoes

1 tablespoon minced coriander

2 tablespoons vegetable oil

2 green chillies, minced

1/2 teaspoon turmeric powder

1/2 teaspoon pepper powder

salt to taste

1/2 cup milk

Method (Egg)

1. Break the eggs into a bowl. Add half a cup of milk and whisk for 3-5 minutes.
2. Chop the onions and tomatoes fine.
3. Heat the oil and add the minced chillies and onions. Fry till the onions are browned, then add the turmeric and pepper powders.
4. Add the tomatoes and fry until they turn soft.
5. Lower the heat, add the beaten eggs and salt, and cook stirring all the while till the eggs are done. Add half the chopped coriander.
6. Transfer the scrambled eggs into a bowl, sprinkle the rest of the coriander, and serve hot with bread and butter.

Method (Paneer)

1. Boil the milk adding the lemon juice till the milk curdles. When the milk has curdled, strain to extract the paneer. Set aside some of the whey for cooking.
2. Follow the same method as above, substituting the paneer for the eggs and cooking the paneer if necessary with some of the whey.

Fried Tomato Slices

Ingredients

4 large tomatoes

salt and pepper to taste

oil or ghee for frying

grated cheese (optional)

Method

1. Cut the tomatoes into thick slices.
2. Shallow fry both sides. Put on a plate, sprinkle some salt, pepper and cheese.

Spinach Cutlets

Ingredients

1 cup channa dal (gram dal)

a large bundle spinach, chopped

4 green chillies

1 small piece ginger

1/2 teaspoon amchoor

1 onion

1/2 teaspoon garam masala powder

2 teaspoons dhania-jeera powder

1/2 teaspoon pepper powder

1/2 teaspoon chilly powder

salt to taste

1 tablespoon flour

bread crumbs

oil for frying

Method

1. Boil the dal in water. When half cooked, add the chopped spinach. While still warm, mash to a rough paste.
2. Chop the chillies, ginger and onion.
3. Heat 2 tablespoons of oil, add the chopped ingredients from Step 2, and fry for a while. Add the mashed dal, the dry masalas and salt, and fry for a few more minutes until the water evaporates. Remove from fire, cool and when cool, shape into cutlets.
4. Mix the flour with some water to a thin paste. Dip the cutlet in this, roll in the bread crumbs and shallow fry both sides until brown. Serve on a plate with the fried tomatoes.

Coconut Pancakes

Ingredients	For the filling
2 eggs	2 cups grated coconut
2 cups flour	1/2 cup sugar
a pinch of salt and baking soda	1 tablespoon raisins
3/4 cup milk and water each to mix	a few drops vanilla essence
oil or vanaspati for frying	1 tablespoon walnuts, chopped (optional)

Method (for the filling)

1. Boil the sugar with 1/4 cup water till a thick syrup is obtained. Add the coconut and stir until the coconut turns transparent. Remove from heat.
2. Add the essence, raisins and nuts. Mix well and set aside until needed.

Method (for the pancakes)

1. Sift the salt, baking soda and flour together into a bowl.
2. Break the eggs and beat the whites separately until fluffy. Add in the yolks, and beat for a few more minutes.
3. Pour the beaten eggs into the flour and gradually mix in the flour with a wooden spoon.
4. Now gradually add the water-milk mixture and continue to beat, ensuring that no lumps are formed. When the batter is of a dropping consistency, beat a little more. Set aside for 30 minutes or so before making the pancakes.
5. Heat a frying pan, pour in 1-2 teaspoons of oil, and allow it to spread evenly.
6. Remove from heat and pour in a ladleful of batter. Tilt the pan so that it spreads evenly in a circle. Put back on fire, cook for a minute or two until it is done.
7. Turn the pancake onto a plate or wooden board and put some of the coconut fillings in the centre. Roll lightly or fold over as desired. Place on a plate, and serve immediately. Note that the pancakes can be made and served plain.

Pancakes without Eggs

The ingredients and method are the same as those for the egg pancakes with one difference. Instead of the eggs, substitute 1 cup sour milk with 1/4 teaspoon baking soda dissolved in it.

Mango Chutney with Vinegar

Refer to Part 6 for this recipe.

—— ⏤ℳenu 6 ——

Vegetable or Egg Florentine or Vegetable Cheese Florentine Potato Croquettes Fried Beet Root and Onion Slices	Bread Rolls Butter Tomato Chutney	**Sweet** Banana Fritters or Malpuras

---

Vegetable or Egg Florentine

Ingredients

2 medium onions
2 medium tomatoes
1 medium capsicum
1 medium potato
1 medium carrot
4 eggs or 2 cups grated cheese

3 green chillies, minced
a handful of coriander, minced
4 tablespoons tomato ketchup
4 tablespoons milk
4 tablespoons vegetable oil
1 teaspoon pepper powder

Method

1. Chop all the vegetables fine, and keep them separate.
2. Beat the eggs with pepper and salt. Add the milk and beat a little more. Set aside.
3. Heat the oil in a frying pan (preferably a non-stick one), add the minced chillies, and fry for half a minute. Add the onions and when browned, add the capsicum and fry for 2 minutes. Add the tomatoes and fry till they turn soft.
4. Add the potato and carrot, and fry for a couple of minutes. Add some salt and water. Cover and cook till the vegetables are done.
5. Add the tomato ketchup, 3/4 of the chopped coriander, and mix well. Spread the vegetables completely so that they fully cover the base of the pan.
6. Now reduce the heat and pour the beaten eggs on to the vegetable layer. Tilt the pan carefully to allow the eggs to spread. Cover the pan tightly and while still on low heat cook the eggs. When done, remove the lid. (When cooked the eggs will have formed a layer on top of the vegetable.) Carefully transfer the Florentine on to a serving plate without disturbing the eggs. Garnish with cheese and the rest of the coriander if desired. Serves 4.
7. Alternately, pour the vegetables into an oven-proof dish, spread the eggs over this, and bake in a moderate oven for 30-40 minutes or until the eggs are set.

Vegetable Cheese Florentine

The ingredients and method are the same as above. When the vegetables are cooked, transfer them to a well greased pie-dish. Sprinkle the cheese evenly all over, place the dish in an oven for the cheese to melt and form a layer. Alternately, serve as is without grilling. (For this half the quantity of cheese will do.)

Fried Beet Root and Onion Slices

Ingredients
2 medium beet roots
2 large onions
salt and pepper to taste

oil or vanaspati for frying
1 egg
bread crumbs

Method
1. Boil the beets, and when cool cut into thick slices.
2. Beat the egg, and add the salt and pepper.
3. Heat the oil. Dip the beet slices in the beaten egg, remove, roll both sides in the bread crumbs, and shallow fry till crisp.
4. Fry the onions.
5. To serve, arrange the fried beet root slices and onions on a plate, and serve hot.

Potato Croquettes

Ingredients
250 gm/9 oz. potatoes
1/4 cup milk
1 medium onion, minced
2 green chillies, minced

1/2 cup flour
salt and pepper to taste
oil or vanaspati for frying

Method
1. Wash, peel and grate the potatoes. Leave in water for a few minutes. Then squeeze out all the water, and put in a bowl.
2. Add the flour, seasonings and enough milk to form a batter of a dropping consistency.
3. Heat the oil in a frying pan, and fry spoonfuls of the batter in it. Serve immediately. Makes 20.

Bread Rolls

Ingredients

3 cups flour

2 teaspoons sugar

1 teaspoon butter or margarine

1 teaspoon salt

1 teaspoon dry yeast

or 2 teaspoons fresh yeast

1/4 cup warm milk

1 cup water

Method

1. Mix the milk with half a cup of warm water, and dissolve the sugar in it. Add the yeast and set aside to ferment.
2. Sift the flour with salt, and rub in the butter.
3. Add the yeast mixture to the flour and knead to a very smooth dough, adding some more water if necessary. Make into a soft elastic ball. Grease a bowl, and put the dough in it. Cover with a wet muslin cloth and leave it aside for at least an hour to allow it to rise. It should double in size.
4. Take out the dough, punch it again and divide into small round balls. Shape the balls into sticks, clovers or leave them plain as desired. Keep these rolls on a greased baking tray and leave again to 'prove'.
5. When about to bake, brush the dough with some milk, water or white of egg if desired. Bake at 230°C/450°F for 7-10 minutes. Serve hot with butter.

Banana Fritters (With Eggs)

Ingredients

2 bananas

1 egg

1 cup flour

a pinch of salt

1 tablespoon sugar

a little milk to mix

ghee or vanaspati for frying

a pinch of grated nutmeg

juice of 1/2 lemon

Method

1. Mash the bananas and add the egg, flour, salt and milk. Mix thoroughly such that the batter is of dropping consistency. If not, add some more milk. Set aside for 15 minutes.
2. Heat the ghee. Pour the batter in, a tablespoon at a time, and deep fry to golden stirring all the while. Drain the fritters and sprinkle some sugar mixed with nutmeg. Serve with a dash of lemon juice.

Malpuras
(Sweet Flour Fritters)

Ingredients

1 1/2 cups maida

1 tablespoon semolina (rava)

1/2 cup sugar

6 almonds

1 cup milk

1 teaspoon cardamom seeds

1 teaspoon fennel seeds

1 teaspoon khus-khus(poppy seeds)

a pinch of baking soda

a pinch of saffron

ghee or vanaspati for frying

Method

1. Warm the milk. Soak the saffron in it, add the sugar, and mix well. Add the baking soda, and stir.

2. Add the flour and semolina, and beat vigorously to form a smooth batter. Set aside for 15 minutes.

3. To the batter add the cardamom, fennel and khus-khus, and mix well. If the batter is thick, add a little more milk to make it of a pouring consistency.

4. Heat the ghee in a kadai (wok). Pour a tablespoon of the batter in, reduce the heat, and cook to a golden brown. Turn over, and cook the other side as well. Drain the excess ghee and serve.

Makes 20.

```
┌─────────────────────────────────────────────────────────────┐
│                      ──── Menu 7 ────                         │
│   Cheese Omelette        Bread            Sweet               │
│   or Vegetarian Omelette Butter           Orange Muffins      │
│   French Fries (optional) Apple Chutney   or Fruits of the    │
│   Seasoned Baked Beans                    Season              │
└─────────────────────────────────────────────────────────────┘
```

Cheese Omelette

Ingredients

4-6 eggs
1 cup grated cheese
salt and pepper to taste
2 tablespoons milk
butter or oil

Mince fine

1 medium tomato
1 onion
2 green chillies
1 teaspoon coriander leaves

Method

1. In 1 tablespoon of butter fry the minced onions and chillies till the onions turn light pink. Add the tomatoes, some salt and fry till they turn soft. Remove from fire and set aside.
2. Separate the egg yolks from the whites. Beat the yolks with the milk till thick and creamy. Add the pepper and salt.
3. Beat the whites stiff, fold into the yolks, and mix well.
4. Heat a frying pan, preferably non-stick. Put in some butter and when hot, pour in half the eggs and allow to spread. Cook on low heat till done covering the pan.
5. Remove the lid and pour into the centre of the omelette half the onion tomato mixture. Sprinkle the coriander and half the cheese. Fold the first third of the omelette over the vegetables, then the remaining third over. Serve piping hot, with toast and apple chutney.
6. Make the second omelette the same way.

Vegetarian Omelette

Ingredients

1 cup thick tomato juice
1 cup gram flour (besan)
3 green chillies, minced
1 small onion, minced
1 tablespoon chopped coriander
1/2 cup grated cheese

salt and pepper to taste
1/2 teaspoon chilly powder
1/4 teaspoon turmeric powder
2 teaspoons sugar
1 tablespoon oil or vanaspati

Method

1. Mix together all the ingredients (except the cheese and oil) adding some water if the batter is too thick.
2. Heat a tava (skillet), or preferably a non-stick pan. Pour in the oil and when hot, pour a ladleful of batter (2 teaspoons). Spread the batter into a round.
3. Pour 1-2 teaspoons of oil all around the edge of the omelette and allow to cook till golden brown in colour. Turn it over and cook the other side as well.
4. Sprinkle some cheese, fold the omelette and serve immediately.
5. Alternately, grease a round pan with oil, pour in the batter mixed with 2 tablespoons of oil into it and bake at 190°C/375°F for 20 minutes or until done. Remove from oven, sprinkle the cheese and grill until the cheese melts. Cut into wedges and serve, with toast and apple chutney.

French Fries

Refer to Part 3, Menu 2 for the recipe. It is found there under the name Potato Fingers.

Seasoned Baked Beans

Ingredients

1 tin of baked beans (200 gm/7 oz.)
1 small onion, minced
1 tablespoon tomato ketchup
2 tablespoons oil
salt and pepper to taste

Seasonings

2 teaspoons chopped coriander
1/2 teaspoon chilly powder
1/4 teaspoon garam masala powder

Method

1. Heat the oil, and fry the onions to a light brown. Add the seasonings, and fry for another minute.
2. Stir in the baked beans, and add the ketchup, some water, salt and pepper. Simmer for a few minutes.

Orange Muffins

Ingredients

1 cup flour
1/2 cup sugar
1/4 cup margarine or vegetable oil
a pinch of baking powder
1 egg
1/4 teaspoon salt

1 tablespoon milk
1 tablespoon orange juice
1 teaspoon orange rind, grated
3 drops orange essence (optional)
muffin pans
1 tablespoon raisins

Method

1. Sift the flour, baking powder and salt.
2. Beat the oil and sugar till blended. Add the egg, and continue to beat for a few minutes.
3. Add the sifted ingredients to the egg along with the milk and orange juice and rind. Mix thoroughly, and add the essence and raisins. The batter should be of a lumpy consistency.
4. Pour the batter three quarters full into the muffin pan and bake at 190°C/375°F for 15 minutes.

Note

If you do not have a muffin pan, bake the muffins in small cups.

PICKLES
AND
CHUTNEYS

PICKLES AND CHUTNEYS

Apple Chutney

Brinjal Pickle

Carrot Pickle

Green Chilly Chutney

Chilly Pickle

North Indian Lime Pickle

South Indian Lime Pickle

North Indian Mango Pickle

North Indian Sweet-Hot Mango Chutney

South Indian Sliced Mango Pickle

South Indian Mango Thokku

Mango Chutney with Vinegar

Vinegar Mangoes

Mixed Vegetable Pickle (Punjabi Style)

Mixed Vegetable Pickle (Gujarati Style)

Radish Pickle

Navaratna Pickle

Tomato Chutney

Tomato Thokku

Tomato Sauce

Apple Chutney

Ingredients

1 kg/2.2 lb apples (cooking variety)
2-3 cups sugar, depending on tartness of apples
250 gm/9 oz. onions
150gm/5 oz. ginger
100 gm/3.5 oz. garlic
15 gm/0.5 oz dried red chillies
or 3 teaspoons chilly powder
2 cups vinegar
40 gm/1.5 oz. salt

Method

1. Clean and grate the apples. Chop the onions, ginger and garlic. Pound the red chillies.
2. Add the chopped ingredients, chilly powder, and 1 cup of vinegar to the grated apples and cook until the apples and onions have become soft and the mixture is almost dry.
3. Now add the sugar, salt and the other cup of vinegar. Cook further until the mixture is of a chutney consistency.
4. Remove from fire, cool and bottle.

Brinjal Pickle

(Eggplant Pickle)

Ingredients

500 gm/1.1 lb brinjal (round purple variety)
30 gm/1 oz. ginger
30 gm/1 oz. garlic
8 green chillies, slit (optional)
30 gm/1 oz. chilly powder or 30 dried red chillies
1 small stick or 2 teaspoons turmeric
1 tablespoon mustard seeds
1 tablespoon cumin seeds
1 teaspoon fenugreek seeds
1 cup oil
1 1/2 cups vinegar
2 tablespoons + 2 teaspoons salt
1/4 cup sugar
3 sprigs curry leaves

Method

1. Wash, wipe, and dry the brinjals. Cut them into large pieces, smear 2 teaspoons salt and set aside for 2-3 hours.
2. Chop half of the ginger and garlic. Grind the other half with the turmeric, cumin and mustard in the vinegar to a smooth paste. If you are using red chillies, soak in half a cup of vinegar for 20 minutes and grind this also with the above.
3. Dry roast the fenugreek seeds, powder and set aside.
4. Fry the slit chillies and curry leaves in some oil. Add the chopped ginger and garlic, and continue to fry for a few minutes. Add the masala paste and fry until the oil surfaces.
5. Remove the brinjals from the salt water, and fry them with the masala. Add the sugar and 2 tablespoons salt and cook until a thick gravy is formed. Add the powdered fenugreek, remove, cool and bottle.

Carrot Pickle

Ingredients

500 gm/1.1 lb carrots	15 dried red chillies
3 teaspoons mustard seeds	1 cup oil
3 teaspoons cumin seeds	1 cup vinegar
1/2 teaspoon methi seeds (fenugreek)	1/4 cup sugar
30 gm/1 oz. ginger	30 gm/1 oz. salt
30 gm/1 oz. garlic	

Method

1. Scrape and cut the carrots into small pieces.
2. Grind all the masalas in 3/4 cup vinegar.
3. Fry the masalas in oil until the oil surfaces. Add the carrots and fry until they are soft. Add the sugar, salt and the remaining vinegar, and cook until the carrots are done and a thick gravy is formed.
4. Remove from heat, cool and bottle.

Green Chilly Chutney

Ingredients
1/2 cup green chillies, chopped
2 cups fresh coriander, chopped
1 lemon sized ball tamarind
3 tablespoons sesame seed (or vegetable) oil
1/2 teaspoon mustard seeds
1 tablespoon salt

Masalas
4 teaspoons sesame seeds
1/2 teaspoon asafoetida
1/2 teaspoon fenugreek

Method
1. Dry roast the sesame seeds in a kadai (wok) and remove. Pour 1 teaspoon of oil, fry the asafoetida and fenugreek, and remove. Powder these ingredients together and set aside.
2. Grind the chillies, coriander, tamarind and salt to a paste without adding any water.
3. Season the mustard in hot oil, and add the ground paste. Fry until almost dry. Add the powdered masala from Step 1 and fry for a couple of minutes. Remove, cool and bottle.

Chilly Pickle

Ingredients
250 gm/9 oz. green chillies
1 teaspoon turmeric powder
1 teaspoon methi (fenugreek) powder
2 teaspoons white mustard seeds
2 teaspoons cumin seeds
6 garlic cloves
1 small piece ginger

2 cups vinegar
1 1/2 cups oil
3 teaspoons sugar
60 gm/2 oz. salt

Method
1. Wash and slit the chillies lengthwise. Add the salt and place in a covered jar for 1 hour.
2. Grind all the masalas in the vinegar using as much vinegar as necessary for grinding.
3. Fry the ground masala in oil until the oil surfaces. Strain the chillies from the salt water, add this to the masala, and fry for a few minutes.
4. Add the remaining vinegar (if any), sugar and as much salt water as necessary. Simmer for 5-10 minutes.
5. Cool and bottle.

North Indian Lime Pickle

Ingredients

25 limes	2 tablespoons mustard
1/2 head garlic (optional)	1 teaspoon fenugreek seeds
25 dried red chillies	1/2 teaspoon turmeric powder
1 tablespoon onion seeds	1 1/2 cups oil
1 tablespoon cumin seeds	6 tablespoons salt

Method

1. Extract the juice from 12 limes, add a pinch of salt and set aside.
2. Boil some water. Add a pinch of turmeric powder, add the rest of the limes, and boil for 2 minutes. Remove the limes from the water. Wipe with a cloth and allow to cool.
3. Dry roast the mustard, fenugreek, onion and cumin seeds. Roast the chillies with a teaspoon of oil, pound all these along with the garlic into a rough powder and set aside.
4. Cut the limes into fours. Mix the masala powder with some oil and add the salt, making it into a dough. Stuff the limes with this and put the stuffed limes into a jar. If any masala remains, put it in as well.
5. Heat and cool the oil. Pour into the jar along with the lime juice. Keep the mouth of the jar covered with a piece of cloth.

South Indian Lime Pickle

Ingredients

6 large limes	1 teaspoon fenugreek seeds
6 teaspoons chilly powder	1 small piece asafoetida
1/2 teaspoon turmeric	2 tablespoons oil
2 teaspoons salt	1 teaspoon mustard

Method

1. Boil sufficient water to cover the limes when immersed. When the water is boiling, add the turmeric powder and the limes, and boil for 2 minutes. Remove from fire, cover vessel, and set aside for a few minutes.
2. When the limes have cooled, remove from water. Cut each one into 8 pieces. Add the salt and mix.
3. Fry the fenugreek and asafoetida in 1 teaspoon of oil in a kadai (wok). Remove, powder and set aside.
4. Cover the lime pieces with the chilly powder. Season the mustard seeds in oil and pour this over the lime pieces. Add the fenugreek and asafoetida powders and mix thoroughly. Cool and bottle.

North Indian Mango Pickle

Ingredients
1 kg/2.2 lb mangoes
2 teaspoons turmeric powder
60 gm/2 oz. salt
2 cups oil
1 lemon-sized ball of jaggery
(optional)

Broil separately
1/2 tablespoon fenugreek seeds
1 tablespoon onion seeds
2 tablespoons mustard seeds
2 tablespoons aniseed
1 small piece asafoetida
30 dried red chillies

Method
1. Cut the mangoes into 8 pieces each, and apply salt and turmeric powder. Leave in the sun for a couple of hours every day for 2-3 days or until the pieces are quite dry.
2. Powder the broiled masalas using a mixer-grinder. Add this powder to the mango pieces. Add some more salt if necessary.
3. Bring the oil to a boil, and pour it over the mixture. Mix well, cool and bottle. (Optionally, a piece of jaggery may be added to the oil while it is being heated.)

North Indian Sweet-Hot Mango Chutney

Ingredients
500 gm/1.1 lb mangoes
250 gm/9 oz. sugar
1 teaspoon cumin seeds
1/2 tablespoon chilly powder

1/2 teaspoon turmeric powder
salt to taste
1 1/2 cups water

Method
1. Dry roast the cumin seeds, powder and set aside.
2. Peel and grate the mangoes. Add 1 teaspoon of salt, turmeric powder and set aside for a couple of hours.
3. Boil the water and sugar together to prepare a syrup of one-thread consistency.
4. Squeeze out the excess water, if any, from the mangoes. Add to the sugar syrup and cook on a very slow fire until the mangoes become soft.
5. Now add the chilly powder, powdered cumin seeds, some more salt, if necessary, and mix. Boil for a minute or two.
6. Remove from fire, cool and bottle.

South Indian Sliced Mango Pickle

Ingredients

6 mangoes
1/2 cup oil
1/2 cup salt
12 green chillies
1/2 tablespoon chilly powder
1/2 tablespoon mustard powder
1 tablespoon sugar (optional)

Dry roast and powder

1 tablespoon sesame seeds
1/4 teaspoon asafoetida
1/2 teaspoon fenugreek seeds

Seasoning

1/2 teaspoon turmeric
1/2 teaspoon mustard seeds
1 sprig curry leaves

Method

1. Clean and peel the mangoes. Cut into thin slices.
2. Chop the chillies.
3. Season the mustard and curry leaves in hot oil. Add the chopped chillies and mango slices, and fry on low heat until the mangoes turn soft. Add the chilly powder, turmeric and salt, and continue to fry until the oil surfaces. At this stage you may add a tablespoon of sugar if the mangoes are too sour. Remove from fire.
4. Add the mustard and masala powders, and mix well.
5. Cool and bottle.

South Indian Mango Thokku

(Grated Mango Chutney)

Ingredients

6 medium mangoes
1/2 cup salt
3 tablespoons chilly powder
1 teaspoon turmeric powder

1 teaspoon mustard seeds
1 teaspoon fenugreek seeds
1/2 teaspoon asafoetida
1 cup oil

Method

1. Wash and grate the mangoes. Add a pinch of turmeric powder, some salt, and set aside.
2. Fry the asafoetida and fenugreek seeds in one teaspoon of oil. Remove, powder and set aside.
3. Squeeze out the water from the grated mangoes. Season the mustard seeds in hot oil, and stir in the mango gratings and turmeric powder. Fry on low heat until the mangoes become soft. Add the salt, chilly powder and continue to fry until the oil surfaces. Remove from heat, add the asafoetida powder, and mix well. Cool and bottle.

Mango Chutney with Vinegar

Ingredients

500 gm/1.1 lb mangoes
150 gm/5 oz. jaggery
25 gm/1 oz. garlic
25 gm/1 oz. ginger
45 gm/1.5 oz. salt
1 teaspoon turmeric powder

1 1/2 teaspoons aniseeds
1 1/2 teaspoons onion seeds
10 dried red chillies
   or 2 tablespoons chilly powder
1 cup vinegar
4 tablespoons oil

Method

1. Pound the red chillies coarse using a pestle and mortar. Add the ginger and garlic, and pound along with the chillies. Pound the jaggery separately.
2. Peel and slice the mangoes into small pieces.
3. Season the aniseeds and onion seeds in hot oil. When done, add the pounded ingredients except the jaggery, turmeric powder and mango slices. Fry for a few minutes until the mangoes turn soft.
4. Add the jaggery, vinegar and salt, and stir on low heat until all the slices are cooked and the chutney is thick.

Vinegar Mangoes

Ingredients

1 kg/2.2 lb mangoes
3 tablespoons sugar
120 gm/4 oz. salt
1 1/2 cups vinegar
1 1/2 cups oil
5 sprigs curry leaves
1 teaspoon turmeric powder

Grind to a paste in vinegar

30 gm/1 oz. garlic
30 gm/1 oz. ginger
1 1/2 tablespoon cumin seeds
2 tablespoons mustard seeds
2 teaspoons pepper
25 dried red chillies

Method

1. Wash, wipe and cut the mangoes into 8 pieces each. Put in a jar and sprinkle half the salt and half of the teaspoon turmeric powder. Keep the jar in the sun for 1-2 days depending on the heat, stirring the contents occasionally. The pieces must not get very dry.
2. Heat the oil and add the curry leaves, ground masala, the rest of the turmeric powder and fry until the oil surfaces.
3. Remove the mango pieces from the salt water. Add it to the mixture and fry for 3-4 minutes. Now add the salt water, the rest of the salt, vinegar and sugar. Cook on low heat for 15-20 minutes.

4. Remove from heat, cool and bottle.

Note

A large lump of jaggery may be substituted for sugar. This imparts a rich colour to the pickle.

Mixed Vegetable Pickle (Punjabi Style)

Ingredients

1 kg/2.2 lb turnips	175 gm/6 oz. mustard powder
1 kg/2.2 lb carrots	175 gm/6 oz. chilly powder
1 kg/2.2 lb cauliflower	1 cup vinegar
150 gm/5 oz. ginger	500 gm/1.1 lb oil
150 gm/5 oz. onion	40 gm/1.5 oz. salt
40 gm/1.5 oz. garlic	250 gm/9 oz. jaggery
1/2 tablespoon freshly powdered garam masala (optional)	

Method

1. Wash, peel and cut the turnips into thick slices. Wash the carrots and cut into inch-long pieces. Clean and break the cauliflower into florets. Tie the vegetables in a clean muslin cloth. Boil some water in a large vessel, immerse the vegetables in it, and allow to simmer for 3-5 minutes. Remove from cloth and spread on a clean, thick sheet to allow all the water to evaporate.
2. Grind the onions, ginger and garlic to a paste with the vinegar.
3. Fry the ground paste in 2 tablespoons of oil until the oil surfaces. Remove from fire and cool.
4. Mix the vegetables, fried masalas, chilly and mustard powders, salt, and half a tablespoon of freshly powdered garam masala in a large stainless steel vessel. Mix all the ingredients well with some oil and put in a jar. Cover the jar with a clean cloth, tie the cloth, and keep the jar in the sun for 2-3 hours every day for 4-5 days.
5. Soak the jaggery in the vinegar and boil to obtain a syrup of a one-thread consistency. Cool, pour this into the jar, and mix well, adding the rest of the oil.
6. Store, making sure that the jar is tightly closed.

Note

For the freshly powdered garam masala, use 6 cloves, 3 cinnamon sticks, 3 large cardamoms and a dash of pepper.

Mixed Vegetable Pickle (Gujarati Style)

Ingredients

150 gm/5 oz. cauliflower
150 gm/5 oz. carrots
30 gm/1 oz. green chillies
30 gm/1 oz. ginger
6 lemons
6 tablespoons oil
a pinch of asafoetida
1/2 teaspoon mustard seeds
1 teaspoon salt

For the pickle masala

1/2 cup red chilly powder
1/2 cup mustard powder
1/2 teaspoon fenugreek
1/2 teaspoon turmeric
1/2 teaspoon asafoetida
1 tablespoon salt
1 teaspoon oil

Method

1. Prepare the pickle masala as follows: heat the oil, add the fenugreek powder and asafoetida, and fry. To this, add the rest of the masalas, salt and mix thoroughly. Set aside until needed.
2. Wash and cut the cauliflower and carrots into small pieces along with the ginger. Put these in a vessel. Add water and salt, and set aside for 3-4 hours.
3. Remove the vegetables from the salted water. Wash thoroughly in cold water, drain, and tie the vegetables in a clean muslin cloth.
4. ·Bring some water in a large saucepan to a boil. Dip the vegetables for 5-7 minutes until they are blanched. Remove from cloth and allow to cool.
5. Extract juice of 4 lemons, and cut the others into small pieces. Cut the chillies into small pieces.
6. Heat the oil. Add the mustard and asafoetida, and when done, add the chillies. Fry for two minutes and add the lemon pieces. Cook for another minute or two and remove from fire. Add the vegetables, pickle masalas and lemon juice, and mix thoroughly.
7. Bottle when cool.

Radish Pickle

Ingredients

1 kg/2.2 lb radish
125 gm/4.5 oz. green chillies
4 large lemons
1/2 cup oil
1/2 cup vinegar
30 gm/1 oz. salt

Broil and powder

50 gm/2 oz. mustard seeds
1 teaspoon turmeric
1 teaspoon fenugreek seeds

Grind to paste

100 gm/3.5 oz. ginger
50 gm/2 oz. garlic

Method

1. Scrape and cut the radishes into thin rounds. Cut each round into fours. Cut the chillies into small pieces. Extract juice from the lemons.
2. Fry the chillies in hot oil and add the ground paste. Continue to fry until the oil surfaces. Remove from fire and cool.
3. Mix the radish slices with the salt, ground paste, powdered masalas, lemon juice and vinegar. Place in a jar. Keep the jar in sunlight for 3-4 days by which time the pickle will be ready to eat.

Navaratna Pickle

(Nine Vegetable Pickle)

Ingredients

1 small beet root	2 tablespoons vegetable/
1 carrot	sesame (til) oil
1/2 cauliflower	1/2 teaspoon fenugreek seeds
1 capsicum (green pepper)	1/2 teaspoon asafoetida
3 cabbage leaves	1/4 teaspoon turmeric
6 green beans	1 teaspoon chilly powder
1/2 cup shelled peas	1/2 teaspoon mustard seeds
2 teaspoons lemon juice	1 - 1 1/2 tablespoons salt
4 green chillies	
1 sprig curry leaves	

Method

1. Wash and dry all the vegetables before cutting. Cut the beet, carrot and capsicum very fine. Chop the cabbage and beans. Cut each chilly into 2-3 pieces. Break the cauliflower into small florets. Put all the vegetables except the chillies in a large steel vessel.
2. Fry the asafoetida and fenugreek seeds in 1 teaspoon of oil in a kadai (wok). Remove, powder and set aside.
3. Pour the rest of the oil into the kadai. Heat and add the mustard seeds. When done, add the chillies and curry leaves, and fry for 1 minute. Remove from fire. Add the chilly powder and turmeric, and mix. Pour this on to the vegetables. Add the salt, lemon juice, fenugreek and asafoetida. Mix well.
4. Cool and store in a refrigerator. This pickle will not keep for more than 2-3 days.

Tomato Chutney

Ingredients

1 kg/2.2 lb tomatoes
6 green chillies, slit
2 teaspoons chilly powder
1/2 teaspoon turmeric powder
1 cup vinegar
1 cup oil
1 1/2 tablespoons salt
1/2 cup sugar

Grind in vinegar to a paste

6 garlic cloves
2.5 cm/1 inch piece ginger
1 tablespoon cumin seeds
1/2 tablespoon mustard seeds

Method

1. Wash, wipe and cut the tomatoes into four or eight pieces each.
2. Heat the oil. Fry the chillies for 1 minute. Add the ground paste and fry until the oil surfaces.
3. Add the tomatoes and fry until they turn soft. Add the salt, sugar, chilly and turmeric powders, and cook for a few minutes. Add the vinegar and simmer on low heat until a thick gravy is formed. Cool and bottle.

Tomato Thokku

(South Indian Tomato Chutney)

Ingredients

1 kg/2.2 lb half-ripe tomatoes
12 green chillies
2 teaspoons chilly powder
1 teaspoon turmeric powder
1 tablespoon salt
1 teaspoon fenugreek seeds
1/2 teaspoon asafoetida
1 teaspoon mustard seeds
7 tablespoons oil
2 sprigs curry leaves

Method

1. Wash and wipe the tomatoes. Grind along with the green chillies and salt in a mixer to a paste.
2. Fry the asafoetida and fenugreek seeds in one teaspoon of oil. Remove, powder and set aside.
3. Pour the rest of the oil and heat. Add the mustard seeds, and when done, the curry leaves. Add the ground paste, turmeric powder, chilly powder, and fry on low heat stirring occasionally. Cook until the oil surfaces. Add the fenugreek and asafoetida powder, and mix well. Remove, cool and bottle.

Tomato Sauce

Ingredients

1 kg/2.2 lb tomatoes
1 cup sugar
1 1/2 cups vinegar
2 tablespoons salt

15 dried red chillies
2.5 cm/1 inch piece ginger
8 cloves garlic

Method

1. Wash and wipe the tomatoes. Cut into fours and leave in a large-mouthed vessel.
2. Grind the chillies, ginger and garlic to a fine paste in half the vinegar. Add this ground masala to the tomatoes and cook until the tomatoes turn soft and the masalas are done. Remove from fire, cool and strain to take out the thick pulp.
3. To the cooked pulp, add the salt, sugar and the rest of the vinegar. Simmer the mixture for 20 minutes or so until it is thick. Remove from fire, cool and bottle.

Note

Some vinegar may be added on top in each bottle. This helps to preserve it.

GLOSSARY

Ajinomoto	This word, originally a name of a company's brand name for MSG (Mono Sodium Glutamate) is now commonly used in India to describe MSG. It is an optional flavouring ingredient in Chinese dishes.
Ajwain	A small seed (botanical name carum) of the caraway family used as a flavouring agent.
Aloo	North Indian term for potato.
Ambat	A lentil preparation made of ground coconut and spices, with or without vegetables, South Indian style.
Amchoor	Dried mango powder, obtained by grinding desiccated unripe mangoes.
Anardana	Pomegranate seeds.
Aniseed	Larger than ajwain, these aromatic seeds are used both as a digestive and a breath-freshener after Indian meals. They are used in cooking too. Also known as Indian Fennel in the West.
Appalam	South Indian term for sun-dried wafer, also known as papad in the North. Served as a snack, or meal accompaniment, either dry roasted or deep fried.
Asafoetida	A distinctively pungent dried gum resin with good digestive properties.
Aval	South Indian term for beaten rice. Also known as poha.
Badam	Indian term for almond.
Badshah	The Indian version of the Greek sweet Baclava, a deep-fried sweet pastry.
Baigan	Aubergine, eggplant. Also known as brinjal.
Balushahi	*See Badshah.*
Basundi	Delicately flavoured dessert comprising of milk, sugar and other ingredients.
Bath, Bhath	Indian term for cooked rice, usually seasoned and mixed with other ingredients such as lemon juice, eggplant, yoghurt, etc.
Batura	Deep-fried leavened bread made of flour mixed with yoghurt.
Bengal gram	The yellow dried chick pea. Also known as channa, this lentil has a dark brown covering and is smaller than the Garbanzo bean (white chick pea).
Bengal gram dal	The husked and split yellow chick pea. Also known as channa dal.
Besan	Yellow chick pea flour, made from Bengal gram. Also known as gram flour.
Bhagara	Seasoned.
Bhajji, Bhajjia	Deep fried fritters, made with a variety of thinly sliced vegetables and besan.
Bhindi	Okra. Known in India as Lady's Finger.
Bhujjia	A semi-solid preparation of lentils and vegetables.
Biryani	A spicy rice preparation, the Mughlai variant of pulav.

Black gram	Also known as urad, the split variety is used in seasonings. *See urad dal.*
Bonda	Deep-fried vegetables in the shape of balls (usually potatoes) dipped in a besan batter.
Brinjal	Aubergine, eggplant.
Burfi	A tea-time sweet made of besan, thickened milk, coconut or other nuts.
Capsicum	Green pepper.
Chakli	Deep fried swirls or sticks made of rice flour.
Channa	Yellow (dried) chick pea. Also known as Bengal gram.
Channa Dal	Husked and split yellow chick pea. Also known as Bengal gram dal.
Chhenna	Fresh Indian cream cheese, used in many Bengali confections.
Chapati	Unleavened bread made from whole wheat flour. Cooked dry, but optionally smeared with ghee or butter immediately after cooking.
Chilly, Chilli	The Indian chilly is usually an unripe green pod, similar in length but much thinner than the Jalapeno pepper seen in American supermarkets. If you are using Jalapeno peppers, substitute 1 Jalapeno for every 2-3 chillies. The dried red chilly is a sun-dried version of the green chilly. Usually available in packets.
Chitranna	Seasoned rice, South Indian style.
Chivda	A fried snack usually made of poha or besan.
Chutney	If fresh, this is made from coconut and other ingredients with or without yoghurt, and is served as a dip for snacks. If used as a pickle, it is cooked in oil or vinegar, and can be preserved for longer periods.
Colocasia	A plant of the arum family with an edible root. Also known as yam.
Cutlet	Vegetable patty made with potatoes as a base, either shallow or deep fried.
Curds	The common Indian term for plain yoghurt.
Curry	A spicy vegetable preparation, often made with garam masala.
Curry Leaf	A fragrant plant of the neem family that grows abundantly in India, this leaf adds a distinctive flavour to Indian dishes. In North America, this can be obtained fresh (best), or dry (in packets) at Indian grocery stores.
Curry Powder	A ground mixture of turmeric, black mustard and other spices.
Dahi	Plain yoghurt.
Dahi vada	Vadas soaked in seasoned yoghurt.
Dal	Generic Indian term for dried lentils or pulses. The most common dals from India include Moong, Masoor, Tuvar, Channa and Urad.

Dhania	Also known as coriander, cilantro or Chinese parsley. The fresh leaves, and the powder are both used extensively in Indian cooking. The powder is best when freshly ground from the coriander seed. Available in many supermarkets.
Dhokla	A Gujarati dish made of fermented besan.
Dosa, Dosai	A savoury pancake made from a fermented mixture of ground urad dal and rice, and shallow fried on a cast iron skillet (tava) or frying pan.
Dum	Curried gravy.
Dumplings	Steamed balls made of flour and added to soup.
Fenugreek	In vegetable form it is leafy green and is used both as a herb and a vegetable. The seed is usually brown, and has a bitter taste. It is known in India as methi.
Florentine	An egg or cheese preparation baked on a layer of vegetables, one of which is spinach.
Gaajar	Carrot.
Garam Masala	A dry roasted mixture usually made with the following ingredients: cinnamon, coriander, cumin, cloves, cardamom and pepper. Garam masala is a generic term, and there are countless variations based on region and individual preference.
Ghee	Clarified butter. Obtained by melting butter until fully clarified and the milk solids separate. The resultant clear liquid is ghee.
Glacé	Covered with icing sugar or glazed.
Gobi	Cauliflower.
Gojju	Sweet and sour chutney made with vegetables, tamarind and jaggery, South Indian style.
Gram Flour	Chick pea flour. *See besan.*
Gujarati	From the state of Gujarat in Western India.
Gulab Jamun	Fried balls made of milk powder and flour in a rose syrup.
Haldi	Turmeric.
Hara Masala	Green masala. This is a fresh masala, made with a combination of one or more of the following ingredients, chopped and ground: onions, ginger, garlic, green chillies, coriander and mint leaves.
Halwa	Semi-solid sweet preparation made of milk and other ingredients served as a dessert or at tea-time.
Idli	A steamed cake made from a fermented mixture of ground urad dal and rice. This highly nutritious dish is very popular as a breakfast food in South India.
Imli	Tamarind.
Jackfruit	A very large fruit with a thick thorny skin, and a fleshy interior.
Jaggery	Unrefined sugar with a unique flavour. Also known in North India as gur, and in Tamil as vellum.

Jeera	Cumin seed, usually white.
Kabab, Kebab	The vegetarian kabab is a vegetable or lentil preparation shallow or deep-fried, and served at tea-time as a snack, or as an accompaniment to a meal.
Kabuli channa	This is a variety of white chick peas, also known as Garbanzo beans in the West.
Kachodi	A thick puri with a vegetable stuffing.
Kachumber	A salad popular in Western India made with cucumber and other fresh vegetables, with a lemon dressing.
Kadai	A vessel used for deep frying or cooking, similar to the Chinese wok.
Kadhi	A lightly seasoned preparation of buttermilk and gram flour seasoned lightly and served with rice, North Indian style.
Katori	Small serving bowl, usually made of stainless steel.
Kedgeree	A steam-cooked mixture of lentils, rice and onions.
Kela	Plantain or banana.
Kesar	Saffron.
Kesari	A halwa made of semolina, South Indian style.
Kewra	A unique flavouring essence from the screw pine tree.
Khandvi	Gram flour rolls, popular in Western India.
Khara Bath	Also known as uppuma, this cream of wheat (semolina) preparation is made with vegetables, and is usually a breakfast or tea-time food.
Khattal	Jackfruit.
Kheema	Curried minced vegetables.
Kheer	An Indian pudding, this is a delicately flavoured dessert comprising of milk, sugar and other ingredients such as rice, lentils, vermicelli, or even some vegetables. Served hot or cold.
Khichadi	A steam-cooked mixture of lentils, rice and onions.
Khoya	Solid residue obtained by boiling milk for an extended period.
Khus khus	White poppy seed.
Kofta	Balls made of vegetables and/or lentils and deep-fried. Usually served in a thick curried gravy.
Kootu	A thick seasoned stew made of mixed vegetables, lentils and ground coconut, South Indian style.
Korma, Kurma	Mixed vegetable curry cooked with ground coconut and yoghurt.
Kosamalli	South Indian term for salad.
Kulfi	Flavoured Indian ice-cream set in moulds.
Kurma	*See Korma.*
Lauki	Green-white marrow. It is a long vegetable which has to be skinned before cooking.

Luchi	Small puris of Eastern India made from maida.
Maida	White wheat flour.
Malai	Cream.
Malpura	A shallow-fried sweet flour fritter.
Masala	Generic Indian term for spice. Usually a combination of powdered or spices ground fine to a paste with water or vinegar (if used in pickles).
Masoor Dal	Split and skinned red lentil, that is actually pinkish in colour.
Mattri	A savoury pastry.
Methi	Fenugreek. Refer to fenugreek for a description.
Milagu	South Indian term for peppercorns.
Moillee	A South Indian curry of vegetables or eggs cooked in coconut milk.
Moong Dal	A variety of lentil, available in two varieties: green moong (whole) and yellow moong (split).
Morkuzhambu	A South Indian dish with a soup like consistency. Can be described as South Indian buttermilk curry with coconut.
Mughlai	Of or relating to the Moghul empire.
Muli	White or red radish.
Musambi	A citrus fruit, slightly larger than an orange family. Known in India as sweet lime.
Mutter	Green peas.
Mysore	A state in Southern India, now known as Karnataka.
Naan	Indian bread baked in a clay oven.
Navaratna	Literally meaning nine gems, this implies a preparation made with nine vegetables.
Omha	*See ajwain.*
Omhapudi	A savoury snack made of chick pea flour.
Pachadi	South Indian term for raita.
Pakoda	Vegetables deep-fried in a spicy gram flour batter.
Palak	Spinach.
Palya	Karnataka term for cooked vegetables.
Panchporan	A mixture of five seeds, e.g. aniseed, cumin, fenugreek, mustard and onion.
Paneer	Known as Indian cream cheese or Indian cottage cheese, it is a fresh cheese obtained by splitting milk.
Pantua	Bengali milk and flour pastry in cardamom syrup.
Papad, Papadam	Crispy thin snack or meal accompaniment, made from sun-dried rice flour and lentils. Served roasted or deep fried.
Paratha	Whole wheat Indian bread, cooked with oil or ghee on an iron griddle.
Paruppu	Generic South Indian term for lentil.

Paruppu curry	A lentil curry made with a combination of vegetables, South Indian style.
Payasam	South Indian term for kheer.
Peda	Milk fudge.
Philouries	Deep fried spiced gram flour fritters.
Phirni	A rice blancmange, this is basically a thick kheer.
Phulka	Thin unleavened whole wheat bread that has been made to puff up over a flame. Served plain or with the application of ghee or butter.
Pista	Pistachio nut.
Poha	Beaten rice.
Poli	A sweet paratha.
Pompom	A deep-fried snack made with cheese and eggs.
Posto	A spicy Bengali curry.
Pottal	A vegetable of the squash family with an edible seed, popular in Eastern India.
Pudina	Mint.
Puffs	Vegetable pastries with a samosa-like filling
Pulav, Pilaf, Pilau	A fried rice dish made with vegetables, and seasoned with spices such as bay leaves, cinnamon, cloves and cumin.
Puri	A deep fried whole wheat bread.
Rabdi	A thick kheer.
Raita	Chopped salad vegetables such as cucumber, onions, or tomatoes in seasoned yoghurt. Usually served as a meal accompaniment.
Rajma	Red kidney beans.
Ras	Syrup.
Ras Malai	Rasagoollas in a cardamom-flavoured creamy syrup.
Rasagoolla	Balls of chhenna in a cardamom syrup.
Rasam	A watery (South Indian) lentil preparation somewhat like a clear soup, heavily spiced and served as an appetizer, or with rice.
Rasapulipitha	A dessert made of coconut and semolina in flavoured, thickened milk.
Rasedar	Curried gravy.
Rava	South Indian term for semolina or cream of wheat.
Rice flour	Ground rice powder.
Rissole	A kabab made of chopped vegetables or lentils rolled in bread crumbs, rolled and fried into a ball or cake.
Roti	Generic Indian term for bread, leavened or unleavened.
Sabudana	Sago.
Sago	A beady substance made from the sago palm. This finds use in making vadas and vadams.

Sagu	South Indian style vegetable curry.
Sambar	A gravy of lentils (usually toovar dal) and vegetables cooked together with ground coconut, spices and tamarind, very popular in South India.
Samosa	A savoury pastry with a vegetable filling.
Sandesh	Milk fudge made of Indian cream cheese.
Semia	Vermicelli.
Semolina	Cream of wheat.
Shahi Tukra	Royal toast. This is an Indian version of French toast, made with nuts and milk.
Shahjeera	Black cumin.
Sind	A region in Southern Pakistan.
Sindhi	From the province of Sind.
Sooji	North Indian term for semolina (cream of wheat). The South Indian term is rava.
Suran	Yam.
Tamarind	Pod of the tamarind tree. Tamarind concentrate can be used as a convenient substitute in the recipes where it is called for.
Tava	A concave iron skillet, usually 25 cm (10 inches) in diameter. Used for making dosas, as well as chapatis and parathas.
Thokku	Mango or tomato chutney, South Indian style.
Tikki	A small vegetable cutlet.
Til	Sesame.
Toovar, Tuvar	Also known as arhar dal, this is a yellow split bean, widely used in Indian cooking. Toovar dal is used in sambar and rasam.
Tuvar	*See Toovar.*
Uppuma	A savoury preparation from semolina or cream of wheat, seasoned and cooked with a variety of vegetables. It is popular as a breakfast or tea-time food.
Urad	Known in English as black gram. Urad dal is a high-protein black lentil, which comes in three categories: whole urad (saabat urad), split urad with the skin (chilke urad), and split urad without the skin. The last two categories of urad find extensive use in idlis, dosas and vadas, and are also used in seasonings.
Vada, Vadai	A South Indian snack made from lentils ground to a batter with seasonings, and then deep fried. Can also be made from semolina or rice flour.
Vadam	South Indian term for a deep-fried snack of various shapes usually served as a meal accompaniment, made from various combinations of rice flour, sago and lentils which have been sun-dried.
Vanaspati	A vegetable shortening, available in India under the brand name 'Dalda'.
Venn Pongal	A South Indian kedgeree, comprising of rice and lentils cooked together.

INDEX

T

U

V

Y